Defending America

DEFENDING AMERICA

Introduction by James R. Schlesinger

Robert Conquest

Theodore Draper

Gregory Grossman

Walter Z. Laqueur

Edward N. Luttwak

Charles Burton Marshall

Paul H. Nitze

Norman Polmar

Eugene V. Rostow

Leonard Schapiro

Paul Seabury

W. Scott Thompson

Albert Wohlstetter

Basic Books, Inc., Publishers   **New York**

The Institute for Contemporary Studies   **San Francisco**

Library of Congress Cataloging in Publication Data

Main entry under title:

Defending America.

Includes index.
1. United States—Foreign relations—1945—
—Addresses, essays, lectures. 2. United States—
Military policy—Addresses, essays, lectures. 3. Russia
—Foreign relations—1945—Addresses, essays,
lectures. 4. Détente—Addresses, essays, lectures.
I. Conquest, Robert.
JX1417.D43   327.73   76-43479
ISBN: 0-465-01585-9

CONTENTS

ABOUT THE AUTHORS   vii

PREFACE   ix

Foreword   xi
    JAMES R. SCHLESINGER

I

Political and Economic Implications of American Policy

1 Appeasement and Détente   3
    THEODORE DRAPER

2 The Projection of Soviet Power   22
    W. SCOTT THOMPSON

3 America and West European Communism   37
    WALTER Z. LAQUEUR

4 The Soviet Threat to Europe Through the Middle East 49
    EUGENE V. ROSTOW

5 The Economics of Détente and American Foreign Policy 65
    GREGORY GROSSMAN

6 National Security: Thoughts on the Intangibles   81
    CHARLES BURTON MARSHALL

II

The United States Military Posture

7 Nuclear Strategy: Détente and American Survival   97
    PAUL H. NITZE

8 Racing Forward or Ambling Back?   110
    ALBERT WOHLSTETTER

9 European Insecurity and American Policy   169
    EDWARD N. LUTTWAK

10 The U.S.–Soviet Naval Balance   187
    NORMAN POLMAR

III

Human Rights and Freedoms

11 The Human Rights Issue   205
    ROBERT CONQUEST

12 The Effects of Détente on the Quality of Life
    in the Soviet Union   217
    LEONARD SCHAPIRO

IV

Epilogue

13 Beyond Détente   233
    PAUL SEABURY

INDEX   245

ABOUT THE AUTHORS

JAMES R. SCHLESINGER is Director of the Federal Energy Administration. He was Acting Director, Office of Management and Budget from 1969 to 1971, and Chairman of the Atomic Energy Commission from 1971 to 1973. For five months he was the Director of the Central Intelligence Agency, and then became the Secretary of Defense, from 1973 to 1975.

THEODORE DRAPER was a member of the School of Historical Studies, Institute for Advanced Study, Princeton University, from 1968 to 1973. He is a member of the Council on Foreign Relations and of the American Academy of Arts and Sciences. His publications include *American Communism and Soviet Russia* and *Abuse of Power*. He is a frequent contributor to national journals in the field of foreign policy.

W. SCOTT THOMPSON has been Associate Professor of International Politics at The Fletcher School of Law and Diplomacy since 1969. He is a member of the Council on Foreign Relations and of the editorial boards of ORBIS and of the *Sage International Handbook of Foreign Policy*. His most recent book is *Unequal Partners: Phillipine and Thai Relations with the United States 1965–75*.

WALTER Z. LAQUEUR is Chairman of the Research Council, Center for Strategic and International Studies, Washington, D.C., and Director, Institute of Contemporary History, and Wiener Library, London. He is also Visiting Professor of History at Harvard. His publications include *Russia and Germany* and *Guerrilla*, the first of a three volume study on guerrilla warfare and terrorism.

EUGENE V. ROSTOW is Sterling Professor of Law and Public Affairs, Yale Law School. He was Under-Secretary of State for Political Affairs from 1966 to 1969, and has been president of the Atlantic Treaty Association since 1973. His most recent books are *Law, Power and the Pursuit of Peace* and *Peace in the Balance*.

GREGORY GROSSMAN is Professor of Economics, University of California, Berkeley, and past President of the Association for Comparative Economics Studies. His works include *Soviet Statistics of Physical Output of Industrial Commodities* and *Economic Systems*.

CHARLES BURTON MARSHALL is Professor of International Studies, Johns Hopkins School of Advanced International Studies. He is a member of the Council on Foreign Relations and the Washington Institute for Foreign Affairs. His publications include *The Cold War: A Concise History* and *Crisis over Rhodesia: A Skeptical View*.

PAUL H. NITZE was Deputy Secretary of Defense from 1967 to 1969, and a member of the U.S. delegation to the Strategic Arms Limitations Talks from 1967 to 1974. His most recent book is *U.S. Foreign Policy 1945–1955.*

NORMAN POLMAR was the American Editor of *Jane's Fighting Ships* from 1967 to 1976. His publications include *Aircraft Carriers: A History of Carrier Aviation and Its Influence on World Events* and *Soviet Naval Power.*

ROBERT CONQUEST is Senior Fellow, Hoover Institution on War, Revolution and Peace, Stanford University. Among his recent books are *Power and Policy in the USSR, Russia after Khrushchev,* and *The Great Terror.*

LEONARD SCHAPIRO is Emeritus Professor of Political Science (with special reference to Russian Studies), London School of Economics and Political Science, University of London. He is a member of the editorial boards of *Soviet Studies, Soviet Survey,* and *Soviet Jewish Affairs.* Among his recent books are *The Government and Politics of Soviet Russia* and *Totalitarianism.*

PAUL SEABURY is Professor of Political Science, University of California, Berkeley. He is a member of the Council on Foreign Relations and the editorial board of ORBIS. His recent publications include *The Rise and Decline of the Cold War, The Balance of Power,* and *The United States in World Affairs.*

ALBERT WOHLSTETTER is the University Professor of Political Science, University of Chicago and Sometime Fellow of All Souls College, Oxford. He is a consultant to various U.S. government agencies and has authored and co-authored numerous articles and several book-length studies, the most recent of which, *Nearing the Bomb,* will be published in 1977 by the University of Chicago Press.

PREFACE

When the policy of détente was formally announced in May 1972, hopes were high that longtime hostilities were over and that a new phase in Soviet-American relations might begin. The reality did not live up to the promise; President Ford finally abandoned the word *détente* in the spring of 1976. Nevertheless, he and Secretary of State Henry Kissinger continued to ask what alternative there was to present policy, and to denounce critics as dangerous cold warriors.

In response to growing public concern about the drift in present policy, the Institute for Contemporary Studies asked thirteen international relations and military policy experts to assess the present state of American foreign and defense policy and to recommend alternative courses. The results are for the reader to judge.

This is the Institute's first venture into international affairs; our previous studies have addressed only domestic issues. We are especially pleased to be associated with Basic Books in this project which, we think, will make an important contribution to the ongoing public debate on the proper direction of American foreign policy.

H. Monroe Browne
President
Institute for Contemporary Studies

November 1976
San Francisco, California

FOREWORD

If the United States lost its inner equilibrium during the later stages of the Southeast Asian conflict, then the end to that conflict (as well as other events) has started this nation along the road toward recovery. American political life appears increasingly devoid of the intensive conflicts of yesteryear. We should welcome both the return to sanity and the clear signs, perhaps kindled by the Bicentennial, of the restoration of the national spirit.

In this new mood we are turning once again to a serious examination of our longer-term interests—as well as to the more or less permanent role that the United States must play in world affairs and the constraints on that role. Just as the incubus of Vietnam has been lifted, so also the false hopes regarding détente—as a kind of ritual incantation that would gradually resolve major problems of international rivalry—are being dissipated. These illusions concerning détente represented the utopian imaginings of a nation that had grown weary and was seeking a surcease to its responsibilities. They also reflected the deep-seated American belief that stability was as natural in the international order as in domestic affairs. Concretely, it was hoped that the Soviets shared our desire for stability, were willing to avoid either sudden departures from the status quo or the quest for marginal advantage, and thus were prepared to resolve many outstanding issues through "linkage."

The Soviets have been reasonably direct in indicating that such aspirations remain a bourgeois fantasy. To become a status-quo power would imply abandonment of the remnants of revolutionary zeal—from which still flow the motivating force behind Soviet policies and the cohesive element binding together the Soviet state and party apparatus. The Soviet faithful are continually reminded that the laws of class warfare are in no way repealed by détente, but continue to operate in their ineluctable manner—with all that this implies. Fortunately, however, these laws no longer seem to require direct military conflict between the superpowers.

Nonetheless, the Soviets have underscored that détente hardly implies the relaxation of tension in the Western sense. On the contrary, détente in the Soviet view requires the intensification of the ideological struggle.

The *intensification* of the ideological *struggle* scarcely seems consistent with the relaxation of tension. The relaxation of tension, to the extent that it has occurred, has thus been one-sided, and reflects the lulling of Western wariness. For the Soviets, détente turns out to be simply another phase in a continuing process of bargaining and conflict. In short, rather than seeking stability, the Soviets remain keenly alert to the benefits of instability—in terms of wrenching from the West economic, political, or military advantages—marginal or otherwise.

This explains why the concept of "linkage" has simply disappeared from our official rhetoric. It also provides a partial explanation for the continuing difficulties in Africa, the Middle East, South Asia, and even Western Europe. Support continues for wars of national liberation—though on a highly selected basis—for these conflicts supposedly reflect social forces unfettered by the restraints of détente. It also explains why arms negotiations, both Strategic Arms Limitations Talks (SALT) and Mutual Balance Force Reductions (MBFR), in no way reflect a shared quest for a systems-analytic concept of stability—understandably sought by arms controllers—but rather separate quests for power advantages obtained through wearing down the patience of the other side. Yet even for such meager results from negotiations, an economic price is demanded in the form of the continuous flow of technology.

The outcome is vastly different from that to which we once aspired. As experience gradually eroded our earlier hopes, the meaning officially ascribed to détente underwent continued revision—thus permitting semantics to keep pace with events. Détente seemingly was reduced to an ever-changing set of verbal formulas. Ultimately the domain of détente shrank to two simple objectives: the imperative to avoid nuclear war and "the containment of Soviet global power." The latter at least gives rise to a feeling of *déjà vu*.

All of this gradually has increased public uneasiness with the entire process of negotiation. Indeed, this is regrettable, for negotiations remain not only a moral obligation for the enlightened powers of the West, but can yield certain concrete and mutually beneficial results. But negotiations must not proceed on expectations that the Soviets have had a change of heart or are willing to embrace our Western beliefs regarding stability. All negotiations must proceed on the basis of a profound understanding of Soviet attitudes and tactics. In the large, the issues raised by these persisting Soviet attitudes and tactics represent the central focus of this excellent volume of essays.

A reader need not necessarily agree with each of the specific points made by every author. But the overall impact is one of compelling arguments, lucidly expressed. The discussion reflects an underlying premise that only the United States has sufficient power to maintain freedom and diversity throughout the world—to the degree necessary for the flourishing of our own social order. Therefore it remains incumbent upon us to be alert to the tactical and strategic objectives of the Soviet Union in all realms—political, economic, military, and societal.

Above all, it is necessary to hold aloft the distinctive values represented by our civilization—which indeed make that civilization worth protecting. In citing the stirring quotation from Milton's *Areopagitica*, "Give me liberty to know, to utter, and to argue freely according to conscience above all liberty," Robert Conquest points compellingly to the credo that ultimately inspires Western civilization.

It is indeed reassuring—though only in a limited respect—that the Soviets, in their continuing drive to shift "the correlation of forces" to their advantage, are seeking to obtain their objectives without war or the penalties of war, as C. B. Marshall makes clear. But that is only an additional motive for our efforts to maintain our guard in such a way that the nations of the West—and those that would ultimately seek to emulate them—can navigate through this difficult period.

Yet surely there is nothing novel or surprising in recognizing that eternal vigilance is the price of freedom. As American political health has returned, and as the national spirit has been restored, we recognize anew this inescapable reality and are preparing to take the necessary steps to give it life. In the course of this reawakening, undue expectations regarding détente have been jettisoned. There is growing recognition that the Soviet concept of "peaceful coexistence among states with different social systems" does not differ markedly from what we earlier defined as cold war attitudes. There is genuine reassurance, to be sure, in Soviet recognition that nuclear war is not inevitable. Yet the Soviet belief in the inevitability of the triumph of their own social order underscores that diplomacy can modify only slightly either the underlying realities of power or deep-seated ideological convictions. It also means that the survival of our civilization will require unremitting attention and effort.

James R. Schlesinger

Washington, D.C.

I

Political and Economic Implications of American Policy

1

THEODORE DRAPER

Appeasement and Détente

I

Appeasement became a dirty word in the 1930s. For several centuries it had been a perfectly clean, even a virtuous term. How could a word that had meant peace and conciliation turn into its opposite? The term was transformed because it was used to describe the concessions to and deals made with fascist dictatorships in the 1930s. The turning point came some time between October 1938 and March 1939. In October 1938 British Prime Minister Neville Chamberlain, just back from Munich where he had agreed to tear off a vital part of Czechoslovakia and hand it over to Hitler's Germany, spoke with satisfaction about "our policy of appeasement" of which the Munich agreement was to be only the first step. The "real triumph," he said, was the execution of "a difficult and delicate operation by discussion instead of by force of arms." [1]

The Munich agreement was the first step, but not the one that Chamberlain had contemplated. In March 1939, only six months later, the remainder of Czechoslovakia came under German rule. Slovakia and Carpatho-Ukraine declared their nominal independence but in fact they became German protectorates—together with Bohemia and Moravia. The Munich agreement, which was supposed to build up "a lasting peace for Europe," as Chamberlain had put it, became nothing more than a license for Hitler to take over Eastern Europe before turning against Western Europe. In another six months force of arms instead of discussion made it almost impossible to say the word *appeasement* without shame and loathing.

The word, of course, was not to blame. But why had it been misused?

Why did it turn into such a ghastly mockery? Clearly the reason was that appeasement could not appease the unappeasable. It would have been bad enough if Czechoslovakia had been dismembered and betrayed by France and Great Britain to buy peace for themselves; but it was criminal folly to give away someone else's freedom only to increase Hitler's territorial appetite. In those circumstances it was capitulation on the installment plan. The stench of the Munich agreement might not have been so sickening if it had been recognized for what it was. What made it so unbearable was its glorification, such as this memorable tribute in the London *Times:* "No conqueror returning from a victory on the battlefield has come home with nobler laurels than Mr. Chamberlain from Munich yesterday." [2]

Détente is another one of those perfectly good words that get a bad name when they are misused. It appears to be a relatively recent importation from the French. The first citation in the *Oxford English Dictionary* is dated 1908. The word is usually defined as a "relaxation of tension" and thus may mean much or little depending on what kind of tension is being relaxed by how much. At the 1974 Senate Foreign Relations Committee hearings on détente, speaker after speaker complained that the word had to be pinned down. Former Ambassador George F. Kennan said that he had "never fully understood the use of the word 'détente' in connection with [Soviet-American relations]." In response, former Senator J. William Fulbright remarked that "détente is a difficult word to have inherited in this connection, but I think we are stuck with it." Former Senator Eugene McCarthy commented that "the meaning has changed every time it is applied." Professor Marshall Shulman referred to "the ambiguities of the word 'détente,'" and Professor Herbert Dinerstein pointed out that "everyone has a different notion about what détente is." Former Secretary of State Dean Rusk said it was a "process," not a "condition." Secretary of State Henry A. Kissinger agreed that "it is a continuing process, not a final condition." [3] An academic definition has made it into "a logical spectrum of relations along which conflict either increases or decreases." [4]

Détente is not only difficult even for experts to define; whatever it is, it appears to be fluctuating and ambiguous. In theory, it has been situated somewhere between cold war and *rapprochement* or even *entente*. Since *détente* moves uneasily between two poles, it occupies a purely relative position without a definite profile of its own. According to this conception, *détente* is always moving away from or toward something else.[5] No wonder, then, that *détente* has been so hard to pin down; by its very nature it is considered to be transitory and volatile.

In practice, however, the current Soviet-American détente should have a much more positive and recognizable character. The materialization of détente was supposed to be the main achievement of the Moscow summit meeting in May 1972, at which the new phase of Soviet-American relations was formally inaugurated by three agreements—military, commercial, and political. The military agreement took the form of SALT I, which provided in principle for quantitative parity in antiballistic missiles. The commercial agreement set up a U.S.-USSR commission to promote trade and development of economic resources. The political agreement was embodied in the "Basic Principles of Relations Between the United States of America and the Union of Soviet Socialist Republics." These three agreements were designed to give this détente some concreteness and delineation. *Détente* could not be all that vague and ambiguous if it had a set of definite "basic principles," no matter what they might be.

II

Détente has been so confusing not because it lacks definitions and interpretations, but because it has too many.

The original American theory of détente was developed largely by Henry Kissinger in 1972. The main concept behind it was the "linkage" of the military, economic, and political. Of these the military linkage represented by SALT I was originally given the biggest buildup. After the Moscow linkage, Dr. Kissinger was euphoric. He extolled SALT I as an "agreement without precedent in all relevant modern history." The summit meeting had been so successful, he reported, that the American side had achieved all that it had planned and had expected to achieve, "give or take 10 percent" [6]—an extraordinary record for any diplomatic conference.

The second thoughts were less ecstatic. SALT I, it became increasingly clear, had been little more than a promissory note. In 1974 Secretary Kissinger himself said that if a more far-reaching follow-up nuclear agreement were not reached "well before 1977, then I believe you will see an explosion of technology and an explosion of numbers" of fearsome proportions.[7] In that same year Professor George B. Kistiakowsky, one of the most eminent and experienced experts in nuclear strategy and arms control, testified: "The SALT I agreements do not inhibit or limit the strategic-arms race. They merely channel it into such directions as each side perceives to be militarily most advantageous to it." [8] Secretary Kissinger's deadline of 1977 showed no signs of being met.

On the American side, it was always recognized that the Soviets were interested in détente primarily for economic reasons.[9] The basic Soviet motive derived from a declining rate of growth and productivity. According to official Soviet data, this rate fell from 10.9 percent in 1950–1958 to 7.2 percent in 1958–1967 to 6.4 percent in 1967–1973. Western recalculations of the Soviet figures show the actual decline to be from 6.4 percent in 1950–1958 to 5.3 percent in 1958–1967 to 3.7 percent in 1967–1973.[10] A key reason for the Soviet problem was their failure to keep up with the advanced technology of the West. At first the Brezhnev regime had tried to overcome this weakness through earlier détentes with France and Germany. But by 1972 the American-Soviet détente made the United States the preferred source of scientific-technological transfer.

There was a hitch, however. The Soviets were unable to pay for what they wanted. They demanded large scale, long term U.S. government credits at abnormally low interest rates. They sought most-favored-nation status without being able to reciprocate. They wanted delivery of entire factories and plants on terms which meant that the Soviet Union would do all the owning and the Western donors would take all the risks. Such an economic relationship is inherently unequal. If all goes well, Americans could benefit through profits and jobs. So far, many deals have failed and a few have succeeded, so that the profits from increased Soviet-American trade have gone to a few favored or fortunate entrepreneurs. The Soviets have an altogether larger stake in the relationship. They want to get from it a structural change in their economy and a bail-out mechanism for their agriculture. This economic exchange is not an ordinary one—the Western contribution to the Soviet economy is heavy with political and potentially military significance.

Professor Marshall I. Goldman's most recent study on how the economic détente has worked is not reassuring. Professor Goldman is not an enemy of détente or of Soviet-American trade—quite the contrary. Yet his final analysis of what has gone on in the name of détente is disturbing:

The types of goods and the types of negotiating tactics the Russians tend to use in purchasing goods from the United States make it possible for the Russians to obtain high technology products for bargain prices that no other buyers could cajole. Moreover, much of the technology and sometimes the products themselves have been heavily subsidized by the American taxpayer. The initial subsidy for development and production, the bargain prices, and the subsidized interest rate of the Export-Import Bank mean that the Russians are often able to obtain a triple subsidy on their American purchases.

These advantages, Professor Goldman adds, have an important political component built into them.[11] One does not have to believe that the Soviets obtain all the benefits to see that this form of détente works mainly in the Soviets' favor.

Indeed it was deliberately intended to work this way. Dr. Kissinger concocted the theory of "incentives" to justify such a peculiarly one-sided economic exchange. According to Dr. Kissinger, the Soviets were advised in 1970 and 1971, in advance of the agreement on détente, that they could get paid off in credits and most-favored-nation treatment "if they engaged in what we considered responsible international behavior." [12] A Kissingerian formulation of the incentive-payment theory specifically applied to the Soviet-American economic relationship: "We see it as a tool to bring about or to reinforce a more moderate orientation of foreign policy and to provide incentives for responsible international behavior and, therefore, it has to be seen in this context." [13]

As late as December 1975, in his private briefing of American ambassadors at a meeting in London, Secretary Kissinger went so far as to say that "we must create the maximum incentives for a moderate Soviet course." [14] Yet at that very moment the Soviet Union was already deeply committed to what Dr. Kissinger considered to be a most immoderate course in Angola.

This once-beguiling Kissingerian theory was strictly one-way. Not the slightest allusion was ever made to Soviet incentives to the United States in return for the latter's responsible international behavior. Not only have the Russians never offered any such incentives; they have sternly denied that they are obliged to pay anything for détente.

The incentive theory acted as the entering wedge of appeasement within the larger sphere of détente. If unilateral concessions represent an essential aspect of appeasement, and the concessions do not even serve the purpose of buying off their recipient, the incentive theory amounted to just such a unilateral concession.

At the same meeting in December 1975 Dr. Kissinger's alter ego Helmut Sonnenfeldt, Counsellor for the State Department, produced a related theory of how to appease the Soviet Union. Most attention to his statement was focused on the odd circumstance that Mr. Sonnenfeldt's mastery of the English language did not include the word "organic." But he used the term, whatever he may have meant by it, in order to get across a line of thinking that cannot be misunderstood. Mr. Sonnenfeldt claimed that the Soviet policy in Eastern Europe had been "an unfortunate historical failure" because it had not been able to "go beyond sheer power." He then offered to help the Soviet Union get a sounder and broader base: "We seek to influence the emergence of the Soviet imperial power by making the base more natural and organic so that it will not remain founded in sheer power alone." This school of thought would do for the Soviets what they allegedly cannot do for themselves—make their influence less unnatural and less inorganic in order to bolster their power with "attractions" they are said to lack.[15] Such unrequited generosity was just what was meant by "appeasement" in the sense that it acquired after the ignominious fate of the Munich agreement.

III

The idea that détente applies simply and solely to the prevention of nuclear war ignores the very charter of the Soviet-American détente—the "Basic Principles" of 29 May 1972. These principles contained among other things the following mutual restraints:

—Prevention of the development of situations capable of causing a dangerous exacerbation of Soviet-American relations.
—Doing the utmost to avoid military confrontations.
—Recognition that efforts to obtain unilateral advantage at the expense of the other—directly or indirectly—are inconsistent with these objectives.
—Special responsibility to do everything possible to avoid conflicts or situations which would serve to increase international tensions.[16]

These principles implied that there were two sides to détente—political and military. The former was designed to prevent situations from developing which might bring on the latter. On ceremonial occasions, such as his speech at the Helsinki conference at the end of July 1975, Brezhnev has paid lip service to this combination of military and political détente.[17]

The "Basic Principles" also signified that détente applied not only to relations between the United States and the Soviet Union, but also to the relations of each with the rest of the world. Dr. Kissinger gave assurances that "we consider Soviet restraint in the Middle East an integral part of détente policy" [18] and that "the principle of restraint is not confined to relations between the U.S. and the USSR, it is explicitly extended to include *all* countries." [19]

There seemed to be agreement, then, on two constituent elements of a true détente: it must apply to the political as well as the military realm, and it must apply to the relations of the United States and the Soviet Union with the rest of the world as well as to their relations with each other.

However, to understand what détente means to the Soviet leaders we must examine the Soviet theories underlying détente, as we have the American. For example, a basic Soviet theory concerns what is called the "new relationship of forces." Brezhnev expressed this theory not long ago in the following formula: "International détente has become possible because a new relationship of forces now exists on the world scene." [20]

What is this "new relationship of forces?" The short answer, spelled out in all Communist and Soviet propaganda, is that the "new relationship of forces" now favors the "socialist world" led by the Soviet Union. The point here is not whether the theory is right or wrong. The point is that—for the Soviet Union and its followers—détente is not an abstract, a historical condition; it is the product of a concrete, historical "relationship of forces" which determines not merely what détente is but— far more important—what détente does.

A second Soviet theory in this connection is that of the "two spheres." An authoritative exposition of this theory was given by Professor Georgi Arbatov, a high-level Soviet spokesman, who is head of the Institute of the U.S.A. of the Academy of Sciences of the USSR:

What is involved here [the policy of détente] is essentially different spheres of political life in our time (though they may influence one another in various ways). One of them is the sphere of social development, which steadily makes headway in any international conditions—whether détente, "cold" war, or even "hot" war. . . . The other is the sphere of inter-state relations, in which other extremely important questions are resolved—questions of war and peace, methods of resolving controversial foreign-policy questions, and possibilities for mutually advantageous international cooperation.

The drawing of a clear line between these two spheres is one of the basic premises of the Leninist foreign policy of peaceful coexistence of states with different social systems.[21]

In the pro-Soviet Communist movement, the theory of "peaceful coexistence" has been promulgated somewhat more clearly and starkly. One version has it that peaceful coexistence "refers exclusively to the domain of inter-state relations between socialist and capitalist countries. It rules out just one form of struggle between socialism and capitalism— the form of direct military collision."[22]

Formerly, as we have seen, détente was supposed to cover anything of
a political or military nature which could exacerbate Soviet-American
relations, give one side unilateral advantage at the expense of the other,
or serve to increase international tension. The theory of the "two spheres"
eliminates a huge political area—under the trade name of "social development"—from the domain of détente. By reducing détente to the
avoidance of "direct military collision" between the United States and
the Soviet Union, it leaves everything else wide open.

This tendency to shunt détente out of the political sphere into a narrow military sphere came to a head with the need to rationalize large-
scale Soviet military intervention in Angola and the use of Cuban troops
as Soviet proxies. Détente was now represented as the best ally the Soviet Union had in its conduct of political warfare around the world. On
29 November 1975 a writer in *Izvestia* insisted that it was impossible to
bring "the sphere of class and national-liberation struggle" within "peaceful coexistence." [23] On 30 November an *Izvestia* correspondent reported
that détente "gave a powerful impulse to the national-liberation movement of colonial and oppressed peoples." [24] On 2 December an *Izvestia*
commentator held that "the process of détente does not mean and
never meant the freezing of the social-political status quo in the world,"
nor could it prevent the Soviet Union from giving "sympathy, com-
passion, and support" to those whom it chose to represent as "fighters for
national independence." [25] On 6 December a writer in *Pravda* boasted:
"Détente created favorable conditions for the new successes of the cause
of national liberation." [26]

By the spring of 1976 Soviet commentators were mainly interested in
restricting the scope of détente. A Soviet journalist who was writing a
book on Soviet-American affairs had planned to call it "Dialogue De-
velops," but had seen fit to change the title to "The Limits of Détente."
An American observer noted that détente had come to mean in the Soviet
view only two things—the prevention of a nuclear disaster and expanded
trade with the West.[27] This 1976 Soviet version of détente was only
distantly related to the more expansive 1972 version as enshrined in the
"Basic Principles."

The Soviets were not the only ones to reinterpret détente in such a way
that it was hardly recognizable any longer. In January 1976 former
President Richard M. Nixon—who had originally sold détente as "a
solid framework for the future development of better American-Soviet
relations" [28]—chided those who overlooked "the fundamental fact that
in a period of détente the risk of war goes down but the risk of conquest
without a war through subversion and covert means goes up geomet-

rically. That has been true for years." [29] If so, it had also been true in 1972, and the geometric increase in the "risk of conquest" was scarcely a "solid framework" for better Soviet-American relations.

In effect, less than four short years after the "Basic Principles" had been promulgated with such optimism and fanfare, almost any action which either side chose to take violating the "Basic Principles"—that is, actions that could cause a dangerous exacerbation of Soviet-American relations, that could obtain direct or indirect unilateral advantage, or that could increase international tension—was now conveniently classified as part of the "class and national liberation struggle" or passed off as an *anticipated* increase in the "risk of conquest" by the Soviet Union.

To be sure, the Soviet Union had long claimed the right to support "national liberation movements." In the heyday of détente, however, this motif had been muted in favor of emphasis on avoiding international friction. That the Soviet political line should be turned around to provide a propaganda screen for military intervention on the west coast of Africa was something new and ominous. If that sort of intervention could be justified in the name of détente, almost anything short of direct conflict with the United States could be made to fit the "Basic Principles."

IV

The concept of détente is like an accordion; it can be stretched out or pulled in. It can be as broad as it seemed to be after the summit meeting of May 1972 or it can be as narrow as it became after the Arab-Israeli war of October 1973. That war proved to be the first real test of the Soviet-American détente. It provided so clear a violation of the "Basic Principles" by the Soviet Union that even Secretary Kissinger had to admit as much, albeit in the relative obscurity of a Senate committee hearing. The violation concerned the message sent by Brezhnev to Algerian President Boumédienne, and apparently to other Arab leaders, telling them that it was their Arab duty to get into the war against Israel. Pressed by Senator Harry F. Byrd, Jr., Secretary Kissinger agreed, "Yes, I would say this was a violation." [30] Kissinger himself, it may be recalled, had testified that Soviet "restraint" in the Middle East was "an integral part of the détente policy." If it did not hold there, it was unlikely to hold wherever American and Soviet interests seriously clashed.

In that case the détente relationship was relegated to taking care of relatively minor matters, leaving the major ones to nuclear alert or rival military interventions.

After the October 1973 war Dr. Kissinger began to stress the schizoid character of détente. To take care of all possible contingencies, as he explained in March 1974, détente was "composed of both competition and cooperation, . . . with profound ambiguities at every stage of this relationship." [31] Later he spoke of détente as if it were merely an improved method of communication, "a means by which a competition which is inevitable—in the nature of present circumstances—is regulated while reducing the danger of nuclear war." [32] Détente had become a profoundly ambiguous means to an evasively contradictory end.

Above all, détente was now largely reduced to limiting "the risks of nuclear war," as Dr. Kissinger put it.[33] Former Senator Fulbright could think of nothing more or better than: "Détente, in its essence, is an agreement not to let these differences [between the two superpowers] explode into nuclear war." [34] Professor Marshall Shulman found that the main business of détente was "to reduce the danger of nuclear war." [35] The case for détente after October 1973 came essentially to rest on its relationship with nuclear war and on little else that was unambiguous and uncontradictory.

We have now come to the heart of the matter—the relationship between détente and nuclear war. Is there a meaningful linkage between nuclear war, economic-incentive payments, and political restraint? The American—or Kissingerian—theory and practice of détente are fundamentally dependent on a positive answer to this question. If the answer should be negative, the entire American policy rests on an insecure foundation.

For the past thirty years, during hot wars, cold wars, and incipient détentes, nuclear weapons were not used. They were not used by the United States when it had a nuclear monopoly—even when its forces were decimated by Chinese Communist troops in Korea; even when the United States suffered defeat in Vietnam in the longest and most humiliating war in its history. There is obviously something about nuclear war that has set it apart from all other forms of warfare in which we still engage. There is something about nuclear weapons which cannot be fitted into hot wars, cold wars, or détentes. The nuclear war must as yet be regarded as *sui generis*. We still have no experience with it; we cannot fathom its bottomless depths of pure nihilism; we cannot imagine a rational use for it.

With the nuclear weapon we have reached the *reductio ad absurdum* of all warfare—a weapon that is *too destructive*. This was already the lesson when the United States still had a monopoly of it. As soon as the Soviet Union became an atomic and then a nuclear power, we achieved a higher stage of military absurdity—a weapon that was *too mutually destructive*. This second stage was reached by the mid-1950s; by the late 1960s, when the United States realized that the Soviet Union would achieve rough nuclear parity, we entered the third stage. The absurdity had now arrived at its final destination—the power of *mutual annihilation*.

In exasperation, Secretary Kissinger once dramatically exclaimed: "And one of the questions which we have to ask ourselves as a country is what, in the name of God, is strategic superiority. What is the significance of it, politically, militarily, operationally, at these levels of numbers? What do you do with it?" [36]

It was, as the saying goes, a good question. It implied that on the level of mutual annihilation it mattered little how much more annihilating a nuclear power could or would become. It also implied that there was no political "significance" to be attached to those incomprehensibly high levels of destructiveness. Nuclear warfare cannot be weighed in political scales or translated into political terms. Politics, so to speak, is subnuclear. Thus Secretary Kissinger himself inferentially cut the ground from under the nuclear-political linkage.

The control of nuclear warfare, then, is of an order so different from the control of "conventional" warfare, let alone the control of political and ideological rivalries, that it must be dealt with as something apart. Just as nuclear warfare resists every calculus of political or economic usefulness, so too it is not amenable to political blandishments or economic payoffs. The enormity of the nuclear problem defies all past human experience. This is not to say that the human race need or should resign itself to the ever-present threat of nuclear annihilation; it means that the threat must be faced on its own terms, without pretending that it can be circumvented through "linkages" of an altogether different order of magnitude. Economic incentives and political phrase-mongering—the tools of détente—are not in the same league as nuclear arms.

The promoters of détente sought to save it by reducing it to a hard core of avoidance of nuclear warfare. They were in fact exposing its essential hollowness. They were giving it, in effect, the selfsame function that the cold war used to have—an alternative to hot war. They were giving détente undeserved credit for an impasse that had been brought about by the mutual destructiveness of nuclear warfare. The linkage of détente with nuclear war betrays a misunderstanding of both concepts. In any case, we have gone very far from the détente of 1972 which, according to Dr. Kissinger, had moved "on a very broad front on many issues." Those who have tried to save détente by moving it on to a very narrow front—the single issue of nuclear warfare—unwittingly have administered its last rites.

Another problem with the narrow, nuclear interpretation of détente is that it puts all the rest of the world's ills and all the other possible forms of conflict outside the realm of détente. If détente is as schizoid as the latest American and Soviet versions make it out to be, one must constantly ask what belongs and what does not belong to the sphere of détente. If, as the Soviet spokesman Arbatov tells us, détente belongs exclusively to the sphere of "inter-state relations" and not at all to the sphere of "social development," the question arises whether the wars in the Middle East or in Angola belong to the former or to the latter. In the Soviet view, the latter is decidedly the case, which tells us how broad the category of "social development" is and how narrowly détente has been confined. If, as Secretary Kissinger has told us, détente is composed of both "competition and cooperation," the question arises: What pertains to competition and what to cooperation? An even more awkward question might be: If cooperation is the real essence of détente, what is the nature of the competition? Isn't it the bad old "cold war"? If we can have competition and cooperation together, why not cold war and détente together? These semantic games are hopelessly muddling and are contaminating all discourse on world affairs today.

V

In July 1975 Secretary Kissinger hurled an angry challenge at critics of détente:

Therefore, critics of détente must answer: what is the alternative that they propose? What precise policies do they want us to change? Are they prepared for a prolonged situation of dramatically increased international danger? Do they wish to return to the constant crises and high arms budgets of the cold war? Does détente encourage repression—or is it détente that has generated the ferment and the demands for openness that we are now witnessing? [37]

He seemed to think that the answers to these questions were crushingly obvious. The answers may be obvious, but they are surely not the ones that he had in mind.

1. *What is the alternative that they propose?* When I first tried to answer this question in *Commentary* of February 1976, I wrote:

One alternative would be to cease and desist from the unconscionable exploitation of the word "détente" or at least to stop waving it as a banner. It has now become an obstacle to thought. It is of little or no use in relation to nuclear war. It is a mockery in relation to such wars as we have, as in the Middle East and Angola. It admittedly does not apply to ideological conflict. It has been defined and redefined virtually out of existence. If it continues to serve as a political shibboleth, it must surely suffer the same fate as "appeasement," if it has not done so already.[38]

Soon after these lines were published, President Ford let it be known that the word *détente* was to be banished from the official vocabulary. Yet it should be made clear that a perfectly good word had been made unusable because it had been perverted in practice. In the present circumstances "nondétente" is not the same as a state of war, any kind of war. The problem is with the perversion, not with the ideal. Indeed, what makes the perversion more difficult to combat is the reiteration of the ideal as if it were the reality. The same problem arose in the case of *appeasement* as long as it was motivated by weakness and fear. The particular concession at Munich was wrong in itself because France and Britain had no business giving away a vital part of another country, particularly a country which was an ally of France. But international diplomacy can hardly exclude concessions in principle. It is always the nature and circumstances of the concession which are in question. The problem is whether the concessions are mutual, or at least stand a good chance of being reciprocated. One-sided concessions do not require any particular diplomatic skill.

2. *What precise policies do they want us to change?* One precise policy that was misconceived from the outset and should be disavowed is that of "incentive" payments to the Soviet Union. It is this policy more than any other which has opened the door to *appeasement* in the guise of *détente*. Arbatov and other Soviet spokesmen have stormed against the idea that the Soviets are expected to make any "payments" to the West.[39] The theory and practice of American incentive premiums are especially misguided in connection with nuclear-weapons negotiations. If the threat of mutual annihilation is not persuasive enough to bring one or the other side to its senses (and here I do not point an accusing finger only at the Soviet Union), immeasurably lesser incentives are at best superfluous and at worst a symptom of futile appeasement. Advance

payments to the Soviet Union for services in the common interest that may or may not be rendered have never worked and even make matters worse. They merely serve to convince the masters of the Soviet Union that the famous "relationship of forces" has changed in their favor.

3. *Are they prepared for a prolonged situation of dramatically increased international danger?* Let us recall that this question was flung out with much unction and indignation in the summer of 1975. In the next few months, the level of tension and danger increased dramatically. The question was plainly addressed to the wrong parties. The Angola crisis was hardly the work of the critics of détente. Some of them may even have seen such dramatically increased danger coming since the Arab-Israeli war of 1973.

4. *Do they wish to return to the constant crises and high arms budgets of the cold war?* To answer this question, it is useful to recall Secretary Kissinger's answer to another question put to him in December of 1974:

SENATOR BYRD: Is it not correct that since 1972, in a period of so-called détente, there has been a methodical improvement and expansion of nuclear and conventional power in the Soviet Union and in Eastern Europe?
SECRETARY KISSINGER: Yes, that is correct.[40]

We have it from Secretary Kissinger, then, that détente in its heyday did nothing to discourage the Soviets from improving and expanding their military power. Whether the same can be said of the United States seems more doubtful, but let us assume that both sides have improved and expanded their nuclear and conventional power in the détente years between 1972 and 1974. It may be argued that the situation would have been even worse without détente. Perhaps—but it certainly did not get any better, and it is most unlikely that more intercontinental missiles and more megatonnage would have significantly changed the nature of the problem. The obvious answer, then, to this question about wishing to return to the constant crises and high arms budgets of the cold war is: No. But what does it have to do with détente? Has détente saved us from crises and high arms budgets? More to the point, the answer is again: No.

5. *Does détente encourage repression—or is it détente that has generated ferment and the demands for openness that we are now witnessing?* This was the most incredible of all Secretary Kissinger's questions. It revealed how much his understanding of the Soviet system had changed since he took up residence in Washington. In one of his major works,

The Necessity for Choice, published in 1961, he had discussed this very question at some length. He had frowned on those who thought that "Western diplomacy should seek to influence Soviet internal developments." He had scoffed at "the tendency to base policy toward the USSR on an assumed change in Soviet society." He had reproached those who saw "in every change of [Soviet] tone a change of heart." He had decried "the persistence with which it has been claimed that the economic needs of the Soviet Union would impose a more conciliatory policy on it." He had severely disapproved of the fact that "whatever aspect of the Soviet system they have considered, many in the West have sought to solve our policy dilemma by making the most favorable assumptions about Soviet trends." He had instructed his readers sagely: "The tendency to justify negotiations by changes in Soviet attitude makes us vulnerable to largely formal Soviet moves." And he had cautioned them that "the possibility of evolution of Soviet policy in a more conciliatory direction may be jeopardized by the eagerness with which it is predicted." [41]

Nothing could illustrate more aptly that these warnings are still timely than the connection between détente and Soviet repression. By the time Dr. Kissinger asked the question "Does détente encourage repression?" in July 1975, repression was already in full swing. The official crackdown on the underground *samizdat* movement took place in 1972, the very first year of détente. The orchestrated vilification of Andrei Sakharov, the Nobel Peace Prize winner, started in August 1973. Aleksandr Solzhenitsyn was arrested and deported in February 1974.

Hedrick Smith, the former Moscow correspondent for the *New York Times,* has by chance directly answered Dr. Kissinger's question in his new book, *The Russians*—an account of his experiences in the Soviet Union from 1971 to 1974, the precise years of détente:

The technology of Soviet repression had become more sophisticated and more effective as détente proceeded. The unexpected irony was that détente, instead of spawning more general ferment among the Soviet intelligentsia, as the West had hoped and the Kremlin had feared, became a reason for tighter controls and sometimes provided new techniques for quieting disaffected intellectuals.[42]

There may be other reasons for pursuing a policy of détente, but discouraging Soviet repression is not one of them. Indeed, détente has been more closely connected with encouraging a climate of appeasement in the United States than with discouraging repression in the Soviet Union. A humiliating and gratuitous climate of appeasement was symbolized by the presidential refusal, no doubt on the advice of the Secretary of State, to receive Solzhenitsyn because the gesture might displease Leonid

Brezhnev. Yet Brezhnev had never refused to meet with any person hostile to the United States and its institutions in order to avoid displeasing Richard Nixon or Gerald Ford. The Soviets consider culture and ideology to be outside the boundaries of détente, but they seem to be the only ones to think so and to act on this premise. Leading American scholars have testified to the culture of appeasement which has infected the scholarly exchange program.[43] This type of appeasement was built into détente when we adapted ourselves to the Soviets but they did not adapt themselves to us. Russian scholars have been treated in the United States as if they were Americans, and American scholars have been treated in the Soviet Union as if they were Russians. In these circumstances, appeasement works silently, automatically, almost unthinkingly. It is the most insidious kind of appeasement because the cards are stacked in the Soviets' favor without any overt effort on their part.

VI

Such have been the acrid fruits of détente. By the end of 1975 the Angola crisis made it impossible to ignore that something had gone wrong. Indeed, Secretary Kissinger's reaction to Soviet policy in Angola cut the theoretical ground from under the already rickety structure of détente—the underlying theory that the Soviet Union had become a status-quo power. This idea was actually the implied premise of the "Basic Principles" of May 1972.

In his press conference on 23 December 1975, however, Secretary Kissinger announced his discovery that the Soviet Union had become a "true superpower" in an expansionist phase. Unfortunately, Dr. Kissinger's exposition of his new theory began with a strange history lesson: "The basic problem in our relation with the Soviet Union is the emergence of the Soviet Union into true superpower status. That fact has become evident only in the 1970s." [44]

This dating of the Soviet Union's "true superpower status" was most convenient for the purpose of justifying both the détente of 1972 and the evident disillusionment with the détente of 1975. In fact, the Soviet Union's superpower status had become evident—even to Dr. Kissinger—quite some time before the 1970s. As long ago as 1964 he had referred to the Soviet Union as a "superpower." [45] In 1968 he had noted that the Soviet Union was one of the two powers which possessed "the full panoply of military might." [46] Did the new status conferred on the Soviet Union by Dr. Kissinger at the end of 1975 mean that it had been an "untrue" superpower in 1964? Or did "true superpower" mean a "super superpower"? How much more of the full panoply of military might, circa 1968, was it necessary for the Soviet Union to possess to be promoted to the rank of "true superpower"? Kissinger's excursion into history was obviously more a political than a historical operation. The new "true superpower" status of the Soviet Union was discovered just in time to explain a crisis in American détente policy, as if the crisis were the result of immanent historical forces of which American policymakers could not have been aware in 1972.

That the crisis for détente had reached a very advanced stage was made plain by Secretary Kissinger in his 23 December news conference:

We do not confuse the relaxation of tension with permitting the Soviet Union to expand its sphere by military means and that is the issue, for example, in Angola. . . .

If the Soviet Union continues action such as Angola, we will without any question resist. . . .

Unless the Soviet Union shows restraint in its foreign-policy actions, the situation in our relationship is bound to become more tense, and there is no question that the United States will not accept Soviet military expansion of any kind.

These fighting words by Secretary Kissinger were to détente what Prime Minister Chamberlain's reaction after 15 March 1939 had been to appeasement. Two days after the German invasion of Czechoslovakia and the establishment of a German protectorate, Chamberlain made a speech in Birmingham in which he asked: "Is this the end of an old adventure, or is it the beginning of a new? . . . Is this, in fact, a step in the direction of an attempt to dominate the world by force?" If the answer proved to be "Yes," Chamberlain intimated, Britain was resolved to resist. Dr. Kissinger asked the same kind of question and gave the same kind of answer on 23 December 1975.

Angola was hardly the right place to test the American resolve to resist. It would be foolhardy to permit the Soviet Union to decide the time and place of every confrontation of this kind. When Secretary Kissinger vowed that "the United States will not accept Soviet military expansion of any kind," he was trying to correct one extreme by going to another extreme. We cannot as yet be sure what the post-Angola world holds for the

United States. But we can be sure that it is imprudent and implausible to conduct a foreign policy based on holding back new Soviet expansionism without getting rid of the last vestiges of the illusions bred by détente.

NOTES

1. Great Britain, *Parliamentary Debates* (Commons), 3 October 1938, cols. 45, 48; ibid., 6 October 1938, col. 552.
2. *The Times* (London), 1 October 1938.
3. U.S. Congress, Senate, Committee on Foreign Relations, *Détente: Hearings* (August-September 1974), 93d Congress, 2d Session, pp. 61, 67, 102, 147, 208, 239, 301.
4. Walter C. Clemens, Jr., "The Impact of Détente on Chinese and Soviet Communism," *Journal of International Affairs* 28, no. 2 (1974):134.
5. Ibid. "If tensions mount, the parties may move toward cold and then hot war. If tensions diminish, the parties move toward détente (whether short- or long-lived); from détente they could move further toward rapprochement or even entente."
6. Henry A. Kissinger, news conference, 29 May 1972, *Department of State Bulletin* 66, no. 1722 (26 June 1972):897.
7. Henry A Kissinger, news conference in Moscow, 3 July 1974, *Department of State Bulletin* 71, no. 1831 (29 July 1974):215.
8. *Détente: Hearings*, pp. 161–62.
9. Robert Ellsworth, *Department of State Bulletin* 63, no. 1639 (23 November 1970):642–43; also Marshall Shulman, "Towards a Western Philosophy of Coexistence," *Foreign Affairs* 52, no. 1 (October 1973):43: "The condition of the Soviet economy is clearly the primary determinant of present Soviet foreign policy."
10. *Détente: Hearings*, p. 32, statement by Dr. Herbert S. Levine.
11. Marshall I. Goldman, *Détente and Dollars* (New York: Basic Books, Inc., 1975), pp. 275–76.
12. U.S. Congress, Senate, Committee on Finance, *Emigration Amendment to the Trade Reform Act of 1974: Hearings* (3 December 1974), 93d Congress, 2d Session, p. 106.
13. Ibid., pp. 96–97.
14. *New York Times*, 7 April 1976.
15. Ibid., 6 April 1976.
16. The full text of "Basic Principles" may be found in *Department of State Bulletin* 68, no. 1722 (26 June 1972):898–99.
17. *Pravda*, 1 August 1975, quoted in *The Current Digest of the Soviet Press 27*, no. 31 (27 August 1975):13.
18. *Emigration Amendment: Hearings*, p. 77.
19. Henry A. Kissinger, statement, 19 September 1974, "Détente with the Soviet Union: The Reality of Competition and the Imperative of Cooperation," *Department of State Bulletin* 71, no. 1842 (14 October 1974):510.
20. *Information Bulletin*, issued by *World Marxist Review* 13, no. 12–15 (1975): 14.
21. Georgi Arbatov, *Izvestia*, 4 September 1975, in *The Current Digest of the Soviet Press* 27, no. 36 (1 October 1975):3.
22. *World Marxist Review* 18, no. 9 (September 1975):59.

23. N. Polyanov, *Izvestia,* 29 November 1975.
24. V. Kobysh, ibid., 30 November 1975.
25. V. Matveyev, ibid., 2 December 1975.
26. Oleg Skalkin, *Pravda,* 6 December 1975.
27. David K. Shipler, *New York Times,* 15 April 1976.
28. Richard M. Nixon, address to joint session of 92d Congress, 2d Session, 1 June 1972.
29. Answers of Richard M. Nixon to Senate Select Committee on Intelligence, 94th Congress, 2d Session, quoted in *New York Times,* 12 March 1976.
30. *Emigration Amendment: Hearings,* p. 89.
31. "Secretary Kissinger Holds News Conference at London," 28 March 1974 *Department of State Bulletin* 70, no. 1817 (22 April 1974):423.
32. Henry A. Kissinger, interview with William F. Buckley, Jr., 13 September 1975, *Department of State Bulletin* 73, no. 1893 (6 October 1975):534.
33. Henry A. Kissinger, interview in Peking, 12 November 1973, *Department of State Bulletin* 69, no. 1798 (10 December 1973):716.
34. U.S. Congress, Senate, *Congressional Record,* 93d Congress, 1st Session, 9 November 1973, p. S–20136.
35. *New York Times,* 10 March 1974.
36. Henry A. Kissinger, news conference in Moscow, 3 July 1974, *Department of State Bulletin* 71, no. 1831 (29 July 1974):215.
37. Henry A. Kissinger, address, 15 July 1975, "The Moral Foundations of Foreign Policy," *Department of State Bulletin* 73, no. 1884 (4 August 1975):166.
38. Theodore Draper, "Appeasement and Détente," *Commentary* 61, no. 2 (February 1976): 27–38.
39. Arbatov, *Izvestia,* 4 September 1975; Polyanov, *Izvestia,* 29 November 1975.
40. *Emigration Amendment: Hearings,* p. 76.
41. Henry A. Kissinger, *The Necessity for Choice* (New York: Harper and Row, 1961), pp. 195–201.
42. Hedrick Smith, *The Russians* (New York: Quadrangle, 1976), p. 439.
43. Robert F. Byrnes and Zbigniew Brzezinski, *Détente,* edited by G. R. Urban (New York: Universe Books, 1976), pp. 80–82, 270–71; also see exchange between Daniel C. Matuszewski, deputy director of International Research and Exchanges Board, and Theodore Draper, *Commentary* 61, no. 6 (June 1976):22–26, and *Commentary* 62, no. 3 (September 1976):22–28.
44. Henry A. Kissinger, 23 December 1975, *Department of State Bulletin* 74, no. 1908 (20 January 1976):70.
45. Henry A. Kissinger, "Coalition Diplomacy in a Nuclear Age," *Foreign Affairs* 42, no. 4 (July 1964):539.
46. Henry A. Kissinger, *Agenda for the Nation* (Washington, D.C.: Brookings Institution, 1968), p. 587.

2

W. SCOTT THOMPSON

The Projection of
Soviet Power

After thirty years of religious wars and the *de facto* break-up of the Holy Roman Empire, in 1648 with the Treaty of Westphalia the powers of that period recognized the small European state, whatever its religion or government, as sovereign and legitimate; and the Western international system was born. Through the age of revolution and two world wars the system progressed to a high point in the late 1940s, when new institutions emerged to help govern the system beyond the norms and customs that had characterized its existence theretofore. These organizations included a universal United Nations to codify Western assumptions of acceptable behavior, an International Monetary Fund to enshrine proper and—in effect—capitalistic assumptions about the world monetary system, and hosts of other ancillary but important institutions.

Within this international system was a Russian Communist enclave which soon was to make its first major expansion into Eastern and Central Europe, and later was to be joined by a separate Chinese Communist enclave which in time became hostile to both Moscow and to the goals of the Western system.[1] Of these two enclaves our focus is on the Soviet one and on its projection of power into the third world in the 1970s.

America's bicentennial year, 1975–1976, is perhaps more significant as a way station to a position the reverse of that in 1945 than as an American anniversary. For by 1975 the international organizations had already become forums for anti-Western and anti-American biases, for opposing democratic political principles and free-market economics—forums where third-world and Communist purposes, usually different in origin, shared a common objective of creating a new international order. Each of these blocs had a different new order in mind, but their intermediate purpose —a common interest in destroying the old—raised enough questions to require Western statesmen to take their challenge seriously.

Even more important, by 1975 the Soviet Union had developed an interconnecting and mutually supportive alliance system to a new stage, cementing its own relations and those of Eastern European satellites with Middle Eastern, Asian, and (most recently) African clients. Thus, for example, on 4 July 1975 Poland and Mongolia signed a significant treaty of friendship guaranteeing their mutual support in time of need [2]—but the presence of North Korean pilots in Iraq, Cuban soldiers throughout Africa, or Vietnamese guerrilla war experts in Algeria was more significant operationally.

From being a Western system with a communist enclave and with a vast hinterland of Western colonies that functioned both as an economic and military-strategic reserve, the Western system had become a beleaguered group of democratic states with a dwindling handful of third-world allies willing to stand upon important issues of principle. Changes in the Middle East, where Egyptian-American relations warmed and Syrian-Soviet ties weakened, buoyed hope that all was well—thus underlining how far the Western system had deteriorated given the base against which our ties in the Middle East were being measured. Access to vital raw materials was threatened by the alliance of Soviet and third-world states, coming together for their separate reasons toward a common intermediate goal. The world, from being an interconnecting Western security system, became a system where Western interconnections disappeared as rapidly as new Communist ones were put into place. And the mutually reinforcing security system which the Soviets created in the Middle East and Asia brought flexibility and multiple options to Soviet military planning.

In such circumstances, momentum accrues to the gainer and accelerates his progress. The appearance of irreversibility in his gains seems to enfeeble one side and stimulate the other all the more: the bandwagon collects those on the sidelines. As witnessed in the collapse of Vietnam in the spring of 1975, once the appearance of irreversibility sticks it becomes hard for the incipient loser to regain momentum. There is an exponential rate of advance by the winning side.[3]

IDEOLOGY AS A STRATEGIC WEAPON

All states seek to have their own behavior generalized; it is in their nature and interest. The American desire to make the world "safe for diversity" thus attempts to sustain the pluralism essential to internal American politics. Likewise, sixty years ago the Russian Marxists believed that their revolution would have to be exported to assure its survival at home. But the Soviet belief was strengthened by an understanding that the ideology of world revolution—which seeks intrinsically to generalize the Soviet system—therefore necessarily conflicts with existing systems.

Viewed in this light, the answer to the old question—whether Soviet foreign policy is driven by ideology or by Russian national interests—does not come easily; it is difficult to separate the two, though one need hardly doubt that where the two could be isolated, interests of state would prevail. Moscow, for example, has never hesitated to scrap the interests of Communist parties with which it has fraternal ties if the greater good of Russian interests is served thereby. A recent example occurred in France, whose Communist party was enraged by Moscow's ill-concealed and plainly expediential preference for Giscard d'Estaing's ticket over Mitterand's popular front with the Communists in 1974.[4] The Kurds and the Communist parties in Iraq and Egypt have been both beneficiaries and victims of Moscow, depending on the larger needs of Soviet Middle Eastern policy.

But ideology is also important, whether intrinsically or as an instrument of national interests. Thus the Soviet Union in recent years has underlined the significance of ideology and made clear in both word and deed that neither détente, nor any other principle of diplomacy practiced towards superpowers, conflicts with the demands of Soviet doctrine, particularly where the latter applies to the third world and its "national liberation" struggles.

Throughout the third world, the Soviets have encouraged the diverse and decentralized ideological centers of radicalism—from Havana to Algiers, from Hanoi to Conakry—to recruit allies and to reinforce the nascent radicalism of other states. They have not bothered much about the masses, ironically, concentrating instead on the leaders. They have captured the semantic symbols of competition: the "progressive" states, all totalitarian and usually retrograde economically, are those states joined in their cause who call for the "liberation" of Puerto Rico but not the liberation of the Tsarist-Soviet Asian or European colonies. Their most potent weapon in the third world has been the Leninist prescription to leaders to maximize power. It became a vastly convenient label for doing what had become quite natural—doing away with opponents, capturing the "commanding heights" of the economy (for furthering party or personal interests),[5] and ensconcing themselves permanently in power until the next "radical" leader can muster a bigger part of the army.

Ideology, used skillfully, economizes on the use of force and can make the use of tanks, for example, almost unnecessary—though, as seen in the case of Angola, tanks can be quite useful both as a way of increasing the price of a Western response and as real instruments of war.

Meantime, American intellectuals have declared an "end of ideology," and fashionable journalists—as if it followed logically—have unilaterally proclaimed the death of the cold war. For détente was always a popular notion in America as it was supposed to encompass an end to the very notion of ideology, something which has always been anathema to pragmatic Americans. The problem is that American interests are diverse throughout the world; few of them are *intrinsically* worth the risk of war. To take even a fairly substantial example, the notion that American marines should fight over Middle Eastern oil can well be considered crass. Yet it is difficult to see how the issue of oil can be separated from the greater issue of European and Japanese economic prosperity and ultimately—if one considers that the health of American institutions depends at least in part on Europe and Japan—of the survival of Western institutions. And the abandonment of what little doctrinal coherence exists in American foreign policy becomes a signal for a piecemeal surrender throughout the globe—because then the parts are not seen to be an intrinsic part of a greater whole. It is in such doctrine that the interrelationship of Western interests and institutions is demonstrated.

The West, in effect, conceded the real competition in the third world before the engagement. Thanks to the shrewd Soviet manipulation of slogans and timely association with third-world goals, an asymmetrical set of assumptions was accepted about the rules of the game. The Soviets could champion the cause of the independence of French, British, and Portuguese colonies, and then work to bring the newly independent and weak states either into their orbit or at least out of the western orbit and into the so-called nonaligned world. It could then work to affect the definition of nonalignment until such came to mean, as it has, "nonaligned against the West," as several members are explicit Soviet allies and many are implicit allies.[6]

But the West was not allowed, and did not ask, to work openly and outrightly for the independence of the Soviet-dominated countries— neither for the satellites in Eastern Europe, nor for the fully independent prizes along the Baltic captured in 1940, much less for the Tsarist colonies of Central Asia acquired at much the same time as those of the French and British in Africa. Yet the differences between these colonies and those of the West hardly reflect well on the Russians: whereas the British and French had, to a great extent, acquired their dependencies peaceably, the Tsars had acquired—and the Soviets had maintained— their territories forcibly; and whereas the Western Europeans have engaged in a not always successful attempt to fashion nation-states out of peoples, the Soviets have attempted to Russify their colonies and thus to destroy states clearly on the path of nation formation.

Only in late 1975 was it finally said in the West that the Soviet Union should not be allowed to have it both ways—that it could not have détente with the United States while mounting such interventions as that in Angola. This became a marginally important slogan in American politics in 1976; but it was a little late, coming as it did at the end of a twelve- month period in which the Indochinese wars were lost to Communist (Moscow-supplied) forces, in which Angola was won by Soviet-financed forces, and in which a core ally, the Portugese Communist party, nearly captured power in the capital of a NATO (North Atlantic Treaty Organi- zation) member.[7] In effect, the concept of détente had simply picked up where a one-sided anticolonialism had left off.

LEARNING FROM PAST MISTAKES

However much ideology has been a general guide, Soviet tactics in the projection of its power have been flexible. The Soviets have been able to learn lessons from their failures, and—like serious people and states every- where—they have been patient and content to accumulate small gains at a time.

Many Western observers of recent Soviet moves have taken comfort from the evident problems the Soviets have faced—some caused by in- herent obstacles in the areas involved, some by the very manner and style of Soviet involvement. These optimistic analysts see in Soviet problems the hope that the Soviets will fare no better than the United States in imposing their own image of the world in these warm climes. That misses the point. The Soviets have had and will continue to have difficulties. But the United States retreated from failure, pretending that the game in which it had engaged and taken so seriously—in Southeast Asia—never really was very important; and it then proceeded to suppress the memories and every attempt to learn from its mistakes. The Soviet Union, in contrast, seems willing and able not only to learn from its own mistakes but to profit from our thirty years of successes and failures in constructing and sustaining an international system. Some examples from Africa—the most current arena of Soviet expansion—are pertinent, if still not equal to the Middle East and South Asia in long-term importance to Moscow.

Take Guinea. In the aftermath of the punitive French withdrawal from Conakry after the colony's rejection of the *Communauté* in 1958, the Soviets moved swiftly to establish relations with the strident regime of West Africa's *enfant terrible*, Sékou Touré. In little more than two years, however, the Soviets were in trouble. Their very senior ambassador, Solod, who had moved to Conakry from Cairo as a signal of Moscow's growing interest in the radical West African state, was invited to leave at the end of 1961 owing to his purported involvement in a plot against the regime. The payoff for the West came a lear later, when Guinea turned down the Soviet request for staging privileges for their (missile-laden) planes en route to Cuba. This strategic loss for Moscow was caused by its own mistakes, compounded by further tactical errors in the mid-1960s.

But the "revolutionary" movement of the third world did not die. Radicalism was sustained in Guinea by Cuba, North Vietnam, and other radical states. When a Portuguese attack on Conakry in 1970 showed the utterly vulnerable (and pitiful) state of the regime, Sékou Touré had nowhere to turn for help; whereupon the Soviets established a naval *cordon* for him in return for access and privileges greater than those requested eight years earlier. By 1975 Conakry had become an ideal staging post for intervention in Angola: cruisers, oilers, destroyers, landing ships, intelligence-collection ships were stationed there and deployed as needed to the coast of Angola. Guinea's leaders, the same group as at independence (minus those hanged along the way), played an important role in pressing other African leaders to join the bandwagon of their Angolan ally, the MPLA (Angolan Popular Liberation Movement), in the name of anti-racism. They had found the Soviets to be indispensable: ultimately a state as radical and threatening to its regional system as was Guinea needed the protection of a great power. The Soviets thus confirmed that they could trade strategic privileges off against the protection they supplied to a "nonaligned" regime and against the flattery to its sensibilities.

In Ghana, they learned another sort of lesson. There, the cost of establishing an intimate relationship—one that was superficial with the leadership and counterproductive with the populace—was greater than in Guinea; after Kwame Nkrumah's overthrow in 1966 more than a thousand Soviet technicians, teachers, and spies were expelled. They have not been invited back en masse, though technical teams recently returned to check on the possibility of completing projects abandoned earlier, at the same time that the regime in Accra rehabilitated Nkrumah's memory.

In fact the Soviets anticipated their own problem, showing how steep was their learning curve in this period of rapid expansion. In 1965 the Soviets attempted to change precisely those features of Nkrumah's regime which led to his overthrow a year later—the "cult of the personality," the economic mess, and so forth. They were in too deep to get out in time and they paid a heavy price for their ephemeral accomplishments.

But again they learned quickly. At a conference of African Communists in Cairo their spokesmen articulated the problem: the Soviets had tried to get a "quick fix," a profitable relationship without homework, without an underlying base, without the structures for making relations between Communist and tropical dual economies feasible. Thereafter the Soviets eschewed opportunities for fashionable relationships, except where short-term goals were sought, and concentrated on those of potentially enduring significance. They sustained regimes dedicated to Marxism-Leninism, of which there were a growing number in Asia and Africa, and they conducted the normal form of opportunistic diplomacy used by all powers with whatever regimes had large weight to bear on regional affairs: hence their cultivation and support of Nigeria during that state's civil war. The payoff came in 1975 when Nigeria played a leading role in obtaining recognition for the MPLA regime in Angola and in "legitimizing" not only Cuban intervention but the notion of a long-term Cuban occupation.

The Soviet regime has always had greater flexibility in dealing with a broad spectrum of groups—whether liberation movements, political parties, or established governments—than has the U.S.; now it has learned how to shift support swiftly from groups on one part of the spectrum to groups on another, in light of the Soviet estimate of the group's ability to further Moscow's interests. For example, in 1961, after a steadily increasing warmth in relations with Ghana, Moscow established a secret camp there for the training of radical insurgents—"freedom fighters" or assassins, depending on one's vantage point. Yet within several months the camp was closed; and the Ghanaians received no further help of this sort until the next year when the Chinese, with fewer "established" friends to offend in the region, picked up where the Russians had left off.[8]

What had happened? The Soviets had sized up the potential of the human material with which they were working and found it wanting. "When treason doth prosper, none dare call it treason." Support some clever insurgents who succeed, and Soviet interests are advanced; should treason fail, not only do the commandos lose their heads, but Soviet interests are damaged at a time when Moscow seeks respectability in Africa. In the mid-1960s Moscow was trying to widen its formal state-to-state relations in the third world to encompass such symbolic capitals of the political status quo—and, ironically, of dynamic economic growth—as the Ivory Coast and Nigeria.

Given the depth and background of Soviet ties that had accumulated in Africa it is a wonder that so many Americans were shocked when a division of Cuban troops—dispatched in September 1975 before the withdrawal of the Portuguese army, and encouraged, financed, and advised by their Russian allies—was able to defeat its more numerous and more broadly based Angolan adversaries in two militarily breathtaking months. However tenuous the Soviet and Cuban hold may be in the long run— and it is by no means clear that the UNITA (National Union for Total Independence of Angola) forces in Southern Angola cannot attempt a comeback—the Communist forces have established a vastly important beachhead for the short- and medium-term future.

Angola marks a new high-water mark of Soviet influence in the third world. The Soviets' approach to that conflict built on and used all the accumulated advantage they had in Africa, and added a new one: the escalation of weaponry. It was the 122mm artillery that proved decisive in the conflict. There was also a background of relations with a local Marxist party through which to establish ideological legitimacy; there was the issue of racism on which they could fasten their crusade; and there was the presence, both in Angola and in the two neighboring states of Zaïre and Zambia, of great reserves of natural resources of vast importance to the Western alliance. Though a modest task force from the Sixth Fleet could have sent it scurrying, the Soviet naval group that operated between Conakry and Luanda became the symbol of Soviet aid to potential allies. None of this even constituted a risk on Moscow's part, given the state of opinion in the United States and the furtiveness of the policy fashioned in the State Department to counteract it. Short-term benefits were immediately apparent: there was the embarrassing deference paid to Fidel Castro by the Canadian prime minister on an official visit to Cuba; more significant, despite his admiration of China and its brand of communism, President Samora Machel of Mozambique in effect opted for Moscow over Peking in the contest of those two powers for premier Communist position in southern Africa.[9]

The pattern in Africa is not isolated. Beyond the borders of Europe maneuver the Soviets and their surrogates—whether Cuban, North Korean, or East German—in South Yemen as in Laos, in Guyana as in Equatorial Guinea, and in Somalia as in Angola. All the familiar tactics of imperial power are now present, even to the gunboats that have appeared in the harbors of Ghana and Libya to intimidate the regime or in those of Guinea and Somalia to intimidate its opponents.

PROJECTION AT THE MARGINS

So the projection of Soviet power and the expansion of the Soviet alliance system have proceded step by step; the Soviets have retreated where necessary, learning always, always persisting, and building exponentially on consolidated gains of the past. The linkage and parallel with the central strategic level can also be seen. "What in the name of God can you do with strategic superiority," the American Secretary of State laments. The response is easy, and it is the lesson of this essay: you project it at the margins. The strategically superior state has enough power left over at the center to provide for the protection (or intimidation) of states at the margin of its previous realm of influence. The same is true at the conventional level: power is projected geographically at the intersection of previously established spheres of influence; and the local power, sensing the change in the balance, alters its behavior accordingly.

There are two extremes on the spectrum of accommodation. At one end, a rare, overt (but superficial) change can occur overnight. In Zambia, the government-directed press, once the defeat of its allies in the Angolan civil war was seen to be irreversible, simply switched the target of its hyperbolic attacks from one side to the other. Having berated the Cubans, the Soviets, and everyone else supporting the MPLA on a daily basis, the Times of Zambia on 13 February 1976 suddenly praised the Cubans and urged them to continue their war of liberation southward. Less dramatic accommodations, taking place after important events, are more familiar—as in the behavior of the non-Communist Southeast Asian states after the dominoes of Indochina fell in 1975. As insurgencies heat up in Thailand and Malaysia, one can presumably expect an intensified struggle between factions of the left and right, further destabilizing the state, as has been happening in Bangkok. Unless those states can elicit great-power support more firm than that of the past, or summon a stronger resolve in themselves, they must accommodate to a Communist power in the region.

More interesting in many ways—and in the long run most important—is the subtle change occurring almost imperceptibly as a result of strategic and conventional shifts in the global balance. Take Turkey, a member of the Atlantic alliance, whose superior power compensated in Ankara's defense calculus for the proximity of the Soviet Union; NATO was its preferred association for reasons of history and political aspirations. Turkey was beyond the margins of the projection of Soviet power, but Moscow cultivated good relations to ensure innocent passage through the straits and in hope of a new strategic balance. As late as 1967 the Turks relented to strong American pressure and did not invade Cyprus to protect the harassed Turkish community there. But as Western capabilities declined in the 1970s the Turks were not only unsusceptible to American pressure in a similar crisis, but were willing to jeopardize the entire American strategic posture toward Russia by closing the American bases in Turkey and by demanding a high price for their reopening.

Few have understood the magnitude of the stakes: no bases have greater importance to us than those in Turkey. The incident occurred because of a change in the balance of power. At best, the Turkish-American relationship will never again be the same; more realistically, Soviet-Turkish relations will improve further while the ability of the West to use Turkish facilities or air space will decline. Such signs as the recent visit of the Turkish Vice Chief of Staff of the Armed Forces to the Soviet Union, or the incredible fact that Turkey was the recipient last year of the largest single grant of Soviet economic aid for the year, are hardly encouraging. Not to put too fine a point on it, the Soviets are out to detach Turkey from NATO. Their first sign of success came in mid-1976 with the illegal passage through the Turkish straits of their new carrier, the *Kiev*, something forbidden by the Montreux convention—and unprotested by Ankara.

THE LOGIC OF WITHDRAWAL

A comparison of Soviet and American capabilities to project power beyond their existing confines and to sustain a worldwide system of alliances ends with the United States in a substantial lead. From most vantage points, the American preeminence is in orders of magnitude. If the Soviets have launched their first carrier, it is less than half the tonnage of the Nimitz-class carriers, and our navy has thirteen. If the Soviets have established impressive facilities in Somalia and Cuba, they are only a fraction of the size of American facilities in the Philippines or Japan.

But is this relevant? One must consider the question in light of our contrasting strategic objectives. America is an island nation and must control the seas in order to protect its far-flung allies and find its markets. The Soviet Union is a great continental land mass, needing only to disrupt our lines of communication to disrupt our system. We are dependent on other countries for a dozen critical minerals; the Soviets depend on none. They are more or less self-sufficient in oil reserves and, with a command economy, they can adjust their consumption more or less at will.

Two other factors vitiate the apparent American advantage: theater capabilities and momentum. We in the West have been the possessors, with the goods that others want. To disrupt our network, the Soviets only have to build up their forces near the Soviet homeland—the Persian Gulf and Western Europe, the two areas absolutely vital to the U.S.-led community. And there are significant differences in our capability to project force in each area.

In Europe, the simple asymmetry of forces is too widely known to need repetition here. General Johannes Steinhoff, the former chairman of the NATO Military Committee, is only one of many to issue dire warnings of NATO's fate in the event of Russian attack; in his words the fighting would last "at most for a few days." Other equally eminent authorities have predicted that Russia would need only ten days to reach the channel. Less widely noted is that the whole Soviet ability to project power anywhere has been well exercised in Europe. The Warsaw Pact has no problem with weapons standardization, yet NATO commanders cannot even talk to each other over secure phone lines because of the dozens of different communications systems used. Warsaw Pact transport, communications, and logistical systems are all geared for Russian intervention, as the Czech case showed so clearly in 1968.[10] Add the growing Soviet capability in chemical and biological warfare, and Moscow poses a formidable threat indeed to Western Europe.

The growth of Communist parties in Italy, France, and Spain compounds the problem. Even assuming that the Italian Communist Party's conversion to democracy is genuine—as is substantially justified by its history and present practice—the problem is that NATO must alter its strategy to satisfy that party (let alone protect its own security) if a *compromisso historico* occurs in Rome. Meantime the rest of Europe would be demoralized by such Communist gains, and Communist parties in France and Spain, where unreconstructed hard-line Moscow loyalists lurk just below the fashionably flexible top line of the leadership, would be the immediate beneficiary.

The other area is the Persian Gulf. The dependence, directly or indirectly, of Europe and Japan (and, increasingly, the United States) on oil from this critical region is virtually absolute and has been so well described elsewhere as to render further emphasis on the region's import unnecessary. Less well known is the extent to which the Soviets have ensconced themselves in a manner that enlarges their control over the egress of gulf oil to Europe and the United States at a time of crisis. Prior to the 1973 war the Soviet willingness to play "oil politics" was doubted in almost all U.S. government circles, and the handful of senior officials who dissented were considered foolish. Almost no one bothered to ask what the Soviet motive was in establishing, at such enormous cost and time, their new positions of influence at *every* critical geographic point of the region: substantial arms deals with Somalia starting in 1969, arming of the Yemeni republicans in the mid-1960s, and the buildup of naval task force tours in the Indian Ocean in the same period.

Western analysts also seemed too impressed by American lift capability. When one calculated the tonnage of net capability available to either side in the mid-1970s, the Americans were shown to be clearly ahead despite their much greater distance from the theater. Our C5As made it *theoretically* possible for us to project more tangible power into the gulf than could the Soviets. Yet such calculations did not take into account Soviet violations of Iranian air space or the possibility of transit across Turkey. They did not take into account the Soviet ability to preposition matériel in the region; and they did not take into account the fact that in a crisis the Soviets would have a firm base in Somalia from which to operate, while American allies (as in 1973) would be too terrified to extend anything more than minimal facilities, if any, to Washington. The gulf, moreover, is little more than four hundred miles across from the Caspian Sea, where in a crisis the Soviets could build up the visible signs of power for psychological effect. Whatever these imponderables added up to, no calculation could give the United States a net lift advantage in 1980, by which time a much enlarged fleet of Soviet Antonov Cock 22s would be in operation.[11]

Momentum has a small and large dimension. The small one is simply what has happened to American projection capabilities abroad. In the past decade, from Wheelus in Libya to Cam Ranh Bay in South Vietnam, literally hundreds of U.S. bases have been closed or surrendered for reasons ranging from "managerial efficiency"—because facilities could be duplicated and consolidated elsewhere—to ignominious military defeat. It is not that the loss of any single base has been crucial, but that the closure of each has removed an *interconnecting link* from a system; and the function of interconnection is often more important than the ostensible primary function of the base itself. Once the process of closure and decline begins and the investigation is undertaken of each individual base function, it is easy to demonstrate the dispensability of any single base. If a great power has a declining purpose, a declining function, and a perceived declining need, then it is possible to justify the closure of any facility.

The case of Thailand is interesting in this regard. Few things seemed so crucial to American policymakers in the 1960s as access to the great Thai bases constructed at the height of Thai-American cooperation in the Vietnamese war. Expansion was its own justification. As that war wound down, retention of the bases in Thailand as the trump card against Hanoi became even more important. By the autumn of 1974 policymakers were looking to the long-term relevance of the bases, whether or not non-Communist Vietnam survived. The October 1973 war in the Middle East had made America's international vulnerabilities clear. Access to the Persian Gulf, it came to be seen, might only be available through the back door—that is, by way of the Pacific—and the Thai bases were necessary stepping stones between Subic Bay and Diego Garcia for such access. But once Vietnam was lost, the desire to hold onto the Thai bases declined even faster than the withdrawal of our troops proceeded.

Withdrawal became its own justification. In the absence of any real pressure within the bureaucracy to retain the bases, the typical ideosyncratic factors that drive decision making—ambition, preoccupation with other matters, lame-duck status, or whatever—can win out, as they did in this case. With no will behind the negotiators, the lawyers could of course do their work. The final position was ironic. Even shortly before the end of negotiations, the official wisdom was that the bases were indispensable and that virtually all of the four thousand troops there were useful. But once the negotiations had collapsed that position became untenable; it could be argued that there was no special reason why so many troops were needed and that, no matter what, we would not go back to the *status quo ante*. The logic of withdrawal had created a new legitimacy. On 14 July 1976 the last American soldiers departed from Bangkok.

On the larger level, momentum also is critical. In either direction, up or down, momentum creates a justification for the expanding or contracting party. For the Soviet Union, with its new military muscle, the tendency is strong to see new facilities and alliances as natural; strategic need is the rationale of every expansion. "Why shouldn't they have bases in the Middle East or in Africa, now that they have a blue-water navy?" it is asked. Why not indeed, unless it is because it is against something so mundane and self-serving as the American interest. And by the same token, as one hears so often these days, why should America have these cumbersome, entangling bases abroad, when it has so much overkill capability and so many unpleasant memories of trying to defend ungrateful and uncooperative allies? The reason of course is simple: because our interests cannot be separated from those of the rest of the non-Communist world. Already the logic of withdrawal has begun generating pessimism —even morbidity in some quarters, particularly European—about our fate; with this fate, the closing of an American intelligence-collection base in Thailand is ultimately as interconnected as is the addition to the Soviet system of a new tender in Conakry harbor.

The creation of a Soviet international system has proceeded much further than is generally realized. The shift in the strategic balance, the conventional buildup at the margins, the adventitious and often fortuitous overlap of Soviet and third-world interests on the issues of "Zionism" and racism, not to mention the accumulation of personal power in these fragile states, have all played their part. No factor, however, has been so important as the collapse of Western will.

A fragile consensus appears to have been rebuilt in the U.S. Congress for maintaining military inventories, which hitherto had been run down in proportion to their prescribed levels as never before in the nation's history. World order, however, is not sustained merely by inventories. It is sustained by a willingness to use them—which the consensus has not moved to recognize. The collapse of will has resulted from the critical failure of Western elites even to recognize the problem and to see the imminence of its consequences. Knowledge here is a vital first step, lest the owl of Minerva once again come at dusk.

NOTES

1. It is interesting to note that Communist states have tended not to join the Western international organizations (though there is some correlation between their degree of radicalism and their willingness to join such), and where they have, as at the UN, they have used their veto power—or their power more generally to obstruct —quite liberally. This is incomprehensible in terms of the inherent conflict between

Communist interests and those of the new institutions as then constituted. By the same token, U.S. vetoes did not become a feature of its UN diplomacy until the conflict between its interests and those of the majority of UN members on many issues had become irreconcilable.

2. A point made by Mr. Avigdor Haselkorn. See also Avigdor Haselkorn, "The Soviet Collective Security System," *ORBIS* 19, no. 1 (Spring 1975):231–54. I am grateful to Mr. Haselkorn for his helpful comments on a draft of this article.

3. Whether such could happen in the other two pertinent theaters, Korea and Western Europe, is a matter of conjecture, as little serious study of it has been undertaken. One person who was concerned about precisely such replication was former Secretary of Defense James Schlesinger, who was fired before the appropriate studies could be undertaken. See also W. Scott Thompson, "Indochinese Debacle and the United States," *ORBIS* 19, no. 3 (Summer 1975):990–1011.

4. Coming so soon after the Guillaume affair, prudence was particularly pertinent for the Soviets, a point I owe to Professor Robert Legvold.

5. Thus Conor Cruise O'Brien has written in an article in the *New Statesman* 70 (30 Dec. 1965), pp. 879–80, of "party demagogues" in Ghana "often with socialist slogans in their mouths and contractors' money in their pockets."

6. It is interesting to note that Vietnam, North Korea, and Cuba were all invited to the nonaligned conference at Colombo, Sri Lanka, in August 1976. Consider also the headline of a recent advertisement in the *New York Times* (1 February 1976): "The Non-Alignment Movement is a Mighty Anti-Imperialist Revolutionary Force of Our Times," by Kim Il Sung.

7. One should recall how fervently it was argued in some circles at the time that the Portuguese Communists would not attempt to seize power. For a retrospective view, see David Binder, "Lisbon Aide Tells of Communist Bid," *New York Times*, 6 June 1976.

8. See W. Scott Thompson, *Ghana's Foreign Policy, 1957–1966* (Princeton: Princeton University Press, 1969).

9. Colin Legum, the distinguished student of African affairs, argues that most analyses of conflict in southern Africa underestimate the import of USSR–PRC competition as a motive for Soviet involvement. It is hard to see what comfort such an argument offers. See Colin Legum, "The Soviet Union, China and the West in Southern Africa," *Foreign Affairs* 34, no. 4 (July 1976):745–62.

10. See William Schneider, Jr., "General Purpose Forces: Army and Air Force," in *Arms, Men and Military Budgets: Issues for Fiscal Year 1977*, edited by William Schneider, Jr., and Francis P. Hoeber (New York: Crane, Russak and Company, 1976).

11. For a description of the AN–22, see *Air Force Magazine* 59, no. 3 (March 1976).

3

WALTER Z. LAQUEUR

America and West European Communism

Communism in Western Europe will be one of the central issues facing U.S. foreign policy in the years to come, perhaps the most important issue. The question of what U.S. policy should be towards West European countries ruled by coalitions in which Communists are represented has already become a major bone of contention. At present the controversy centers on Italy; in 1978 it could be France; and in a longer perspective, Spain and perhaps Greece.

To understand the issues, one must be aware of recent ideological pronouncements made by the European Communist parties. The new slogans popularized in 1976 after the last congress of the French Communist party "sound positively Jeffersonian" to the *Washington Post*, which adds: "It is poor taste to jeer at other people's sudden conversion." This is very true, provided, of course, we face a genuine conversion and not the first exhibition of a "new look" at a political fashion show. It is most important to ask to what extent—if at all—we can take these declarations at face value and, above all, to ponder what the Communist parties will do once they join a governing coalition.

IDEOLOGICAL DIVISIONS IN
EUROPEAN COMMUNISM

It is well known that ideological differences exist between the European
Communists and the Russians. The Russians regard the dictatorship of the
proletariat as the "supreme form of democracy," while the Italians and
French—to Moscow's chagrin—have dropped the concept. The Russians
stress proletarian internationalism—meaning obedience to Moscow—
whereas the Italians emphasize "critical solidarity," and the French, at
their recent party congress, proclaimed *socialisme aux couleurs de la
France*. The Spanish have declared that the old style internationalism is
dead altogether and that they alone will be responsible for the "Spanish
march to socialism."

According to Santiago Carillo, socialism in Western Europe and the
USSR are bound to be different because of Europe's different—meaning
more democratic—historical tradition; this, he said, "is not a question of
tactics and propaganda." The Italian and Spanish Communists do not
oppose the EEC (European Economic Community) and they have even
modified their attitude towards NATO. Only a few years ago they said
that NATO had to be fought to destroy the Western alliance and liberate
Europe from U.S. hegemony. More recently they have taken the position
that the dissolution of power blocs could not possibly be the precondition, only the result, of détente; and meanwhile there should be no rever-
sals of alliances. Again, to quote Carillo: "One day the Americans will
leave Spain, but this should be envisaged only when the Russians withdraw from Czechoslovakia."

Above all, Western Communists have emphasized their devotion to
democratic values. According to George Marchais, present head of the
French Communist party, neither democracy nor liberty can exist without
a plurality of political parties and freedom of speech. The economic and
social programs of the Western Communist parties are anything but
revolutionary. The Italians do not insist on immediate large-scale nationalization, which may not be surprising since about half of Italy's major
industries now belong to the state anyway. The French Socialists' program in some respects is more radical than that of the Communists, and
the same is true of the Spanish Socialists.

All these developments are very interesting. They would be even more
reassuring if they were not repeat performances. When the French Communists entered the Popular Front in the 1930s, and again in 1945, they
were very discreet about the dictatorship of the proletariat. In 1946

Maurice Thorez, in an interview with *The Times* (London), announced that France would not follow the Russian road to socialism, but that the French people, "rich in glorious tradition," would find its own way. However, the glorious traditions did not prevent the West European Communists from embracing Stalinism again soon after.

There is no denying that the Communist parties have learned from past mistakes; they have undoubtedly become more modern and more pragmatic in their approach. But they have not become more democratic, and it is difficult to imagine that parties still strictly authoritarian in their structure could possibly be guardians of liberty in national politics. When Carillo was asked in a recent interview what differences remained between his party and the Social Democrats in view of the doctrinal changes, he answered quite truthfully that in the final analysis his party was Leninist. This is of course the crux of the matter: thus far there exists no known case of a Leninist party transforming to democratic socialism. Great hopes were put on Yugoslavia in the mid-1950s, but it has not become more liberal in the last two decades. Internal control and repression in Rumania is as stringent as in the Soviet Union. If there was any relaxation in French communism, it took place under Waldeck-Rochet rather than under Marchais. If the Italian party has become more liberal and democratic from Togliatti to Berlinguer, the progress is hardly visible to the naked eye. True, three or four different trends (*correnti*) have appeared in the Italian party since the early 1960s, but such factions also existed in the Soviet party before Stalin and, for all one knows, may exist even now.

Nor is the meaning of the doctrinal innovations at all clear. The Russians, to do them justice, have never insisted that other Communist parties should "slavishly imitate" the Russian pattern. They have always conceded at least in theory that "national peculiarities" should be taken into account. But they have stressed even more forcefully that all Communist parties must learn from the Soviet experience gained in the progress towards socialism. The question whether the "national peculiarities" or the "Soviet lessons" are more important has thus been left open.

Having dropped the concept of the dictatorship of the proletariat, the French have replaced it with a new notion—the "hegemony of the working class"—and it may take much semantic effort to sort out the differences. The Italians have vowed their attachment to pluralism; yet Gian Carlo Pajetta, one of their more enlightened leaders, in an anticlimactic mood praised the multiparty systems of East Germany and Poland. (Only specialists will recall that in these countries, as in Czechoslovakia and Hungary, three or four "non-Communist" parties exist to this day—with political influence roughly comparable to that of the foreign ministry of the White Russian Soviet Republic.) Even Santiago Carillo has declared that while his party should remain in the *Junta Democratica*, everyone will go his own way once the immediate objectives are reached, and that today's friends will be tomorrow's enemies. The Italian Communists have expressed warm support for European cooperation—very much in contrast to the French, who, in early 1976, bitterly attacked the Polish prime minister for praising the EEC. But even the Italians have said that they would like to transform the "small" into a "big" Europe, with a neutral position between East and West, and that it should ultimately become a regional economic organization within the U.N. (Amendola).

In view of these and many other ambiguities, the question invariably arises whether Western observers, forever in search of the cloud's silver lining, have not overrated the significance of recent ideological changes. It is impossible to give a clear answer, partly because Communist statements have been contradictory, partly because conditions vary from country to country. The French party is the most orthodox and its foreign policy is still by and large dictated by Moscow—except on rare occasions when it is angered by what it considers excessive Soviet professions of friendship towards the French government. The Italians are more independent; they find little to admire in the Soviet system and comments made in private by some of their leaders have been very outspoken indeed.

The Spanish are even more extreme in this respect. Carillo once said that if Russia were to attack Spain as it had attacked Czechoslovakia, he would not hesitate for a moment to give the order to resist. Up to the late 1950s the Spanish party was quite orthodox (it opposed, for instance, Khrushchev's conciliatory policy vis-à-vis Czechoslovakia). But more and more it came to resent the overbearing attitude of the Russians, who on frequent occasions impressed on the Spanish comrades that their own views hardly counted since they were a small and uninfluential party. The Spanish were the first to become *pluripartistas*, whereupon the Russians tried to split the PCE, which did not improve relations between the two parties either.

Italy

It is true that the Italian Communists (like the French and Spanish) no more want Soviet bases on Italian soil than they want a repetition of the recent earthquake; and there would be no dancing in the streets of Rome and Milan if Moscow regained its foothold in Yugoslavia and Albania. If Italy were isolated from the storms of the world politics, it is not inconceivable that over a long period the Communist party there would develop toward democratic socialism and adhere to the ground rules of democracy, which prescribe that a party defeated in free elections has to accept the popular verdict.

But the Italian party of today is not yet such a party; there is no reason to assume it would use its influence in government to strengthen democracy. Moreover, Italy happens to be located on the critical southern flank of NATO. It has been argued that an Italian government with Communist participation may well pursue Italian interests more forcefully; however, this is about the last thing that is needed at a time when little if any momentum remains in the movement towards European political cooperation. At best, the Communists would perpetuate this stagnation; more likely, they would undermine the fragile balance of power which at present constitutes the sole guarantee of Europe's relative immunity to Soviet pressure.

When Berlinguer talked about the "iron link" uniting the Communist party of Italy with the Soviet Union and when he proclaimed that those who expect a "break between us and the Soviet Union will forever be disappointed," he merely expressed the political exigencies of Italy's domestic and foreign situation. Internally, despite all its reservations, the legitimacy of the Communist party rests on the social connection; a break would split the party, in part because the rank and file are considerably more fundamentalist in their political convictions than the leadership. (This explains the apparent paradox that the erstwhile "right wing" critics of the Soviet Union, such as Amendola and Pajetta, are now much more restrained in their approach—in contrast to Ingrao, head of the left wing faction, who is more outspoken vis-à-vis the senior partner in the Communist camp.)

The Italians will need the backing of the Communist camp in the years to come in view of the difficulties facing them. The Communists now rule all major Italian cities, but it is not at all clear whether they will be able to cope with the enormous problems facing them. Naples has 140,000 unemployed and Milan 80,000, and the municipal deficits of these cities are almost on the New York scale, ranging from 1 to 1.5 billion *lire*.

If on the national level the Communists one day share responsibility with other parties, they must fear erosion of their mass support, which at present rests largely on protest against Christian Democratic misrule. Thus at some future date they may find themselves in an awkward position—under pressure by their right wing partners, outflanked on the left by extremist groups, forced to adopt more radical (and unpopular) measures which would be without mass support.

In short, the Italian crisis would not end once the Communists enter the government; it will simply be the beginning of a new, more complicated and severe stage in the crisis. These circumstances are unlikely to strengthen the democratic trend in Italian communism or to reduce its dependence on comrades abroad.

France

The relation of forces in France is of course altogether different. There is on the one hand the prospect of an electoral victory with the Socialists in 1978 on the basis of the *program commun*. But the French Communists are now junior partners in the alliance; unlike the Italians, they have been unable to break out of the working-class ghetto. Their share of the electorate has declined from 28 percent in 1946 to 20 percent or perhaps even less today, whereas the Socialist party has made an astonishing recovery in recent years. At the same time, the Socialists have far less cohesion and discipline than the Communists, and the attachment of their radical wing (*Comité d'études régionales et sociales* [CERES]) to parliamentary democracy is not above suspicion. Moreover, there is always the chance of a split, with a minority of Socialists joining forces with the Communists.

Although the non-Communist structures in Italy are in a state of decomposition, this is not so in France, where the democratic tradition is considerably stronger and not limited to political parties. Nor has the French Communist leadership shown a political acumen equal to that of their Italian comrades.

Spain

Predicting the fortunes of Spanish communism is difficult because everything depends on the outcome of the present struggle for power there. We have noted the moderation shown by the Spanish Communist leadership; but, as in Italy, the moderates are challenged by more radical elements among the rank and file, particularly in Catalonia and the Basque region. In recent months Spanish politics have witnessed both growing polarization between right-wing and leftist forces and an almost incredible fragmentation of parties, groups, and *groupuscules*. The country may move gradually towards a more liberal regime; but it could relapse as easily into anarchy, which would lead to some new form of dictatorship. The Communists' popular base is still relatively narrow, but they dominate the trade unions and have made considerable inroads among the intellectuals and the media.

AMERICAN ATTITUDES TOWARD EUROPEAN COMMUNISM

Much advice has been freely offered on how America should deal with the new offensive of West European communism. Some of the scenarios need not be taken seriously—for instance, the idea that the advance of Western communism could be highly beneficial since in historical perspective it is bound to strengthen the liberal trend in world communism and inside the Soviet Union. Needless to say, these trends will have no impact on the Soviet Union. It is possible but quite unlikely that the deviations of Western communism could influence some East European countries, forcing Soviet leaders again to be preoccupied with restoring order in their own backyard. On the other hand, whether this will necessarily limit their forward operations in other parts of the globe is a different question altogether.

In an interview with the Italian weekly *L'Espresso,* Professor Z. Brzezinski has argued that a new American government will interpret the recent changes in Europe as positive signs, not as symptoms of decadence and crisis. Writing in the *New York Times,* Mr. Z. Nagorski of the Council of Foreign Relations has claimed that a new Europe is emerging and that America is failing to adjust itself to it. Europe's democratic institutions, he says,

> require new concepts and new flexibility. They also need to be overhauled in view of the rising demands of highly developed, highly structured, highly stratified societies. . . . The new power levers are about to move that country [Italy] either away from us or closer to the Atlantic Alliance. . . . It is time to look toward the new European political and social requirements leading toward a different world.

The American proclivity to generalize about Europe as if it were like the United States—one country, one nation, one society—always leads to confusion. The problems facing Spain have nothing in common with those confronting Scandinavia. The present trend in Italy is to the left; in

Britain, West Germany, and Sweden it is to the right—or perhaps more correctly, to the center. It is regrettable, no doubt, that generalizations about Europe are invariably wrong; it is, in fact, part of the European problem. But it is meaningless to call for an American adjustment to the new European political and social requirements, when various parts of Europe are moving in different directions.

The same lack of specificity applies to the complaints that America has not shown sufficient sympathy for the forces of democratic socialism in Europe. Broadly speaking, the complaint is not true, except perhaps for the fact that Mrs. Thatcher was invited to the White House while M. Mitterand was not. On the other hand, U.S. relations with the Social Democrats in Bonn and London have always been closer than with right-of-center governments in Paris. In authoritarian countries it is not easy to be on equally good terms with government and opposition at the same time; even the Russians have found this out by trial and error. In any case, the problem facing the United States in Europe is not the need to refrain from showing favoritism in the confrontation between left and right; it is that some of those parties are nondemocratic and have Russian connections.

More specifically, it has been claimed that American intransigence toward the Italian Communists will drive them back into Moscow's arms and that sections of the Italian public and elite opinion, formerly pro-American, will be alienated. This may or may not be true; all that can be said is that past experience, paradoxically, seems to point the other way: American attitudes towards China in the 1950s were excessively hostile, but this did not prevent the Sino-Soviet split. With the possible exception of Albania, until 1948 the Western powers considered Yugoslavia the most hostile Soviet satellite, yet the Yugoslavian and Albanian leaders quarrelled with the Kremlin anyway. American sympathies for Castro, on the other hand, did not prevent rapid deterioration in Soviet-Cuban relations.

Warnings about the alienation of formerly pro-American sectors in Italian elite opinion more often emanate from New York and Washington than from Rome and Milan. Close observers of the Italian domestic scene such as Enzo Bettiza, editor of *Il Giornale Nuovo*, have declared that, on the contrary, Italian opinion leaders have been convinced by American newspapers like the *Washington Post* and the *New York Times* "that public opinion in the U.S. about the credibility of the Italian Communist Party has fundamentally changed." (In Mr. George Ball's interview with the weekly *Il Mondo:* "we cannot change a process that is now irreversible.") It is easy to imagine the effect of such a prediction at a time when the demand for postdated Communist party membership books has been on the increase anyway. Who wants to resist an inevitable and irresistible historical process?

It has been said quite rightly that Italy is first and foremost a European problem which would be far easier to solve if Europe were united. But Europe is not united, and it would be unrealistic to expect any major initiative from these quarters. On the contrary, Chancellor Schmidt's comments on the Italian situation have caused a minicrisis. The Italian Christian Democrats have resented the aspersions which the German chancellor should have cast specifically at the Italian Socialists, whose inability to provide a viable alternative to Christian Democratic rule is at the bottom of the present crisis.

The issue most frequently discussed is the future of Italy in NATO—and the future of NATO in general. It has been noted that Iceland remained in NATO even under a coalition which included the Communists, and that Communists are not in key positions related to national security. But Italy is not Iceland, and in the modern world few ministerial offices are not related to defense in one way or another. These include directly the ministries of foreign affairs, interior, and national defense, and of course the prime ministership. But the ministries of communication and industry are also sensitive positions and it is unlikely that a party as strong as the PCI would be satisfied with the department of health and social welfare if invited to join a government coalition.

The future of NATO depends of course on its functions. If one regards it as no more than a club or a trading company with limited liability, there are indeed no insurmountable difficulties ahead. But if it is to be a defense alliance based, as in the past, on the assumption that an attack against one is an attack against all—and if it is recalled that Italy, *inter alia,* is a member of the Nuclear Planning Group—then the complications become immediately apparent. It may be assumed that, even with a coalition comprising the Communists, Italy will still want to remain under the NATO umbrella; and if something untoward should happen to Yugoslavia the desire may become even stronger. But what active part will Italy play in the alliance? And to what extent will the other members of NATO trust its representatives?

Some commentators have argued all along that NATO may no longer be needed since détente is so deeply rooted, since military power does not really count in the modern world, and since the Soviet Union is so preoccupied with its East European allies. Those who maintained only recently that the danger of Finlandization in Europe was a figment of imagination now claim that, everything considered, Finland is not doing so badly after all. Others less remote from the realities of the European scene suggest the establishment of an inner and outer circle in NATO —with, say, Western Germany and Britain as the core and other countries more loosely associated. But the technical difficulties involved would be tremendous. Such a transformation would certainly weaken the alliance, and it would also again increase pressure in the U.S. for withdrawal of American troops from Europe. For even if a new Western European Communist power center should emerge as a counterweight against Soviet pressure—a most unlikely proposition in the foreseeable future—it may not be easy to persuade the citizens of Iowa or Colorado or New York that one kind of Communist bloc should be defended against another.

Lastly, it is argued that Italy is different, that Americans are too crude and ignorant to understand the intricacies of Italian politics, that they are unaccustomed to coalition governments and therefore fail to see the difference between a *putsch* and power sharing. This in a way is Kissinger's "gulliversation" concept, but it has not worked too well vis-à-vis the Soviet Union and Italy. The Italian Communists may be sucked into the quagmire of Italian intrigues, as so many well-meaning politicians before them; perhaps their élan will be wasted in the long battle of attrition facing them. There has always been something slightly suspect about Italian revolutionary heroes; as Carlyle told Mazzini—"you talk too much." Admirable in many respects, capable of heroic deeds and self-sacrifice, Italian revolutionaries have but seldom shown an equal measure of perseverance and hard work. However, the Italian Communists ought to be measured not by absolute standards, but against their present rivals, and at present the competition is not overwhelming.

Perhaps in time the Italian Communists will become pillars of democracy; perhaps their financial dependence on the Soviet Union will be reduced once they enter the government. We are advised, in short, to rely not so much on the moderation and liberal character of Italian communism, but on the changes that will set in once the party becomes part of the "system." Given the facts of Italian life—the civilized level of political intercourse on the one hand, the corrosive impact of intrigues and corruption on the other—such a possibility cannot be ruled out. But it is no more than a possibility; and it ought to be said immediately that whatever prospect exists in Italy, the chances for a development on similar lines in France or Spain—or indeed in any other European country—are minimal.

TRENDS AND PROSPECTS FOR AMERICAN POLICY

During the past year two different concepts have emerged in American policy toward West European communism. Dr. Kissinger articulated one of them in his London speech to the U.S. ambassadors in December 1975 —the line of conciliation towards the Soviet Union and harshness towards Communist parties in Western Europe. The concept has a certain logic, since détente rests on the existence of a given balance of power; and once the balance is upset in Western Europe, the political consequences can be easily foreseen.

Pierre Hassner and others have criticized this approach on both moral and pragmatic terms: isn't it paradoxical to regard the Soviet Union as a power like all others with which one can exercise a certain condominium, whilst considering the more liberal Italian communism as an incarnation of evil with which one must avoid all contact? Furthermore, they argue, this approach is unrealistic because America cannot control the situation in Italy and because change cannot be prevented anyway.

These arguments deserve serious consideration even though they tend to exaggerate the moment of inevitability. Dr. Kissinger's critics suggest greater vigilance vis-à-vis Soviet military power on the one hand and more tolerance and elasticity toward West European communism on the other. This presumably refers to showing less readiness to concede unilateral military advantages to the Soviet Union, either in the context of SALT II or with regard to the cruise missile or the transfer of technology that could be of military significance. To this extent the critique is of course perfectly justified; and under some pressure, it has influenced American policy of late.

But this does not offer a solution for the problems of NATO. The suggestions that the alliance be diversified both by task and region should certainly be explored, but we must be concerned that this may be no more than an elegant retreat, contributing little to the maintenance of the West-East balance.

The rise of communism in Italy may not have the domino effect that some have predicted. On the contrary, it could provide the salutary shock needed to galvanize other European countries into greater individual and collective efforts. In this regard, the French decision to build up their defenses may be a first straw in the wind. The Italian Communists, very much in contrast to their Portuguese comrades, will no doubt be on their best behavior in the months to come, in order to improve further their image as a democratic force at home and to maintain their responsibilities toward the other European Communist parties. But it will take much more to quiet the suspicions of Italy's neighbors.

Europe faces a crisis, but not every crisis is fatal. There may be coalition governments in the years to come in one or two West European governments in which the Communists will be represented. But there is nothing inevitable about this process, and through its continued military and political presence America certainly has the power to guarantee that the process will not be irreversible. In recent years American attitudes toward Europe have ignored the danger signals with a misplaced optimism which in retrospect was relatively harmless because it did not lead to any major political errors. The present swing toward defeatism is therefore psychologically understandable. But it should be resisted because it is again based on a misreading of the European situation and—above all—because it could lead to fatal mistakes of commission and omission in American foreign policy.

4

EUGENE V. ROSTOW

The Soviet Threat to Europe Through the Middle East

I

What used to be called "the Eastern Question" has bedeviled European politics for millennia. Long tides of war and diplomacy, from Salamis to Agadir, underscore the geopolitical importance of the Middle East to the security of Europe. The Ottoman empire was a difficult problem for Europe when Turkey was strong, and even more difficult when it was weak. In our time the oil, the people, and the space of the Middle East are more obviously a key to the control of Europe than at any previous point of history.

This view of the nature of things is deeply embedded in the Russian mind; for reasons of geography, it is more nearly self-evident to Russians than to Americans. And it has long been a critical element in Russian and now in Soviet foreign policy. The Czars never stopped pushing toward the Mediterranean and the Persian Gulf, as well as toward the Balkans, the Baltic, Korea, and Afghanistan; the nominal cause of the Crimean war, after all, was the unsettled condition of Palestine. Even before World War II was over, the Soviets tried to obtain a trusteeship for Libya from the Allies as they had sought a special position in Egypt and Iran from the Germans a few years before. The first skirmishes of the cold war concerned Iran, Turkey, Greece, and Yugoslavia. During the tempestuous struggle at the end of the British mandate for Palestine—culminating in the birth of Israel and Jordan and the first Arab-Israeli war of 1948–1949 —the Soviets gave indispensable assistance to Israel as a way to reduce British influence in the area and to enhance their own.

By the early 1950s Soviet policy in the Middle East had taken on an altogether different cast. It was no longer an almost absentminded matter of taking advantage of every opportunity for expansion—of "pushing at open doors," as the Russians say—but something far more formidable and ambitious.

During the immediate postwar years the Soviets were checked in Europe by effective Western help to Greece, Turkey, and Yugoslavia, the Berlin airlift, and the formation of NATO and the European Economic Community (EEC). Their riposte in Korea, which began in June 1950, was successfully resisted. In the age-old style of Russian diplomacy, they sought to flow around the obstacles and resume the struggle on another front.

The Soviet strategic goal in the West was and remains the control of Europe; for the Soviets to achieve that goal would transform the balance of power irreversibly in their favor and leave the United States isolated and vulnerable. If Western Europe should come under Soviet control, the lesson for China and Japan would be nearly compelling. The Atlantic Alliance is thus necessarily the first principle of modern American security policy, as was the Monroe Doctrine a century ago.

Starting in the 1950s the Soviets chose a Middle Eastern strategy as their principal means to the end of conquering Western Europe. They thought that by gaining a position of dominance in the Mediterranean, North Africa, and the Middle East, they could reduce Europe without even invading it—as they nearly did in 1973. It would be sufficient to use intimidation and threats, both directly and through the exploitation of the oil weapon.

Abandoning their 1947–1949 policy of support for Israel, the Soviets embraced Arab nationalism and began to intervene not only in the Arab-Israeli conflict, but in the iridescent rivalries among Arab sects, states, parties, and leaders as well. For twenty-five years, as the British, French, Belgian, and Portugese empires of the Middle East and Africa evaporated one after another, the Soviets have been clumping heavily into the vacuums they had often helped to create, sometimes gaining, sometimes losing—but always pressing forward in the confident pattern of a clear policy addressed to the long run.

Impelled by the traditional aspirations of the Czars and by the newer ambitions of their Communist ideology, the Soviets still live in the imperial mood of the eighteenth and nineteenth centuries—a mood which the Western nations have rejected with relief and conviction. Anyone interested in the relation between reality and the perceptions of reality that possess the human mind must wonder whether the Soviet government has yet discovered the fallacy in Lenin's theory of imperialism. Hobson and Lenin assumed that imperialism paid vast profits to the imperialist "exploiters." The Soviet Union is now discovering what Bentham and Norman Angell knew in the past—that imperialism is expensive, and that all the older imperial states had to subsidize their colonies on a large scale. One can readily imagine a Soviet statistician measuring the cost to the Soviet Union of its relation to Cuba, say, or to Egypt—and being sent to Siberia for heresy.

Always cautious and suspicious, and wary of surprises, the Russians have been taught by centuries of experience to respect the acuity of Britain, France, and Germany, and to fear China. And they have been impressed—nearly dazzled—by the recent history of the United States. Thus, as they expected, their early postwar probes were vigorously contained by the West, although they were allowed to take control of Eastern Europe—despite the agreements of Yalta and Potsdam—and to make gains in the Middle East, Africa, and East Asia.

But as time passed and the Soviets continued to test the possibilities for expansion in one soft spot after another, they discovered that the climate of opinion in the West was changing. In 1950 the idea of Western collective resistance to the attack on South Korea seemed obviously the wise and necessary course—a proper application of the lesson the nations should have learned from their failure to protect Ethiopia against Italy in 1935. But the long, bitter war in Korea became unpopular, and the longer and even more bitter war in Indochina became even more unpopular. Men in the West began to wonder if there were not some better way to protect their safety—some alternative to the concept of collective security that they could accept as the major premise of their foreign policy. While no one in the West has yet produced a rival principle for foreign policy, an agitated and emotional debate took place, seeming to weaken or reject the older view without replacing it. Public opinion and the public policy based on it became confused, uncertain, and finally paralyzed.

The Soviets found that the Western withdrawal from the principles of collective security embodied in the United Nations Charter showed signs of becoming a withdrawal from reality. Bored with war and riddled with guilt, the Western nations seemed to have stopped thinking about politics altogether, as they had done in the 1930s. What some Russians began to perceive as the final Marxist or Spenglerian decline of Western will and intelligence in the early 1970s created new and dramatic opportunities for them—opportunities for mutation rather than for incremental change—beyond the wildest dreams of the Czars. For a long time they could not bring themselves to believe that golden transformations on this scale had actually become feasible. But it was difficult even for prudent Russians to resist this hypothesis as they witnessed the reaction of the United States and Europe to the final stages of the Vietnam experience, and to its aftermath in the Middle East. Somewhere in the middle of 1973 the Soviets began to realize that the conjuncture of political circumstances is like that of 1914, 1917, 1936, and 1945—offering revolutionaries a chance to take a Great Leap Forward, seemingly without risk: if in retrospect the Kaiser and Hitler misjudged the opportunities open to them, this could not be said of Lenin, Stalin, or Mao.

II

To understand the intensification of the Soviet effort in the Middle East since the spring or summer of 1973, we must go back twenty years to the beginning of President Eisenhower's administration, when the Soviet Union began its new career as the champion of Arab nationalism. Nasser had come to power in Egypt following Egypt's defeat in 1948–1949 and the military coup which ended the monarchy in 1952. A new collective leadership was exercising authority in the Soviet Union after Stalin's death in 1953. The Korean war dragged on, accompanied by interminable negotiations to be finished, finally, at the Geneva Conference of 1954.

In the Middle East the basic military array of the early 1950s still seemed to be that of the placid prewar period. The appearance was an illusion, of course, but French and British forces were for the moment supreme in the area, backed by the American Sixth Fleet. France still controlled Morocco and Algeria, Britain guarded the Suez Canal, Aden, and a number of other key points, and there were no serious military establishments opposing the existing order. As late as 1958 Britain and the United States intervened without incident in Lebanon and Jordan, ending by their gesture a Soviet thrust for control of the region. A massive Soviet presence in the Mediterranean was for the future.

Britain, France, and the United States had issued a Tripartite Declaration in 1950 guaranteeing the political independence and territorial integrity of all the states in the area. They doled out arms to the newly independent Arab states and to Israel, in ways which were intended to minimize the fever of ambition and the danger of war. There were no other arms suppliers for the region until February 1955, when the Soviet Union finally succeeded in making a military aid agreement with Egypt. The Soviet-Egyptian agreement was soon followed by comparable agreements with Syria and Iraq, and later with Algeria, the smaller states of the Arabian peninsula, and then—much later—with Libya.

The diplomacy of the Soviet arms negotiation with Egypt in 1954 and 1955 has been discussed often, usually in terms of the mistakes John Foster Dulles is supposed to have made in rebuffing Egyptian requests for arms and in somehow mishandling the Aswan Dam negotiations. These criticisms—typical of American habits of self-reproach—miss the point. Nasser sought arms from the Soviet Union the moment the British left Suez in 1954 because he wanted to purchase military equipment on a scale which the United States, Britain, and France could not have approved. Dulles is often accused of having driven the Egyptians into the embrace of the Soviets by turning down an Egyptian request for American help in building the Aswan Dam. The exact opposite is the case. The United States had to reject the Aswan Dam project in October 1955 because the Egyptians had made an arms contract with the Soviets in February, and announced it in September. Either at that time or later one could not imagine Congress or the executive branch of the American government solemnly building a huge dam for Egypt while Egypt undertook campaigns of aggression in the area as a Soviet proxy, ally, and satellite.

Nasser's political goals were incompatible with a close and cooperative relationship with the United States and Western Europe. Nasser flatly refused to join in the American plan for a Middle Eastern alliance system to supplement NATO by containing the Soviet Union from the south. He sought the military means to fulfill his aspiration to become the leader of the Arab nation—and indeed the leader of the Muslim world—by taking over Lebanon, Jordan, and the weak states of the Persian Gulf and the Arabian peninsula. By dominating these important geographical positions and their oil resources, Egyptian control over Iran would finally be achieved. Above all Nasser wanted to destroy Israel and vindicate the Arab belief that the establishment of the Israeli state was an injustice to the Arab nation, beyond the rightful authority of the League of Nations and the United Nations.

Nasser and his fellow officers came to power in Egypt to avenge the Arab defeat in 1948–1949. That yearning was the passion which nurtured all the other passions of Nasser's Egypt: the Pan-Arabism; the soaring ambition; the ambiguous relationship with the Soviets, with the Chinese, and with his fellow members of the Club of the Non-Aligned—Nehru, Tito, Nkrumah, and Sukarno; and the long and costly campaign to conquer the Persian Gulf region via the Yemen, where 70,000 of his troops were hopelessly mired in 1967.

During the early 1950s Nasser led the Arabs in the strategy of refusing to recognize, negotiate, or make peace with Israel. In 1949 the Israelis would not stop fighting until Nasser agreed not only to a cease-fire, but to an armistice—and then, at a later stage, to peace. Fighting alone, without allies and with five divisions defeated and encircled, the Egyptians finally agreed to go to Rhodes, and did sign an armistice agreement with Israel—an event which permitted Jordan, Lebanon, and Syria to enter into comparable agreements.

The Arabs then made a remarkable discovery. The UN Security Council had ordered the Arabs to make peace with Israel and had set up a conciliation commission to facilitate the negotiation of peace. It had ruled that the armistice agreements of 1949 established a legal regime of "nonbelligerency" which would last until the parties made peace. Under those agreements, the Security Council ruled, the Arabs could not claim belligerent rights nor bar the Suez Canal to Israeli ships or shipping. In the early 1950s, however, the Arabs discovered that they could defy mandatory decisions of the Security Council without penalty. They were told in 1951 that they could not shut the Suez Canal to the Israelis. But they did, and nothing happened. They were told they had to make peace with Israel. They refused, insisted that they were still at war with Israel, and that they had "belligerent rights"; again, the Security Council did nothing to enforce its rulings.

True, the Israelis treated the territory they held under the armistice agreements as their own; gradually even the Arabs came to regard the armistice demarcation lines of 1949 as true boundaries between the Arab and the Jewish parts of Palestine—although the armistice agreements provided otherwise (to be discussed presently). But the Western powers showed no appetite for the task of requiring the Arab nations to make peace with Israel. As a result, the deep-seated Arab conviction that the existence of Israel was an aggression against Arab rights became a political force.

By 1951 or 1952 the Soviets began to understand that they could use this conviction among the Arabs as a weapon in their campaign to bring Europe under their control and to split Europe from North America. No Arab statesman, however moderate, can dissociate himself from the call to a holy war—a *jihad*—against Israel. With massive arms supplies, political backing, and the deterrent threat of some Soviet military protection, the Soviets dangled before the eyes of the Arabs the irresistible temptation of an opportunity to drive out the Israelis, as the Crusaders had been driven out many centuries before. Radical forces within Arab politics were aroused by beating the anti-Israeli drum, organizing diplomatic and economic boycotts, guerrilla attacks, and occasional wars against Israel; and one regime after another has been forced to follow the example of Syria, Iraq, and Libya. Under the pressure of escalating hostility, the Arab states are drawn into acts of aggression not only against Israel, but against the Western states as well—for example, the nationalization of foreign concessions, the punitive increase in the price of oil, and the oil embargoes of 1956, 1967, and 1973. With every step down this path, Arab dependence on the Soviet Union is deepened and confirmed.

For more than twenty years the Soviets have pursued the policy of enveloping Europe and NATO from the south, and have pursued it with great skill. In the course of conducting that campaign they have exploited not only the Arab hostility toward Israel, but many other regional quarrels which would weaken the Western orientation of Arab politics and strengthen the hand of their friends.

The Soviet effort in the Middle East has brought them extraordinary rewards. They are now installed in Syria, Iraq, Egypt, Libya, Algeria, Somalia, Aden, and a number of other bases and strong points in the Middle East and Africa. They have supported the Arabs in three major wars against Israel—those of 1956, 1967, and 1973—the war of attrition of 1969–1970, and ongoing campaigns of guerrilla activity, political and economic pressure, and near war. They have been able to exploit and influence the conflict over Cyprus in ways which weaken NATO. The Soviets do not always win. They suffer setbacks occasionally, as they did in Ghana and Portugal. But their policy remains calm and constant despite such reverses.

III

The greatest achievement of Soviet policy in the Middle East so far has been its impact on the Middle Eastern policies of Western Europe and the United States. Bewildered, frightened, and leaderless, Europe and

America have stood by in impotent silence while Arab proxies, with full Soviet support, have destroyed one Western position after another throughout the region, have brought the industrialized nations to their knees by raising the price of oil and threatening further embargoes, and have deliberately produced what they hope will be revolutionary situations in the third world through increases in the price of oil and other raw materials. The West did nothing to protect the ancient Christian community of Lebanon from destruction by Muslim forces deliberately aided by the Soviet Union, whose bold and brutal policy in the area goes almost unremarked by Western politicians or the Western press.

The United States and its NATO partners have identical interests in the Middle East. They share responsibility for the existence and survival of Israel. And they are equally threatened by the possibility of Soviet hegemony in the area, a position of dominance that would permit the Soviets—perhaps by intimidation rather than war—to require the dissolution of NATO, the retreat of the United States from Europe and the Mediterranean, and the reduction of Western Europe to the status of Finland or Poland.

The first question raised by this situation goes beyond the realm of power politics to the true sources of our being, to the ultimate and abiding question: what manner of men are we? Israel came into being in reliance on the solemn promises of the world community, led by the states of Europe and the United States. Depending upon those pledges, nearly three million people, refugees and idealists from the ends of the earth, have come together in Israel. They have forged a living democratic community, state, and nation. The Security Council and International Court of Justice of the United Nations have reiterated over and over again that Israel exists of right; and the Security Council has ruled —most recently in its mandatory decision of 23 October 1973—that the Arabs must at long last make peace with Israel. It is morally and politically unthinkable that the United States and its allies, and many other nations as well, could stand by and allow Israel to be destroyed. Such an event would represent the utter bankruptcy of the West and the disappearance of the last shred of its pride. Before so great a catastrophe, the treaties and other commitments of the United States would cease to have any deterrent influence. One could expect an overwhelming outbreak of aggression within six months at most of a tragedy and a betrayal so terrible. But no student of modern political pathology and no politician who must live by his forecasts can face this critical question without reflecting on the fate of Lebanon.

The second aspect of our national and NATO interest in the destiny of Israel is the use the Soviets have made of the Arab-Israeli conflict in their programs for gaining control of Western Europe. The Middle Eastern wars of 1956, 1967, 1969–1970, and 1973 could never have taken place without Soviet support for Arab policy. And the astonishing gains of the Soviets throughout the region could never have been achieved without the successive Arab-Israeli wars.

Our political and strategic goal in the Arab-Israeli conflict, therefore, should be to convince the Arabs that their flirtation with Soviet policy can bring them nothing but tragedy, and to insist on a fair and even-handed peace. The Soviet interest is to prolong and envenom the Arab-Israeli dispute as long as possible, provided the risks do not become excessive. The interests of the United States and its allies in the Middle East will not be automatically safeguarded by peace between Israel and its Arab neighbors. Many other complex and difficult programs will be required to assure that end. But our common interests in the entire region cannot be safeguarded without an Arab-Israeli peace. This has been a principal theme of our Middle East policy and of Allied policy—whenever there was one—since 1948.

In 1967 the Soviets agreed to a Security Council resolution which sought to obtain agreements of peace in the Middle East. Supplied and egged on by the Soviets, the Arabs had blockaded Israel from the south, mobilized great armies against her, and announced a holy war. To this combination of pressures Israel reacted with explosive force in the Six-Day War, and completely defeated the armed forces of Jordan, Syria, and Egypt—an action it was entitled to take by way of self-defense under Article 51 of the United Nations Charter. On the first day of the war the United States announced that the goal of its policy was "peace," and that it would settle for nothing less than peace.

The Soviets struggled against this policy for five months in 1967, trying both in the Security Council and in the General Assembly to obtain a vote condemning Israel as the aggressor, and calling on Israel to withdraw to the armistice demarcation lines as they stood before the war, without peace. The United States and its allies, united for once on a Middle Eastern issue, prevailed in the diplomatic battle, largely because they had persuaded the Israelis to withdraw without peace in 1957 in exchange for a long series of promises Nasser had made to the United States and then broken. This time, the allies said, Israel could remain in occupation of the territories it conquered in 1967 until the Arabs made peace. The Soviets finally had no alternative but to accept, and thus prevent the outbreak of a new round of war which might have threat-

ened their influence in the Arab world or drawn them into a confrontation with the United States.

Between 1967 and 1973 the structure and dynamics of world politics
were deeply changed. The Soviet Union continued to build up both its
strategic and its conventional military forces on a scale without parallel
in modern history, developing both a blue-water navy and a remarkable
airlift capacity to permit the projection of its influence anywhere in the
world. Soviet spokesmen have often said that the USSR's military program is designed to achieve "preponderance," as the predicate for a
process of continuing political expansion, based on the neutralization of
United States nuclear and nonnuclear forces by superior Soviet force in
every category. The Soviets, enlarging their presence in Southern and
Southeastern Asia, also built up their military presence on the Siberian
border from four to more than forty divisions—a formidable development
which forced China to negotiate a rapprochement with the United States
in 1972 for the most primitive reasons of national survival. To this move,
with its implicit and indeed explicit threat of a Sino-American alliance
under certain circumstances, the Soviets reacted with maximum hostility. Moving swiftly, carefully, and on a very large scale, they planned
the complete defeat of American policy in Southeast Asia, and a massive strategic blow at the relationship of Europe and the United States
through the Middle Eastern war of October 1973.

Both in Asia and in Europe, the Soviet operation was conducted behind the screen of "détente," with sensitive appreciation for the state of
U.S. politics and the American yearning—after Korea and Vietnam—for
relief from the burdens which the effort to contain Soviet expansion had
required since 1947. The Soviet Union wished at all costs to minimize
the risk of arousing Europe and America once again, as Britain had
finally been aroused in 1940. Its program of war was therefore dressed in
the costume of conciliation.

President Nixon's trip to Peking, culminating in the Shanghai communiqué, took place in February 1972. In the Shanghai communiqué,
issued on 27 February, both the Chinese and the American governments
announced that

neither should seek hegemony in the Asia-Pacific region, and each is opposed
to efforts by any other country or group of countries to establish such hegemony.
Both sides are of the view that it would be against the interests of the peoples
of the world for any major country to collude with another against other
countries, or for major countries to divide up the world into spheres of interest.

Nixon's visit to the Soviet Union occurred three months later. It was
greeted with an all-out North Vietnamese offensive in South Vietnam,

designed to put Nixon on his knees in Moscow. The offensive was defeated in the field, and the president's visit was conducted at a different level. The overall goal of the Soviets was to make quite certain that China and the United States were not in fact secretly allied against the Soviet Union. In this setting, the brave promises of Soviet-American détente were made in May of 1972. The declaration of "Basic Principles" and the communiqué issued at that time proclaimed that in conducting their relations the two governments would proceed from the common determination that in the nuclear age there is no alternative to peaceful coexistence. To fulfill that principle, they promised to work together to achieve peaceful solutions for situations of tension in many parts of the world, to exercise restraint in their mutual relations, and to negotiate and settle all differences by peaceful means. Specifically, both nations undertook to bring peace to Indochina, and the Soviet Union promised to cooperate fully with Ambassador Jarring in negotiating a political settlement of the Arab-Israeli conflict in the Middle East pursuant to the principles and provisions of the Security Council's Resolution 242 of 22 November 1967.

The state of tension in the Soviet-Chinese-American triangle and the success of our military efforts and those of the South Vietnamese forces during 1972 led to the Indochina cease-fire agreements of January 1973, which were guaranteed by the major powers—including the Soviet Union —in the Declaration of Paris in March 1973. From the American point of view, those agreements were entirely satisfactory—on paper. Despite a few minor ambiguities around the edges, they confirmed the positions for which the United States and other nations had suffered so bitterly in attempting to carry out their obligations under the SEATO Treaty and the Charter of the United Nations: North Vietnam and South Vietnam were separate states, and the war in Indochina was therefore an international war, like the Korean War, not a civil war. North Vietnam would evacuate Laos and Cambodia, withdraw in effect from South Vietnam, and refrain from any interference, military or political, in the affairs of South Vietnam. That condition being met, the United States should withdraw from South Vietnam, and peace would return to that tortured land on the basis of a political agreement among all the South Vietnamese parties. The Soviet Union promised once again to carry out the agreement it had made with us in 1962—the agreement finally to get the North Vietnamese out of Laos and Cambodia.

The Soviets have never pretended that the 1973 agreements for peace in Indochina were carried out. And our government, weak and uncertain, did not even protest strongly against the fact that it was being

cynically double-crossed by the Soviet Union as well as by the North
Vietnamese. In the shadow of Watergate, Nixon and Kissinger were
prisoners of their own "détente" rhetoric. They remained silent and
hoped for the best. In the grim Watergate summer of 1973 President
Nixon even signed the resolution forbidding all bombing or other military activity in Indochina. Thus ended the last vestige of deterrent
uncertainty about America's will to insist on the enforcement of the
agreements for peace in Indochina. On a trip to East Asia during that
summer, I found that to be the first question on the mind of every government in the region.

The only modern analogy for Soviet behavior in relation to the Indochina agreements of 1973 is the invasion of Czechoslovakia in contempt
of the Munich agreements of 1938. That dire event was a clear signal of
Hitler's intentions in the 1930s. The fate of the Indochina agreements
of 1973 has the same significance to the policy problems we face
today.

At some point during 1973, once we had withdrawn our troops from
Vietnam—perhaps not until the late summer, when Congress had passed
and the president had signed the resolution forbidding all American
military activity in Indochina—the Soviets decided that the paralysis of
the United States government over Watergate was so complete that they
could safely carry through the plans for a decisive attack against Israel
that they had made with President Sadat in 1972. According to President
Sadat, the Soviet Union agreed to support the Arab aggression against
Israel in April 1972, a month *before* Nixon's visit and a month *before* the
Soviet public pledge to cooperate with the United States and Ambassador Jarring in an effort to reach a political settlement.

From the Soviet point of view, the Yom Kippur War was a decisive
answer to China's new relation with the United States. If China's rapprochement with the U.S. tipped the balance of world power in favor
of the latter, separating Europe from the United States could force the
pendulum to swing in the other direction. Such an event would inevitably have a profound impact on Chinese and Japanese expectations
and, in the long run, on their policies.

Of course, the 1973 war did not go according to the Egyptian-Soviet
plan. The Israelis won a brilliant victory, and the United States demonstrated that it was far less paralyzed by Watergate than the Soviets had
thought and hoped. While certain aspects of our diplomacy in 1973 and
thereafter are subject to criticism, President Nixon's support of Israel
was effective and indispensable, and our refusal of any cease-fire unless
the Security Council ordered the parties to make peace in accordance

with Resolution 242 was, in terms at least, the most important achievement of our diplomacy in the whole history of the Arab-Israeli dispute.

The Soviets' behavior before, during, and since the Middle East war of October 1973, like the failure to carry out their promises with regard to Indochina, made nonsense of the pledges of détente given to Nixon during his Moscow visit of May 1972 and their later reiteration of those pledges. Instead of pressing for a diplomatic settlement in the Middle East in accordance with the Security Council resolution as they had promised, the Soviets helped to prepare and equip the Arab aggression of 6 October 1973. They did nothing to inform the United States that the war was coming, thus violating the 1972 declaration of "Basic Principles." The Soviets fully supported the Arab oil embargo and urged distant states to enter the fray. And they are reliably reported to have moved nuclear warheads into the Sinai in the final phases of the war, and to have threatened to intervene in order to prevent the total destruction of the Egyptian and Syrian armed forces.

Again, as they did in Indochina, Nixon and Kissinger concealed what was happening from the American people. In order to preserve the illusion of détente they covered up the Soviet role in the October war both by what they said and by what they did not say. Mr. Kissinger told us that Soviet behavior before, during, and after the October war was "not unreasonable" and "less obstructive than in 1967," and that our "détente" relations with the Soviet Union contributed to an agreed settlement. This, too, is from the theater of the absurd.

Since October 1973 the United States has pursued an active diplomatic effort in the Middle East. Its goal, very properly from our point of view, was to prevent further Soviet penetration of the Middle East, the Mediterranean basin, and East Africa—and, in the long run, to induce Egypt and other Arab states to give up their connection with the Soviet Union. In order to accomplish this goal, the United States—for a time at least—abandoned its reliance on the twin Security Council resolutions which provide the only possible political and legal framework for reaching peace in the Middle East.

Those resolutions rest on twenty-seven years of bitter experience, as well as on principles of international law upon which every state insists for its own protection. They provide that the Israelis need not withdraw one inch from the cease-fire lines until there is a firm and binding agreement of peace, negotiated by the parties and signed by them. This is the famous "package deal" of Resolution 242, which Resolution 338, adopted on 22 October 1973, made mandatory. The provisions of the 1967 package deal reflect the fact that in 1957, after the Suez crisis, we had negotiated a series of secret and informal understandings between Egypt and Israel on the basis of which Israel withdrew from the Sinai. The promises Egypt made to us in order to obtain that withdrawal were not kept. The final straw was Nasser's reckless closing of the Strait of Tiran in 1967. It had been understood in 1957 that if this were done, the Israelis would be justified in using force in self-defense. This is why no majority could be mustered in 1967, either in the Security Council or in the General Assembly, to declare Israel the aggressor.

The second key provision of Resolution 242 was that the secure and recognized boundaries to which Israel would withdraw pursuant to an agreement of peace need not be the same as the armistice demarcation lines of 1949. The armistice agreements specifically provide that those lines are not political boundaries, and can be changed by agreement when the parties move from armistice to peace.

In negotiating the military disengagement agreements between Egypt and Israel, our government gave up its strongest and most important negotiating position, and a fundamental principle as well. And it profoundly misjudged the nature of the issues in the conflict.

The Arab states have turned to the Soviet Union for help in order to destroy Israel. We will have no chance of weaning them away from their Soviet connection until they have made a genuine peace with Israel and the dream of destroying Israel begins to recede into history. By pressing Israel to give up some of the occupied territories without peace, we have allowed the Arab states to continue to hope that somehow, someday, with Soviet help, they will be able to liquidate Israel.

Our strategy therefore put the cart before the horse. By postponing peace and demonstrating that Israel could be made to withdraw without peace, as it did in 1957, we helped to perpetuate the Arab interest in Soviet assistance. American policy revealed a lack of understanding on our part of the nature of law, and of the role it plays in human affairs. By abandoning the principles of international law and a binding resolution of the Security Council, we abandoned a force of incalculable influence in the minds of men.

IV

As this paper is being prepared, the outcome of the struggle is in the balance. The Soviet Union continues to press its campaign in the Middle East with energy and imagination. For the Soviet Union, the Middle

East is a front of strategic as well as tactical importance. It is a front on which we could lose not merely a battle, as we did in Vietnam, but the war itself. For what is at stake in the Middle East is not alone the survival of Israel, Jordan, Lebanon, and many other states and peoples, but the independence of Europe, and therefore the world balance of power. If we are driven from Europe and the Mediterranean—if Europe becomes Finlandized or Polandized, in James Schlesinger's telling phrase —China and Japan would necessarily make their own accommodations with the Soviet Union and we would be alone in an ominous world, as Britain was after the fall of France in 1940.

There would be a great difference, however, between our situation in such an event and that of Britain in 1940. In 1940 it was always reasonable for Britain to expect that the Soviet Union and the United States would be drawn into the war, and that Hitler would be overthrown. If we fail promptly to restore our position in Europe and the Middle East, and to protect our relations with China and Japan, there would be no potential allies to join us in the resultant struggle. We would be truly alone in a hostile, bitter, and disillusioned world—a world nearly beyond hope, like Russia itself.

Under those circumstances, would we arm to the teeth, to prepare for the worst, or would we accept the role which is the essence of the Soviet concept of détente—that we and Western Europe should faithfully supply the Soviet Union with food, consumer goods, and high technology on favorable credit terms, and leave the serious business of world politics to Moscow?

We are in the midst of one of those strange illnesses of the spirit, like that which afflicted the West during the 1930s, when we find it nearly impossible to accept what our minds disclose about the state of the world. As the Atlantic Treaty Association pointed out in October 1975, "the Soviet threat to the Alliance has increased" but "the perception of it in Western opinion has diminished." President Nixon told the Western world over and over again that the cold war was over; that negotiation had replaced confrontation in the relationship between the Soviet Union and the West; and that "détente" was not a goal we had sought since 1933, but a condition his diplomacy had fully achieved. Americans and Europeans are naturally reluctant to conclude that Nixon's view, like the Spirit of Camp David and so many earlier moments of summit euphoria, has no relationship to the reality of Soviet policy.

But there has been no change in the nature of Soviet policy, and no improvement in Soviet-American relations. On the contrary, Soviet policy is more ominous than at any earlier period; it is sustained by a far larger and more threatening armory, and by a political will more ruthless and more reckless than that of Stalin. Soviet foreign policy is designed and carried out, after all, by the same men who planned the Gulag Archipelago.

Together, the United States, its Atlantic and Pacific allies, China, and a number of associated nations have more than enough strength to deal with the Soviet threat through deterrent diplomacy. The question—the ultimate question, on which the shape of the future depends—is whether they have the political will and acumen to do so effectively, and in time.

5

GREGORY GROSSMAN

The Economics of Détente and American Foreign Policy

The basic fact of economic relations between the United States and the Soviet Union is the marked asymmetry of their national interests. The USSR needs fairly developed economic relations; we don't—except for the problematic opportunity to obtain certain quantities of some key commodities. Our foreign policy should therefore aim at trading economic advantages to the USSR for political benefits to us and the rest of the West—known in current parlance as "linkage." The Soviet interest is to avoid linkage and obtain economic benefits at little or no political cost.

THE UNITED STATES INTEREST

First a look at our side. In foreign affairs—as in environmental protection, resource conservation, or quality of life—private gain need not correspond to national (social) interest. The issue here is not that our producers, traders, shippers, and bankers already derive and may well continue to derive private gain from doing business with the Soviets. It is true, as many have pointed out, that dealing with the Soviet bureaucracy is often frustrating and costly; and what starts as a bonanza can end as a bust. But on the whole, as long as the Soviets seek trade with the West, we can count on them to ensure that at least some satisfactory profits are made by American and other Western businessmen. Nor is the small scale of Soviet-American trade (even under optimistic assumptions) sufficient reason to spurn it from a national standpoint.

The issue is rather that even the greatest economic benefits we realistically can expect from doing business with the USSR become insignificant before the totality of our political and strategic relations and their implications for the world at large. Entirely legitimate and innocent pursuit of private business with the Soviets may eventually entail for the United States—and the West in general—significant political or strategic risks. Among them are contributions to Soviet military power; potential political blackmail through threat of default on repayment of capital or on delivery of important materials; or the fostering of vested domestic interests that might with time encumber the proper functioning of our foreign policy in relation to the USSR. Some of these things have already happened. For a quarter of a century the Soviets refused to pay anything on their acknowledged lend-lease debt to the U.S. government until they obtained promises of trade and credits in return. As for vested interests, we have only recently witnessed the fierce opposition of farm interests to *any* use of grain as an instrument of U.S. policy toward the Soviet Union, and the effect of this opposition on the president's speeches during the primary electoral campaign of 1976. Moreover, in the course of doing normal business, private American firms can hardly be expected to collect for the United States and the West in general the political and strategic concessions that may be obtainable from the Soviets in return.

For these reasons the U.S. government must maintain a close involvement in economic relations with the USSR and other communist countries. The government's role is not only to prevent the transfer of strategically important equipment and know-how to a potential military adversary, as has been frequently assumed, but to aim at a broad linkage between economic relations and the overall problem of dealing with the Kremlin. The government can then afford to take on principle a benign view of normal trading relations.

False Arguments

Several dubious or even fallacious arguments supporting U.S.-Soviet economic relations are frequently voiced on grounds of national interest. It is asserted, for example, that sales to the Soviets are good for our balance of payments, though the exact meaning of the statement is often left vague. This is not the place for a treatise on the theory of international economics. Suffice it to say that to be consistent, those who so argue must simultaneously oppose imports from the USSR. Moreover, they should be indifferent to exports financed by our own credits, because exports on credit do nothing for the balance of payments until the credits come to be repaid, and possibly not even then. In any event, given the currently prevailing flexible exchange rates, the chief consequence of additional *net cash* sales to the Soviets is not a balance of payments surplus but a rise in the external value of the U.S. dollar, which may or may not be desirable at any particular point.

Large increments in exports to the Soviets, however, are unlikely in the near future except as financed by large, long-term credits. Whatever appeal they may have for other reasons, such credits to the Soviets raise serious problems.[1] The capital would be of great help to the Soviet economy, and it is therefore reasonable for the United States to expect an appropriate *quid pro quo* in excess of the purely financial compensation, say, in political terms. Second and no less important, our capital in Kremlin hands gives the USSR long-term opportunities for diplomatic pressure and for exploiting our domestic vested interests—a risk that we should not take lightly.

It is sometimes argued that sales to the Russians create jobs in the U.S. Again, this can be so only insofar as net sales result to the world at large; i.e., any consequent reduction of our net sales to other countries —which may occur, owing to the above-mentioned effect on the external value of the dollar—must be subtracted from the increase caused by Soviet trade to ascertain the net employment benefit. But the proper answer to the argument is simply that we do not need exports to create additional jobs; we can do this ourselves through domestic economic measures.[2] If we can achieve the employment effect ourselves, it is hardly prudent to depend on the Soviets to do it for us, while complicating our relations with them and inviting the attendant risks. Why use our capital to build up Siberia when we can use it to improve our own cities and with much greater employment effect?

Key Commodities

The U.S. does have one economic interest, mentioned at the outset of this discussion, relating to the prospect of broadening our foreign sources of supply of certain key commodities by importing more of them from the Soviet Union. In the foreseeable future energy carriers, particularly natural gas and petroleum, are the most important commodity group in question. For several years Soviet authorities and a few American firms have sporadically discussed joint projects for tapping the large natural-gas fields in both western and eastern Siberia and transporting the gas in liquified form from Soviet to American ports. The schemes call for the use of American equipment, technology, expertise, and billions of dollars' worth of capital, with the repayment taking place in kind (the so-called "product payback" method).

So far, these schemes have floundered on economic, technical, and political grounds. Although the gas would not reach the United States for the better part of a decade after such a project is launched, nonetheless this country could derive considerable potential economic benefit —including diversification of energy supply sources, likely downward pressure on world energy prices, conservation of our domestic energy resources, and possibly others as well. But the risks are also substantial. Besides the aforementioned risks involved in any large, long-term loans to the USSR, there is an additional danger that the Soviets may sever the flow of gas or oil ("turning off the tap," as it is often referred to). While the gas and/or oil from Soviet sources will not likely supply more than a small fraction of our energy needs for the remainder of this century, nevertheless at certain times—such as during another Arab embargo —we may find ourselves quite vulnerable to a Soviet threat to turn off the tap. Should we find it on balance desirable to import significant and stable quantities of Soviet gas and/or oil in order to diversify our sources of supply, much is to be said for inducing the Soviets (as by means of long-term purchase contracts) to develop the corresponding resources and facilities with their own capital. As these lines were written the Western press reports revival of the "North Star" (West Siberian) project for exportable liquified natural gas, this time with the investment of German, French, and British capital—rather than American—within the USSR.[3] The possibility of inducing the Soviets to use their own capital is not to be ruled out, given their need for additional stable earnings of hard currency.

THE SOVIET INTEREST

Soviet eagerness for broadened economic relations with the West is of course nothing new. It isn't even uniquely Soviet. Over the centuries the Tsarist state repeatedly turned to the West for the technology, equipment, know-how, and capital necessary to promote its pressing politico-economic objectives, and particularly to confront the West in power terms. Nor for this reason have Soviet leaders, from Lenin through Stalin and Khrushchev to Brezhnev, shown much embarrassment on ideological grounds, as the imagination of some Western writers would make us believe.

Western Technology

Indeed, from the start, Western technology has been one of the three key ingredients in the Soviet formula for industrialization. The other two—to which we shall return presently—are: (1) rapid transfer of labor from the village and the kitchen into modern sectors of the economy, together with massive education and training of the labor, and (2) plowing back (i.e., reinvesting) a very high proportion of the national product for the sake of further rapid growth. It is not unfair to say that Soviet industrialization and economic development have proceeded almost entirely on the basis of Western technology. The role of truly indigenous technology has been minimal hitherto (except possibly in the military and space sectors), despite the enormous numbers and resources devoted to engineering in the USSR.[4]

The technology has been obtained in many ways: much of it by importing nearly every relevant scrap of printed information, but much also —depending on the period in question—by purchasing, licenses, bringing in Western experts in person, buying prototypes for "reverse engineering," espionage, and of course importing billions of dollars' worth of equipment, sometimes in the form of "turnkey" projects. This prodigious effort in technology acquisition has pursued a set of closely interrelated objectives—including rapid industrialization (with emphasis on the "heavy" industries and the military), catching up with the United States in industrial might and overtaking it, raising the material standard of living (an objective that in earlier decades was frequently sacrificed to the others), and the attainment of economic self-sufficiency (autarky).

Autarky

The goal of autarky does not necessarily signify the cessation of international trade. On the contrary, it may trigger—as it has repeatedly done in the Soviet case—a considerable jump in imports in the short run for the sake of becoming largely free of imports later on. Furthermore, despite strenuous efforts on its behalf, the attainment of autarky has proved for

the Soviets to be something of a will-o'-the-wisp. They have repeatedly
been close to achieving it, only to have it elude them; as world technology leaped ahead and the relative importance of industries and products changed over time, their efforts toward self-sufficiency had to be
started anew. There has even been a touch of irony in this, for the very
singlemindedness and strenuousness of the quest for autarky caused the
Soviets to excel at mastering yesterday's technology, thereby minimizing
their ability to keep abreast with today's and anticipate tomorrow's.[5]
And so, repeatedly, new impetus had to be given to trade with the West;
the latest technologies and equipment again had to be bought abroad,
exports had to be enlarged to pay for them, and credits had to be sought.
In the first half of the 1970s we may have witnessed another such phase
in the Soviets' periodic reaching for economic and technological self-
sufficiency. But this time the need to import and to borrow has been
seriously aggravated by certain longer-term tendencies.

Whether the Soviet regime continues to pursue a basically autarkic
policy is crucial not only for its own decisions but also for the West to
understand the Soviet attitude toward détente. Since the early days of
détente an impression has been fostered in the West by official Soviet
pronouncements—and is apparently shared in the highest places of our
administration—that the USSR has given up its traditional autarkic bias
and is ready to partake widely of normal international division of labor
in a sustained manner. Yet the evidence for this conclusion is not clear.
True, Soviet purchases in the West rose sharply in recent years (see
table 1), as did Soviet purchases during the First Five-Year Plan, which
was the classic autarkic supereffort of Soviet history. The answer therefore must be sought in places other than the recent trade statistics—
namely, in specific Soviet behavior in foreign trade, and in the institu-
tional arrangements in the economy which may take advantage of
opportunities in international commerce in a broad and regular fashion.

As to behavior, Soviet imports from the West—apart from the large
imports of grain dictated by dire necessity—have continued to be concentrated on capital goods and associated technology. In other words,
the Soviets have apparently followed their traditional pattern of filling
gaps in industrial capacity with a view to self-sufficiency. In economic
arrangements, there has been no indication yet of any significant insti-
tutional changes which would be necessary steps for serious abandonment
of autarky—such as linking domestic prices with external prices, setting
more meaningful exchange rates, or decentralizing foreign-trade decisions. These changes have been undertaken by smaller East European
countries for some ten years. In one important respect, the supply of

TABLE 1

USSR: Trade with and Indebtedness to Western Industrially Advanced Countries
1966–1976
(in millions of U.S. dollars [a])

	IMPORTS		EXPORTS [b]		IMPORT SURPLUS [c]		Hard-currency debt outstanding, end of period [d]
	From All W.I.A.C.	From U.S.	To All W.I.A.C.	To U.S.	With All W.I.A.C.	With U.S.	
1966	1,779	63	1,756	47	23	16	505
1966–70, average	2,225	83	2,093	51	132	32	1,722
1973	6,119	1,364 [e]	5,000	184	1,119	1,180	3,645
1974	8,195	753 [e]	8,343	236	–149	517	4,465
1975	12,933	1,949 [e]	8,185	183	4,748	1,766	7,489 [f]
1976, Jan.–Sept.	11,005	2,172 [e]	7,668	203	3,337	1,969	10,000 [f]

SOURCE: Official Soviet foreign-trade statistics, except when noted otherwise.

[a] Converted from foreign trade rubles as follows: 1966–70, IR. = $1,111; 1973–76, IR. = $1,333. (Valuation as of USSR's border.) Data in the last column are in U.S. dollars in the source.

[b] Excluding gold.

[c] Because much Soviet merchandise is transported in Soviet bottoms, the import surplus derived from Soviet statistics overstates the foreign-currency drain, while that derived from U.S. statistics ($1,556 million) understates it.

[d] SOURCE: U.S. Central Intelligence Agency, "Recent Developments in Soviet Hard Currency Trade," ER 76-10015, January 1976, processed, table 4; and U.S. Congress, Joint Economic Committee, *Soviet Economy in a New Perspective* (Washington, D.C., U.S. GPO), p. 738. Data in U.S. dollars in the sources. Comprises known medium- and long-term debt. Does not include indebtedness to U.S. government on lend-lease account.

[e] Of which, grain imports were (in millions): 1973–$917; 1974–$302; 1975–$1,128; Jan.–Sept. 1976–$1,100.

[f] Includes the following indebtedness to U.S.: $550 million to Commodity Credit Corporation for grain-sales credit, $174.4 million to Export-Import Bank (of $469 million authorized prior to suspension of new credits to USSR), presumably also $174.4 million to private entities in conjunction with Eximbank loans and guaranteed by same, and perhaps around $1 billion of additional indebtedness to private entities—altogether something close to $2 billion. (Sources: Paul Marer, ed., *U.S. Financing of East-West Trade*, Studies in Development, n. 22. [Bloomington, Ind., Indiana University Press]; in press. International Development Research Center, "Study in East European and Soviet Planning, Development and Trade," no. 22, pp. 26, 210, 393 [this is an excellent source on its subject]; and [U.S.] East-West Foreign Trade Board, *Fourth Quarterly Report* [Washington, D.C.: Government Printing Office, 1976], p. 26.)

grains and livestock products, the USSR is currently bending every effort at very high cost to regain self-sufficiency. No criticism is meant; it is the USSR's sovereign right to persist in its autarkic policy if it chooses. However, the contrary impression, so widely held in the West, appears to have little foundation in observable evidence.

Yet the fact remains that the period of détente to date has coincided with a marked expansion in economic relations between the USSR and the industrialized West, including the U.S., as table 1 shows. The increase has been especially sharp for Soviet imports, and therefore also—indeed, more so—for the amount of Soviet indebtedness to the West. By 1975 imports from the industrial West, swelled by grain shipments in that year, reached 36 percent of total Soviet imports. This figure compares with 24 percent in 1970 and 20 percent in 1965. These percentages surely understate the relative importance to the Soviet economy of imports from the West. Over one-third of 1975 imports, worth nearly $5 billion, were not covered by exports to the industrial West and were mostly financed by net borrowing.[6]

THE ECONOMIC BASIS OF SOVIET INTEREST IN DÉTENTE

The marked increases in imports and credits from the West coincide historically both with détente and with certain major longer-term developments in the Soviet domestic economy. It is an interesting question whether these internal economic tendencies did not give a significant impetus to the Soviet interest in détente, insofar as they increased the need for Western economic assistance to solve domestic economic problems. It was apparently in the late 1960s that the Soviet leaders decided to advance from "peaceful coexistence" to the more intense involvement with major Western powers, especially West Germany and the United States, that came to be known as détente. It was at about the same time that Soviet industrial growth began to run out of steam and that the economy, though probably unforeseen, was about to suffer from two disastrous crop failures in 1972 and 1975.

Decline in Soviet Growth

We have already noted that in addition to Western technology the key ingredients of the Soviet industrialization formula have traditionally been a high rate of investment out of the gross national product (ensuring a high growth rate of capital) and a rapid increase in the nonagricultural labor force. During the 1960s industrial and overall economic growth had already slowed somewhat from the Khrushchevian boom in the 1950s, manifesting a drop in the growth of what economists call "total factor productivity"; but the rate of gross investment continued high (more than 30 percent of GNP) and the expansion of the nonagricultural labor force was also well maintained.

Nonagricultural employment began flagging as the 1960s gave way to the 1970s. Between 1950 and 1970 it increased 3.9 percent per year, and industrial employment 3.7 percent. But between 1970 and 1975 these respective annual average rates of increase were only 2.5 and 1.3 percent, and for 1976–1980 the rate of increase in industrial employment is planned at less than 1 percent per year. After 1980 the rate is expected to slow even further.[7]

At the same time, while capital formation continued at a rather high rate, for various reasons the pressures on investible capital were mounting. It became increasingly necessary to turn for natural resources to the more remote and less manageable parts of the country, where capital needs per unit of capacity are usually much higher than in the older areas. Even before the crop failures of 1972 and 1975 agriculture was claiming an ever larger share of total capital formation. Motorization of the country, a decision taken soon after Krushchev's fall, required growing investments in infrastructure as well as in the vehicle-manufacturing facilities themselves. And as elsewhere, environmental protection and resource conservation suddenly became expensive matters in the USSR.

Other Problems

Still other concurrent developments should be noted. By the end of the 1960s the leadership most probably had already perceived that the 1965 economic reform, a minimal measure to begin with, would not yield any substantial fruit in terms of the system's efficiency or dynamics. There was little evidence that "technological gap" vis-à-vis the leading industrial nations of the West was being compressed, despite very large and costly efforts to overcome it. The reasons for its persistence are many, but the gap is generally grounded in the economic system itself with its bureaucratic structure of planning and management, its inadequate and often perverse incentives, and the lack of competition among producers.

In addition, certain other rigidities rose in importance. One of them relates to public expectations of steadily rising levels of consumption.

Noteworthy is the rapid growth of demand for high-value foodstuffs, especially for meat, which places great and ever-growing pressure on agricultural capacity, so that today agriculture (together with supporting industries) receives over one-third of total gross fixed investment in the economy.[8] The public's large and rapidly growing liquid savings, which cannot be easily neutralized without political damage, support consumer expectations with effective purchasing power. In these circumstances the authorities find themselves severely limited in their freedom of maneuver with the economy's resources—a fact of which they were most recently reminded by the popular disturbances in Poland in June 1976. No longer can they use consumption to cushion the plan's miscalculations and the economy's shortfalls and setbacks, as in the bad old days. Military spending provides another serious constraint on the freedom of maneuver with resources.[9] Consequently, investment now takes up much of the shortfall in resources, with inevitable negative effects on the growth rate.

The tenth five-year plan (FYP) (1976–1980), a summary of which was first released in December 1975, strikingly reflects the joint effects of the longer-term retardatory tendencies and the shock of the catastrophic crop failure. These effects can clearly be seen in table 2, in which the tenth FYP guidelines [10] are compared with the results of the eighth (1966–1970) and the ninth (1971–1975). It is important to note that the ninth FYP results were adversely affected by the crop failures of 1972 and 1975 but were helped by sharp rises in raw material and gold prices and by credits from the West.

(The 1976 grain crop turned out to be a very good one by Soviet

TABLE 2

Indicators of Soviet Economic Growth, 1965–1980

	Eighth FYP [a]	Ninth FYP [a]	Tenth FYP
	1970 actual (1965 = 100)	1975 actual (1970 = 100)	1980 target (1975 = 100)
National income utilized, Soviet definition	141	128	126
Industrial gross output, total	150	143	136
Consumer goods	150	137	132
Industrial labor employment	115	107	104 [c]
Agricultural output, gross [b]	121	113	116
Real income per capita	133	124	121
Retail sales, in current rubles	148	136	129
Investment, gross fixed [b]	143	142	126

[a] The data on actual results are generally believed by Western students to be overstated.
[b] Ratios (percent) of five-year totals to preceding five-year totals.
[c] Estimated.

claims—224 million metric tons [*The New York Times*, 6 January 1977, p. 39]. This should be a considerable boon to the consumer, the balance of payments, and the Soviet economy generally. However, it does not appear to have significantly raised Soviet sights for the current Five-Year Plan [to 1980], and would seem to leave the argument in this chapter essentially unaffected.)

The table shows quite vividly the retardation of growth in the Soviet economy since 1965. It is far from certain, of course, that the targets of the tenth FYP will be met. Historically, the actual results of the FYPs have generally fallen far short of the targets, a fact that official over-statement of results often obscures.

Special note should be taken of the marked drop in the rate of increase in gross fixed investment foreseen in the tenth FYP, which presages a corresponding decline in the growth rate of the capital stock. Together with the sharp decline in the growth of nonagricultural employment, and in view of the already mentioned rising pressure on investible re-sources, this indicates that the momentum of Soviet growth will most likely be much weaker in the next decade than in the 1950s and 1960s. It is not surprising, therefore, that at the 25th Congress of the Com-munist Party of the Soviet Union (February–March 1976) the documents and speeches ushering in the new FYP also placed unprecedently great emphasis on the importance of foreign economic relations "in solving economic problems and accelerating scientific and technical progress" in the near future. Nor is it unreasonable to assume that the anticipation of inevitable slow-down in economic growth may have greatly influenced the Soviet leadership toward their détente policy as a means, *inter alia*, of securing greater economic assistance from the West just as it was be-coming more clearly needed.

Moreover, the guidelines for the tenth FYP (of which a fuller text is not available at this writing) leave little doubt that significant economic reforms—in the sense of enhancing the systems's flexibility and thereby raising its efficiency—are not in the offing. We may therefore expect that the economy's operating characteristics will persist into the near future—among them, sluggishness in research and development and resistance to innovation. Consequently, we may also expect Soviet interest in Amer-ican and other Western technology to remain lively for some time to come and the USSR to continue to buy large amounts of capital equip-ment and to borrow from the West (though possibly with ups and downs as dictated by both domestic and international considerations). The de-sire to borrow sizeable amounts at long term from the West will also continue to derive from the ambitiousness of plans in relation to disposable resources at given levels of technology and organization—a phenomenon caused not just by planners' whimsy or doctrinal rigidity, but by internal political realities. Lastly, despite prodigious efforts, Soviet agricultural output will hardly catch up with rapidly growing domestic demand for some years, taking the good years with the bad. Hence, ready access to American grain supplies larger than the eight million tons per year virtually guaranteed to the USSR until 1981 in the 1975 agreement will remain a vital necessity for the Soviet government.[11]

In sum, given the economic realities—and especially the need for Western (in considerable measure American) grain, technology, and capital—we expect that the Soviets will continue to advocate *détente* for its economic benefits, even in the face of occasional reverses (such as the termination of U.S. government credit and credit guarantees following Soviet nullification of the 1972 trade agreement) and growing political skepticism in the United States and other leading Western countries.[12]

LESSONS FOR AMERICAN POLICY

Whatever verdict history will bestow on the Jackson amendment episode, one valuable conclusion already has emerged from the experience: at that time at least, though it may not have expected the attendant publicity, the Kremlin *did* pay a considerable political price for the economic benefits that it sought from the United States.[13] From the Soviet viewpoint probably the most desirable of these benefits was long-term, large-scale credit, and not the most-favored-nation privilege which received the lion's share of the publicity at the time, and which economically means rather little for likely Soviet exports to the U.S. It should also be noted that termination of the 1972 agreement occurred before the disastrous 1975 crop failure and the general sharp retardation of the Soviet economy, as reflected in the data for the tenth FYP cited in table 2.

The Soviets' nullification of the 1972 trade agreement came almost immediately after Congress (in December 1974) limited Export-Import Bank credit to the USSR to the puny sum of $75 million per year for four years, with additional severe limits on lending for energy development. Thus the Kremlin's move to nullify was quite rational: it had swallowed a bitter political pill over the Jackson amendment and lost much face both at home and abroad in the attendant publicity—only to see the expected big prize, credit, slip out of its hands. By nullifying, moreover, the Soviets relieved themselves of the obligation (which was part of the 1972 agreement) to repay nearly $700 million on lend-lease account—thereby also retrieving a bargaining card for future use.

On the other hand, we have no strong reasons to wring our hands over the nullification of the 1972 agreement, either. We did not so much lose a trade agreement—or even potential trade—as regain some freedom of diplomatic action. Apart from making the (predictable) appropriate rumbles, the Soviets have shown little loss of interest in American goods and technology following that demarche, though of course they can buy considerably less than if the large credits were still forthcoming. But extending the credits without adequate political *quid pro quo* is hardly in our interest. As previously argued, such action invites various major long-term risks without the political benefits that we might get in return. The fault of the 1972 agreement was that it had bargained nothing concrete in return; its demise therefore affords us a welcome new attempt at proper linkage.

In the administration's view, it should be noted, the 1972 trade agreement did represent linkage, in that the economic concessions acknowledged the progress in U.S.-Soviet relations to that point and offered an incentive to continue on the same path. Moreover, it was hoped that the broadening of economic ties would create a set of common interests and a web of mutual involvement that would help shape future Soviet choices and lead the Kremlin toward further lessening of international tensions.[14] In this sense, however, *linkage* carries a rather different meaning —not one of trading economic for political benefit, but one of exchanging fairly definite and immediate economic benefits for rather uncertain expectations and hopes about future Soviet conduct. To say that such an approach leaves many questions unanswered and doubts unresolved is probably no more than to state the obvious. Without addressing ourselves to these questions and doubts, we merely reiterate that, in addition to other Soviet concerns such as China, the Kremlin's interest in broadened economic relations with the United States seems to be such as to preclude the need for general inducements to continue with its détente policy.

CONCLUSION

Consideration of the specific political benefits that the U.S. may wish to obtain in exchange for economic benefits is beyond the purview of this article; there is no dearth of these in our complex and perilous world. But we may nonetheless venture a few general observations here as a summary and conclusion.

The first is that, in principle, economic relations with the Soviet Union should be regarded as a normal matter—up to a point, for the Soviet Union is not just another country. But in regarding them as a normal matter we should not delude ourselves with the comforting thought that "trade is the road to peace"; the converse is more correct, if history is an indication.

As noted at the start, the salient fact about economic relations between the U.S. and the USSR is the asymmetry in their interests. The Soviets need grain, capital goods, technology, and capital from us; but our economic interest in the relationship is small—except possibly for energy and a few other key commodities, where imports from the USSR would either constitute minor additions to our supplies in the foreseeable future or raise serious questions regarding our strategic security. This asymmetry provides an opportunity of exchanging economic for political benefits. To the possible objections of the squeamish we may reply that the West's economic power is its strongest instrument—perhaps its only instrument—in dealing with the Soviets short of force, which no one wants to invoke—although in the final analysis no nonviolent instrument can be effective unless the user is militarily strong enough to deter the other side's temptation to resort to force.

It follows that the object of our economic policy toward another superpower should not only be—as it generally has been after World War II—to impede the growth of its military power. We clearly cannot dismiss this objective so long as the world is what it is, but a major purpose should be to provide our diplomacy with effective bargaining instruments.

In trading economic benefits we must recognize certain risks, such as those implicit in creating domestic vested interests subject to pressure by the Soviets, or in affording leverage to them by dint of their indebtedness to us. Where we create a major vested interest, the U.S. government may have to interpose itself so as to retain freedom of action in foreign policy. For instance, if grain is to be used as a diplomatic bargaining tool, the government must find ways of guaranteeing prices to our farmers regardless of the outcome. This much is prompted by considerations of equity at home as well as efficacy in foreign policy. The 1975 grain agreement with the Soviets unfortunately falls short on both these grounds.

We ought not turn to the Soviets to do for us what we can quite well do for ourselves, such as create jobs in the United States. And the more and faster we reduce our dependency on imported energy, the less exposed our position vis-à-vis the USSR.

An active policy of linkage would not be easy for us to pursue. In addition to formulating a consistent strategy and suitable tactics, it would require reassuring certain domestic interests, coordinating steps with the other major industrial countries in the West, taking note of the transnational nature of our major producers of goods and technology, paying due heed to the complexities within the East, and countering the inevitable Soviet outcries. The last task may be the least difficult; the Soviets have shown considerable ability to understand their opponents' realistic self-interest and to negotiate accordingly. Particularly in light of their economic needs, there is little reason to doubt that negotiate they will. Whether the result will still be détente is purely a matter of semantics; it would, however, continue the improvement of East-West relations on the firmer foundation of economic reality.

NOTES

1. We are here referring to credit on normal terms and conditions commensurate with the nature of the transaction and the credit worthiness of the borrower, and not to credit on preferential terms, which is frequently sought by the USSR. There seems to be little justification for the granting of preferential terms to the USSR, except against some adequate *quid pro quo* outside the financial transaction itself.

2. It may be retorted that domestic expansionary measures are inflationary. But for a given employment effect, net sales abroad are (or are not) just as inflationary as is an increment in domestic demand, keeping certain monetary variables constant.

3. See *Barron's*, 31 May 1976, p. 9.

4. The most forthright defense of this position is to be found in the virtually encyclopedic three-volume work of Antony C. Sutton, *Western Technology and Soviet Development, 1917–1930, 1930–1945, 1945–1965* (Stanford, Cal.: Hoover Institution, 1968, 1971, 1973).

5. An exception may have to be made here for some aspects of military and space technology, though Sutton (ibid.) argues that in these regards, too, the Soviets have been primarily imitative.

6. Cf. CIA, "The Soviet Economy: Performance in 1975 and Prospects for 1976," ER–7610296, May 1976 (processed), pp. 16–18; *The Economist* (London), 29 May 1976, p. 95. Note that "Western industrially advanced countries" and "hard-currency countries" are not identical categories: for example, Finland, a major trade partner, falls into the former category but not into the latter because of clearing arrangements with the USSR. The CIA estimates the 1975 hard-currency deficit to have been more than $5 billion. This was financed by $800 million to $1 billion in gold sales and by medium- and long-term borrowing from the West of some $3

billion (including some $750 million in Eurodollars), plus earning on nonmerchandise accounts.

7. For these and other data for the 1970s and their sources, see Gregory Grossman, "An Economy at Middle Age," *Problems of Communism* 25, no. 2 (March-April 1976):18–33; also Abram Bergson, "Russia's Economic Planning Shift," *The Wall Street Journal*, 17 May 1976.

8. The proportion of total gross fixed investment devoted to agriculture in the broadest sense (including investment in industries serving agriculture, in housing for agricultural labor, etc.) is planned for 1976 at 36 percent. Narrowing the concept down to gross fixed investment in agricultural production capital, one would probably arrive at around 27 percent, still a very high fraction both historically for the USSR and by comparison with other advanced countries.

9. In the present context we assume military outlay to be essentially inflexible in the short run, whether for domestic, political, or external reasons. Military outlay is estimated currently to be 11 to 13 percent of the Soviet gross national product (estimate by the CIA as reported in the *New York Times*, 19 May 1976).

10. See Grossman, "An Economy at Middle Age"; Bergson, "Russia's Economic Planning Shift."

11. The text of the grain agreement is in *Weekly Compilation of Presidential Documents* 11, no. 43 (27 October 1975):1187–88. The guarantee does not apply if total U.S. grain supply falls below 225 million metric tons, as defined in Article V of the agreement.

12. It is sometimes pointed out that the Soviet economy's benefit from the importation of Western equipment and technology is not as great as might appear at first glance, owing to poor utilization and slow diffusion. This may well be so, but this fact need not reduce the USSR's appetite for such things; it may even increase it.

13. See the letter from Secretary of State Henry M. Kissinger to Senator Henry M. Jackson dated 18 October 1974, released to the press the same day.

14. "Secretary Kissinger's Statement on U.S.-Soviet Relations before the Senate Foreign Relations Committee, 19 September 1974," Department of State, Bureau of Public Affairs, *Special Report No. 6*, p. 9: "Over time, trade and investment may leaven the autarkic tendencies of the Soviet system, invite gradual association of the Soviet economy with the world economy, and foster a degree of interdependence that adds an element of stability to the political equation." See also the excerpts from Dr. Kissinger's writings and public statements assembled by Warren G. Nutter, and the latter's commentary in Warren G. Nutter, *Kissinger's Grand Design*, Foreign Affairs Study 27 (Washington, D.C.: American Institute for Public Policy Research, October 1975), pp. 19, 23, 77–78. Franklyn D. Holzman and Robert Legvold, "The Economics and Politics of East-West Relations," *International Organization* 29, no. 1 (Winter 1975):275–320, contains an extensive discussion of the economic and political problems associated with an increase in U.S.-Soviet economic interdependence and the issue of linkage; although this treatment is a sophisticated one, the authors seem to underrate the intensity of Soviet interest in American goods, capital, and technology.

6

CHARLES BURTON MARSHALL

National Security: Thoughts on the Intangibles

My topic, having to do with the common defense, does not bear on palpable matters such as money, inventions, force structures, and deployments. It concerns ideas. It concerns, moreover, ideas not merely within the executive magistracy, the legislative branch, or the Pentagon, important as they are, but ideas entertained in the body politic as a whole. What people think, and how their thoughts constrain the nation's ability strategically to maintain itself as a going enterprise in an exacting world, are my concern here.

My subject pertains to policy. All policy focuses on futurity. The ever-implicit adverb is *henceforth*. The verb linked to the common defense in the Constitution—*provide*, derived from a Latin root meaning to see ahead—conveys the same thought. So one must begin with prediction. How far ahead? The outer limit for this kind of policy is fifteen years. With what precision? Well, with fair assurance, it is feasible to identify important forces likely to have roles in the shaping of events, but emphatically the interval will not be a static prolongation of the present pattern.

This province of life's affairs is akin to navigating in thick weather: one must look intently ahead precisely because it is impossible to see ahead. Particulars are beyond pondering. To illustrate—a similar projection in 1961 would probably have missed the Cuban missile crisis, the ensuing Soviet military build-up, the war in Vietnam and its outcome, the rise of terrorism, the Middle East wars of 1967 and 1973, the petroleum embargo, pervasive inflation, the strategic arms negotiations, the Greek-Turkish quarrel over Cyprus and its destructive consequences for alliance strength in the Eastern Mediterranean, the Portuguese collapse in Africa, the leftward drift in Western European politics, numerous discontinuities in political leadership and especially in the American presidency, and the weakening of executive authority in the United States.

Yet one can venture some prophecy. Trends in the external realm will surely be more ominous, threats to the United States more formidable, and challenges more exigent than those experienced in the three decades since the onset of the strategic rivalry called the cold war. Premises long basic to United States policy will continue to be overturned by emerging realities. The relationship between the United States and the Soviet Union—and this is a point of cardinal import—will continue to set the great strategic frame. A multiplicity of political forces unrelated in origin to that relationship will contend on the world scene, but the United States-Soviet strategic equation—and how it is viewed by the principals and by others, however aligned—will have pervasive effects on the interplay of those forces.

According to Moscow's assertions—and the point is at once impossible either to prove or to refute—the Soviet Union's achievement of proximate strategic parity with the United States provided the essential setting, the indispensable circumstance, for the 1973 petroleum embargo. In a similar way, many developments in the years ahead will hinge on how the strategic equation between the superpowers is discerned. One cannot presage the developments because one cannot foretell what that equation will be or will be seen to be.

This observation introduces the most significant unknown in an attempt to look ahead in world affairs to 1990. The clouded factor of which I speak is how firmly, and over what scope, the United States will remain in strategic contention. A central element in the answer—the will to act effectively in face of perceived circumstances—must await the test of events. The factor of means, which must inevitably constrain will in face of challenges not now foreseeable, cannot wait on events but must be settled in advance on the basis of estimates of what the course of events will probably be. Thus the problem involves reciprocal contingencies and tends to go around in circles. It would be pointless to deplore the logical difficulties, because much of life—and foreign policy in particular—abounds with such puzzles. The important thing here is to understand the meaning of being in strategic contention.

Conducting policy in times of formal peace under the necessity of having the contingencies of war continuously in mind is a relative novelty—dating back only three decades—in the American experience. Except in occasional intervals of war, the longer past provided exemption from considerations of strategy.

Thinking about the contingencies of war involves notionally sorting countries in the external realm into friends, putative enemies, and in-betweens. In event of hostilities, who would be in? On what side? Who would stay out—with what effect? What forces would be used? What weapons? In what environment—land, sea, undersea, air, and space? Against what targets? With what destructive effects? For what duration? With what impact on material structures, people, and national will to persevere? To what final result? Equally important, what are the presumed adversary's answers to those questions? What are his perceptions of the answers on this side and of this side's estimate of that side's perceptions? Peacetime policy conducted in strategic terms is played out against a background of notions about the answers to such questions. In saying this, I neither deplore nor exalt the circumstance. Such a mental process as I have described is basic to discerning the threshold of war. On such a base one derives judgments of how seriously to rate a threat, how far one can safely press an issue, or when it will be prudent to temporize. These judgments in turn are essential for keeping highly contested issues from precipitating hostilities. Thus the process of calculation is not necessarily and inherently bellicose but also has to do with preserving peace.

A basic discrepancy between the respective sides' discernments on such questions in a charged situation—so that each side sees itself a winner and believes the other side agrees—presents a high potential for war. In contrast, war is relatively improbable when the adversaries' perceptions of the outcome agree. Another distinction is called for. Suppose one side feels sure of being a hypothetical winner and is rightly confident of being so rated by the adversary. Then the advantage accrues to that side. The other side is under disproportionate constraint and more susceptible to pressure. With the hypothetical outcome seen by both sides to be in doubt, constraints and susceptibilities to pressure are intrinsically even.

At the onset of the cold war the United States' general condition was excellent, largely in consequence of the course and outcome of World War II. Accumulated assets in capital plant, agricultural productivity and food reserves, and financial resourcefulness exceeded anything in any nation's experience. The country was the sole appreciable source of international credit, with a steady currency which set the standard of value in world trade. The government's credibility was high, civil morale was intact, and military morale was attuned to victory. The country was in position to assure access to energy for its own and its allies' needs, was unchallengeably ascendant in military aviation and in naval power for every strategic ocean, and had a short-term monopoly and a longer-term headstart in nuclear strategic power.

Such an array of assets—and especially the nuclear capability—afforded the United States the edge in all assessments of the outcome of a hypothetical war and so in the calculations of political contention. In what came to be known as the containment policy, that advantage was conveyed vicariously to a multiplicity of allies bound to the United States through miscellaneous commitments and ventures of scope and expense unequaled in any nation's experience. The aim was to instill within the Soviet ruling group itself as well as among the United States' various allies a strong belief in the probability of successful counteraction to any use or threat of Soviet coercion, direct or vicarious—thereby offsetting the Soviet Union's potential for intimidation. In turn, the Soviet Union strove to undermine the containment policy by wearing down the United States' will to persevere in it and by sapping confidence in American resolution among the United States' allies.

Disproportionate constraint on the Soviet Union operated to the United States' benefit at numerous junctures of the ensuing contest—notably during the Cuban missile crisis of 1962. I say notably because in that episode the United States' principal policymakers were awed to find themselves in possession of the strategic superiority which had enabled them to manage through to a flawed success. Astonishing as it may be, a psychic consequence of the experience was an impulsion to let the margin in strategic nuclear power slip away. Some components of the country's once considerable strategic preponderance were bound to dissipate. Others were debased through various defaults. The nuclear advantage was volunteered away in the hope of establishing the precondition for contracting a strategic standoff with the Soviet Union.

The resulting intricate and arcane negotiations, under way at last in 1969, have in seven years of intermittent effort produced accords on quantitative limits and some qualitative restrictions affecting capacity for intercontinental nuclear volleys. Rather than arresting strategic competition, the results can be said more accurately to set some gross bounds within which to wage the contest. The divergencies between the United States and the Soviet Union revealed in the negotiations hugely exceed in significance the agreements registered. The two sides' purposes simply are not reciprocal.

The American aim is to eliminate strategic contention. The following postulates underlie the American case. A war between the nuclear-armed superpowers would be mutually annihilative and would spell the end of civilized existence. At that level of destruction both sides would be losers. In superpower terms a war-winning capability is impossible. The paramount concern must be to avert war. Nuclear strategic strength must become neutralized and nugatory. Diplomatic processes must henceforth be disjoined from them.

In the Soviet attitude, a war between the superpowers might be annihilative for one side but not necessarily for both and would not mark a finish to civilized life. There must still be winners and losers. A war-winning capability remains a cogent concept. The inherent concern of Soviet policy must be to prevail—not to trail off into stalemate. Diplomatic settlements cannot be disjoined from ratios of strategic strength and the image of war. So what is called for is preponderance in combination with a will to bring it to bear. In its way, then, the Soviet outlook also would end strategic contention—not by establishing a perpetual equipoise but by achieving an irreversible imbalance.

Soviet military efforts match the concept and words. Besides a significant build-up of ground forces and a navy designed to contest United States control of the seas in war, the Soviet Union is proliferating shorter-range nuclear delivery systems to provide unchallengeable hitting power for a distance approaching 2,000 miles beyond the Soviet periphery. Within the agreed limits on intercontinental striking power, the Soviet Union is intent on achieving a manifest edge in destructive capability sufficient to make a nuclear riposte implausible—thereby nullifying the United States' nuclear deterrent.

The hopes entertained by the United States in letting its nuclear advantage slip away were—and are—unfounded. The Soviet Union has no intention of settling for strategic stalemate. What it is after is strategic paramountcy. Soviet Foreign Minister Andrei Gromyko's recent words heralding "a visibly increased preponderance" calculated "to lay down the direction of international politics" articulate the notion. The Soviet Union's aim is to have its way without having to fight. The aim requires intimidatory power. A plausible willingness to invoke war is a necessary constituent of such power. What logically follow from this are Soviet endeavors to bring about and amplify an imbalance of threat to be brought to bear in furthering Soviet purposes.

Here an appraisal of bellicosity and peaceableness in the Soviet outlook is important—especially so in view of the emphasis placed upon the idea of the United States' and the Soviet Union's common interest in peace by persons disposed to deplore the superpowers' strategic rivalry and theretofore to shrug off attendant issues as spurious.

Neither the Soviet attitude nor the concrete facts evidence a design to foment wars. I do not doubt the Soviet government's firm desire to avoid large-scale nuclear hostilities. The rift between World War II's preeminent victors did not—and does not—really pit a predilection for peace against an ambition for war. The contention is more complex than that. A dialogue in *The Second Book of Kings* expresses the kernel: "Joram . . . said, Is it peace Jehu? And he answered, What peace?" The division concerns conflicted responses to the query: What peace?

The sides are alike—a superficial resemblance—in postulating peace as normal and viewing war therefore as a deviancy, a breakdown. The rub is this. In the Americans' outlook, the sources of war are assumed to be relatively simple defects, readily rectifiable by improved procedures, closer communication among nations, and embellished cooperation in the form of trade, cultural interchange, and so on. In the Soviet view, conflict is blamed exclusively on other societies. Its causes are seen as faults built into their structures and knotted into their thought patterns. Thus these societies must be totally refashioned, and their modes of thought systematically altered, to match the Marxist-Leninist paradigm in a process dictated by historic necessity, with the Soviet Union its custodian, interpreter, and agent. Peace as a general condition must await an indefinite tomorrow, but meanwhile the term serves as a tag for whatever purpose the Soviet Union may be promoting at any juncture while unremittingly, though opportunely, sustaining its enmity.

Those who are disposed to dismiss the long contention between the superpowers as uncalled-for interpret Soviet conduct as defensive and pragmatic. In answer—for state conduct as for personal life—being hard to get along with may indeed signify defensiveness. States' aggressions, like those of individual persons, generally are linked to felt insecurity. What counts is behavior, not the psychic springs. A ruling group entertaining animosities far and wide is likely to feel insecurity in matching measure. As to the cast of the Soviet hierarchs' beliefs, innermost affirmations are hard to determine. Practice is what counts. The regime's asserted role as the agent of historic necessity is indispensable to its claim of internal legitimacy. Were it to abandon this rationale, the regime would be renouncing its very title to existence. The regime is indeed pragmatic, but this term denotes a method of going about achieving one's purposes rather than the content of those purposes. Like being opportune, to be pragmatic is to eschew futility, to proceed expediently, and to prefer concentrating effort on endeavors that are likely to succeed—an approach indisputably characteristic of Soviet conduct.

An incident recollected from a news item which I once read—concerning how an old couple running a grocery store resisted and slew a bandit who came after their money—suggests an appropriate distinction in terms. Interest in possessing the money might be said to have been common to the bandit and the old couple—hence the contention. The old couple's interest was joint—a big difference. The enduring trouble in United States-Soviet relations has centered on lack of joint interest in peace. That circumstance, which explains and justifies the contest begun three decades ago, persists—notwithstanding the atmospherics of détente concurrent with the tedious negotiations about strategic arms.

The point gives a clue to the consequences of permitting the Soviet Union to acquire irreversible strategic preponderance. With a situation in which a resort to war is implausible in American perceptions but plausible in Soviet premises—and with both principals aware of the mismatch—the burden of constraint obviously must fall disproportionately on the United States. Crisis management inevitably becomes a process for licensing the Soviet Union to whip up crises to suit its purposes and putting pressure on the United States to manage a way out. Disproportionate psychological effects would shape the results of every transaction. Stage by stage, acquiescence would become a habit. Because no combination of nations capable of standing up to Soviet pressure is possible without the United States' participation, the effects would reverberate everywhere. The vision illuminates Minister Gromyko's words about coming into position "to lay down the direction of international politics."

Could not the United States survive in such circumstances? At this point many people pose precisely this question—in tones indicating that if the reply is affirmative, all is well for the common defense. A reasonable answer might be: yes, or at least probably. An entity called the United States, with its actual territorial domain unpenetrated, might go on for a long time in that situation. Beleaguerment would weigh upon it, however. Accesses to sources of raw materials important for national well-being would be jeopardized. The polity would have lost its long-treasured sense of being free from exterior intimidation. In James R. Schlesinger's phrase, the Americans might become "a mean-spirited nation," for it is bad for a people to come to a time of having to think of better days in the past tense. To the extent that such considerations count, national security would be impaired. Beyond that, the nation at some juncture might be pressed to a choice between capitulation to a resolute adversary's designs and war at great disadvantage—a juncture which I cannot foresee but cannot rule out.

Strategic preponderance is presumably irrecoverable for this side. The residual and essential question, then, is whether the United States will do whatever is necessary to ensure strategic equilibrium and thus to prevent the Soviet Union from solidifying a strategic preponderance weighted in its favor.

What is called for on the part of the United States concerns attitudes as well as wherewithal. The problem of national security is not susceptible of being attended to merely by deciding to allocate the necessary resources. Conversely, at any real crux of events, in the absence of forehanded action to provide a strategic base credible in material terms, will and nerve alone will not avail.

The connection deserves emphasis. Strategic strength is too often thought of as if it were inert substance whose very existence ensures against its ever having to be activated. Something akin to the reverse is true. Without there being a plausible, practical possibility of activating it, strategic strength is delusory. I recall prudent advice given me by a serious-minded old-timer when I was growing up in West Texas more than a half century ago—good counsel as applicable for strategic power as for six-shooters. He said it would be bad practice for me to go armed if I was not prepared to draw and absolutely bad practice to draw if I was afraid to shoot. Mere possession of hardware would provide little, if any, security. Mere gestures of courage unsupported by actual resolution would surely bring trouble.

The late Ambassador Charles E. Bohlen concluded: "Unhappily, the United States is not ready for the continuous struggle of wills and never-ending diplomatic crises that we face with the Soviet Union." I incline to that judgment. In explaining his dour estimate, Bohlen blamed a want of "the discipline and patience to prevail," but that explanation only prompts one to look for deeper sources in the national psyche.

Whichever of these concentric circles is involved in pertinent decision making—the president and his immediate advisers who constitute the core, the legislative branch in the next wider compass, and finally a determining number of the citizenry as a whole—there will never be time enough for canvassing every question in all its complexity back to the beginning. In order to reach coherent conclusions—even leaving aside the question of whether such conclusions are adequate or inadequate— there must already be in force a whole array of axioms, proverbial norms, and general premises. Such mental baggage is sometimes referred to as ideology. Because not all such ideas are technically ideological, I prefer Nathan Leites's phrase—"an operational code."

Portions of a society's operational code may be mere social hunches— truths held to be self-evident without being rigorously thought out or empirically demonstrated. Even mischievously misleading hunches are likely to have some foundation in experience. What is fallacious in them may result from construing a lesson of history from one or only a small number of experiences or attributing eternal truth to a maxim which was appropriate for only one occasion or period. What counts is that such ideas mark the accepted approach in general discourse. Doubters are more likely than not to forebear arguing. Thus a president or a secretary of state would routinely accept such ideas in a speech draft. Editors and commentators echo the notions. The ideas are authenticated by repetition and take on the apparent solidity of facts.

The inherent nature of peace, for example, is a concept firmly fixed in the American operational code. Its lineage runs back to the eighteenth-century Enlightenment, a source of so many of our unexamined but generally accepted ideas. The concept was seemingly verified during a long interval of privileged remoteness from serious exterior challenge, following the withdrawal of European military power from the United States' environs in the Napoleonic epoch. The version of peace in the American mind was nonstrategic. Perhaps inevitably, as Geoffrey Blainey observes in *The Causes of War,* Americans who thought about the matter at all tended to attribute the country's strategic noninvolvement to prevailing beliefs, rather than vice versa.

A vision of abolishing war through worldwide application of the American coded norms prompted American sponsorship of what Herbert Butterfield in *Christianity and History* calls "that cruel hoax of the twentieth century"—the idea of fighting the one final war, whereupon "the world can be cleansed, and we can start building paradise." In the sequel to each of the wars to end war—first in the League of Nations Covenant, which the United States renounced, and then in the United Nations Charter, to which the United States still adheres—the formula for lasting peace consisted of those norms globalized, with a perpetual intergovernmental conference to enforce them. The concept of security, still documented in the United Nations Charter, is that of a nonstrategic condition sparing every state from being pressed by enemies, for all would be foresworn against enmity. More importantly, peace would be maintained through an unchallengeable coalition of power confronting any backslider —an awesome certainty calculated to deter all transgressions and thus to obviate forever the need to think of peace strategically.

That dream still haunts the national psyche. The country's shift to a strategic approach to peace at the outset of the cold war three decades ago was provisional, as if merely temporary adjustments to transient realities were being made. That sense of tentativeness endures. The reason is comprehensible: a nation's operational code is not so readily alterable. What is especially difficult, to the point of impossibility, is for a people believing that peace is an inherent condition to come to terms with the existence of an enduring adversary both too important to be ignored and devoted to opposed purposes linked to a code irreconcilable with their own. If the choice of war is ruled out, then the options are reduced either to acquiescing in the other side's purposes or to becoming reconciled to the rigors and dangers of a protracted struggle—a troublesome choice.

In the conduct of external affairs, as in so much of life, the will to believe is potent, and believing is seeing. Harsh conclusions inevitably follow from accepting the obduracy of Soviet purposes. The difficulty in accepting harsh reality encourages one to perceive—or to believe that one perceives—practical possibilities of molding Soviet attitudes regarding conditions of peace to conform to the United States' preferences. The persistent goal of the containment policy—in Eugene Rostow's words—has been "to deter Soviet expansion in areas vital to our security, and, on that indispensable foundation, to persuade the Soviet Union finally to accept the rules of the Charter respecting the international use of force." In varying degrees of conviction six Presidents, from Truman to Ford, and innumerable subordinate expositors, including eight or nine secretaries of state, have accounted for the United States' multifarious commitments in terms of the hope of promoting through strategy a metamorphosis to a nonstrategic world order.

Thus the cold war came confusedly to be portrayed as an epilogue of sorts to World War II—a second effort, as it were, to vindicate the traditional American dream of a nonstrategic world order. With the alleged lapse of the cold war, the basic confusion between the explicit finiteness of a balance-of-power concept and the boundlessness of collective security called for in the Charter persists. The result is a certain derivative asymmetry in the enduring contest.

United States policy, and the general beliefs whence it is derived, remain preoccupied with a goal of achieving globally that nonstrategic version of peace experienced by Americans in a now departed past. This purpose entails the neutralization of strategic factors. Such a neutralization requires the United States to persuade the Soviet Union to renounce its own basic norms concerning peace and war—in other words, to undergo a sort of conversion. In Robert Conquest's words, the approach must assume the Soviet state to be "just another foreign state, a powerful rival no doubt, but little more: a country whose rulers certainly conduct their internal affairs in a way we can only deplore, but . . . in the international field are to be regarded as more or less like anyone else." Thus the pursuit of that hope requires seeing the Soviet Union as it really is not.

Meanwhile, as it concentrates on amplifying strategic preponderance as a condition essential to realizing a contrasting version of world order, the Soviet Union is in position to see this nation as it really is. For Soviet purposes, converting the United States is not required. The Soviet Union can garner advantage from this country's long-established norms concerning peace and war and the nexus between them. It can count upon the Americans' reluctance to recognize the enduring reality of confrontation with an implacable ideological adversary. The tentativeness and tenuousness of the American adaptation to a strategic view of peace, and the prevailing uneasiness with the burdens of maintaining that strategic approach, also work to Soviet advantage. A belief in the Americans' exemption from the vicissitudes of historic existence, a sense that nothing truly terrible can ever overtake the United States from abroad, underlies all of these attitudes. The attitudes are susceptibilities for the Soviet regime to play on in trying, with constancy and no small success, to ease the United States away from the containment policy.

One other set of notions more or less firmly fixed in the American operational code—but pertaining to the nation's view of itself rather than to its perspective on relations with the vast external realm—impresses me as relevant. I refer to an array of bright expectations linked to the doctrine of progress. Here again I shall explain my terms.

Progress is an optimist's word for change. The doctrine of progress—a tenet of historical faith in vogue among nineteenth-century intellectuals—postulates that the momentum of events is inherently upward and forward, not merely in the counting of time but also in the reckoning of human benefits. According to the theory, information accumulating with the passage of years and centuries must crystallize into more and more knowledge, whence steady additions to human wisdom are engendered, with the result that human efficacy and character are steadily enhanced. J. B. Bury's critique, *The Idea of Progress*, likens this notion to the Tower of Pisa, a magnificent edifice tilted at a precarious angle on shaky foundations. Whatever its logical weaknesses, however, the idea was commonly accepted in America as nowhere else, the country being a place where the occupation of a vast national domain endowed with matchless unvested wealth offered ample supporting data for faith in endless progress.

The great depression of forty-five years ago, with its combination of a faltering economy and a baffled government, temporarily shook the nation's confidence in the doctrine. Franklin D. Roosevelt's New Deal, with its bustling and dramatic activities, helped revive flagging spirits, but whether real momentum was actually being restored in those years is a moot question, for World War II intervened.

The war, that second great discontinuity to overtake the American people within a decade, proved to be the occasion of many and colossal successes—a theme ably portrayed in Geoffrey Perrett's *Days of Sadness, Years of Triumph*. Military plans took effect in great campaigns that moved on schedule to indisputable triumphs. Final victory was militarily unequivocal. Against unmistakable and visible enemies, the nation was united as seldom or never in the past. Grand policy, simplified in explanation, enjoyed support from nongovernmental opinion leaders and from the media. Huge reservoirs of talent of all kinds were tapped. Multitudes of people adapted readily to new and unaccustomed tasks. Invention flourished. Production in agriculture and manufacturing spurted. Civil consumption rose in phase with military requirements, and millions of Americans, despite shortages, lived better than ever. Upward social mobility was stimulated as never before. Thanks to economic controls, inflation was kept substantially in check.

The subsequent effects of those combined successes were tremendous. One, already noted, was the superb power base underlying the United States' strategic ascendancy in earlier stages of the cold war. A second and less tangible effect, of special moment here, was restoration of faith in the tenet of historic progress—thenceforth linked to policy. "America can do anything," I remember hearing a Congressman declaim in 1947. Without thinking about the matter searchingly or systematically, and with only occasional relapses into doubt, the vast majority of Americans would have concurred with him. The potential for producing prodigies simply by means of the right policy seemed to be self-evident. The perverse tendency of policy to bring about unintended results was scarcely taken into account. Resolve, supplemented by money, could supposedly always work wonders.

That affirmative spirit was to lead the United States into some of its greatest achievements in foreign affairs but also into the Vietnam debacle, which above all other experiences has undercut people's faith in the nation's capacity for coping with external challenges. Here, however, I am concerned with the impact on domestic expectations. In internal matters, confidence in the inherent capacity of policy to achieve every desideratum remains prevalent.

As a corollary of this belief, nonachievement comes to be seen as a withholding, therefore a deprivation, and by logical extension an abridgement of rights. Thus to an unprecedented degree the concept of rights becomes a notion of entitlement to the satisfaction of any ambition or appetite whatever, and frustration constitutes its own warrant for what-ever recourse a sufferer of its pangs may undertake. The citizen's abid-ing identity is as a user of goods, whether by purchase or grant, to the exclusion of being a producer or even a possessor. Profusion of goods is taken as a bestowed circumstance. Conditions conducive to production are assumed as inherent. Hence one's concern with policy properly re-lates only to distribution, which is simpler than production just as slicing watermelons is less bother than growing them. Society's beneficence is tested by its ensuring of more and more—translatable into better and bet-ter. The citizen's good will toward the polity, inherently contingent, must be wooed. Government, as wooer, tends to become a service enterprise.

Expectations demanding fulfillment by governmental policy include psychic satisfaction along with tangible benefits. Significance—or recog-nized worth—is supposed to be one's inherent due. Everyone's role in life must be meaningful—whatever the word means. Expectations linked to upward mobility become accelerated. Advances from generation to gen-eration—so that each generation stands figuratively on its predecessor's shoulders—no longer satisfy demands for progress. Increments must be manifested over the productive span of each individual life. Levels of livelihood and psychic enjoyment must continually surpass themselves, and anyone not making headway from year to year is entitled to feel deprived. Egalitarianism—distinguishable from equality, which denotes a precept for dealing justly among incommensurable human beings—enters. Evenness is assumed as a circumstance bestowed by nature, so that any disparity becomes a proof of denial. Average becomes a testing point for justice. A situation of being graded below average, by whatever testing process, signifies failure, generates grievance, and summons policy to give redress. A formula for infinite inflation—of wages, honors, titles, ranks, and grades—thus becomes established.

Persons sharing particular ambitions defined as rights—this point gets to the heart of the matter—are aggregated as minorities. Any person may have a plural number of such fractional identities. I was first made aware of that possibility in reading an exposition by Aaron Wildavsky, where-upon, appraising my own identities, I was astonished to learn that I be-longed to four minorities. To me the idea of a society consisting of clamorous fractions in a sum total far greater than the whole population came as an awesome revelation.

What prompts me to these reflections is an essay by Walter T. Ridder —in the *New York Times*, 29 July 1976—concerning the regnancy of frac-tions in the American society. "In some ways," he writes, "it seems to me that we have suddenly gone off on a binge in regard to so-called minorities. . . . In recent times, we seem to have discovered all kinds of minorities, some of which we had never even heard of until their loud claims for recognition shattered our ears."

The relevant circumstance inherent in these phenomena is this: the general welfare, in a hugely expanded version, has become a claimant against the common defense. One must wonder whether a people reduced to a collection of exigent fractions can function effectively as a nation defining its role in history and doing what is necessary to maintain itself to perform that role. It will be difficult to persuade the nation to transcend its particular interests—especially so in view of its historic predilection for a nonstrategic approach to peace. I can imagine a president saying the words to disenthrall the nation and rally it to the courses necessary to keep the United States effectively in strategic contention. He might candidly dwell upon the futility of trying to convert the adversary and the necessity instead of converting ourselves. I am only romancing. I have no expectations.

However pessimistic these thoughts may seem, I offer them in no spirit of defeatism. In the late Joseph A. Schumpeter's words,

I deny entirely that this term is applicable to a piece of analysis. Defeatism denotes a certain psychic state that has meaning only in reference to action. Facts in themselves and inferences from them can never be defeatist or the opposite whatever that might be. The report that a given ship is sinking is not defeatist. Only the spirit in which this report is received can be defeatist: The crew can sit down and drink. But it can also rush to the pumps.

II

*The United States
Military Posture*

7

PAUL H. NITZE

Nuclear Strategy:
Détente and
American Survival*

I

During much of the period of Dr. Kissinger's dominance of U.S. foreign policy, détente with the Soviet Union has been the centerpiece of that policy. U.S. military strength was viewed as being necessary to make détente work, rather than to make possible actual defense of ourselves or our allies against Soviet military pressure (Dr. Kissinger said war with the Soviet Union is unthinkable).

This view was supported by the proposition that any war between the Soviet Union and ourselves would be nuclear and would inevitably result in hundreds of millions of casualties on both sides. This, in turn, implied that it makes little difference, within limitations of the type contemplated by the Vladivostok Accord, whether the Soviet side comes to have more or bigger offensive warheads; the degree to which they improve their weapons technologically; the extent of the asymmetrically better Soviet defenses, both active and passive; or whether one side or the other strikes first, provided only that we maintain strategic offensive forces for retaliation approximately as numerous and powerful as those the U.S. now has and has programmed for the future.

No more serious question faces this country than whether these proposi-

*This chapter first appeared as "Deterring Our Deterrent," in *Foreign Policy* magazine (Winter 1976-1977).

tions are true or false. To assess the probable truth or falsity, three sets of considerations are pertinent: One has to do with the interaction of policy and military strategy; the second has to do with the various methods of assessing relative capabilities; the third has to do with the interaction between the perceived strategic balance and foreign policy, including détente.

II

Twenty years ago, in an article entitled "Atoms, Strategy and Policy," published in *Foreign Affairs*, I included the following thoughts: [1]

A strong case can be made that no rational body of men would initiate a general atomic war unless they believed that the power of their initial attack and its immediate effects on the enemy would be so great as to assure that the subsequent phases of the war would be substantially one-sided. In order to achieve such a one-sided result, the attacking side (either Russia in an initial attack, or the West in response to the aggression by Russia or China which could be met only by general war) would logically concentrate the full power of its initial atomic attack on the military—primarily the retaliatory—capabilities of the other side. The attacker's object would be to destroy, in the initial blow, a large proportion of the base structure from which the defender must launch his retaliatory action (including the planes or missiles on the bases and the submarines and carriers which might support the main retaliatory action). The attacker would attempt to destroy a sufficiently large proportion of this base structure to reduce the power of the defender's retaliatory action to a level which the attacker's own defense system could contain. If he should succeed in this attempt he will have assured that the remaining phases of the war will be substantially one-sided. Once he has gained effective control of the intercontinental air space, then his adversary's entire country, including cities, industries, means of communication and remaining military capabilities, will lie open to his will. He will presumably have much in mind the postwar problem of building a world which he can control and manage. He will want destruction of that world to be held within reasonable limits. He will wish his own country to be spared as far as possible. He will also want to destroy only as much of the enemy territory as is necessary for him to impose his will and get on with the job of making of the world what he wants and can make of it.

The side which has lost effective control of the intercontinental air spaces will face a truly agonizing decision. It may still have the capability of destroying a few of the enemy's cities. But the damage it could inflict would be indecisive and out of all proportion to the annihilation which its own cities could expect to receive in return.

Today some of the phrases in that passage seem out of date, but I believe the central points remain valid, particularly those which emphasize that the objective of military strategy under the circumstance of actual conflict would be to bring the war to an end under conditions less disastrous than other possible outcomes.

A much more succinct and elliptical formulation appeared in the November 1975 issue of *Communist of the Armed Forces*, the leading Soviet military publication: [2]

The premise of Marxism-Leninism on war as a continuation of policy by military means remains true in an atmosphere of fundamental changes in military matters. The attempt of certain bourgeois ideologists to prove that nuclear missile weapons leave war outside the framework of policy and that nuclear war moves beyond the control of policy, ceases to be an instrument of policy and does not constitute its continuation is theoretically incorrect and politically reactionary.

This statement clearly indicates the Soviet view that a war involving nuclear missiles can and should be an extension of policy. A suicidal war would not be such an extension of policy; therefore the military forces should not be limited in capability only to those actions which are more likely to result in mutual destruction. The force requirements for meeting the criterion of being an extension of policy are reasonably obvious, and include the following:

a. A powerful counterforce capability—one sufficient to reduce the enemy's offensive and defensive capabilities significantly and progressively below one's own;
b. Forces sufficiently hardened, dispersed, mobile, or defended as to make disadvantageous a possible counterforce response by the other side—that is, such a response would progressively weaken the relative position of the responder;
c. Sufficient survivable reserve forces even in the event of such a counterforce response to hold the enemy's population and industry hostage;
d. Active and passive defense measures, including civil defense and hardened and dispersed command and control facilities, sufficient to ensure survival and control even if the enemy response to the initial counterforce attack were an immediate retaliatory strike on one's population and industry;
e. The means and the determination not to let the other side get in the first blow—i.e., to preempt if necessary.

An examination of the Soviets' strategic nuclear program and their military doctrinal literature indicates clearly that they are indeed attempting to achieve capabilities consistent with fulfilling all five requirements. One cannot prove, of course, that this is the Soviet reasoning. But the programs begun about 1962 and continued at a high level of effort since that time seem to reflect a fundamental state of mind on the Soviet side that contains no doubt as to the desirability of a force which can meet this set of criteria.

III

That the Soviets are making rapid and significant progress in their strategic force programs is clear. However, to assess the degree of Soviet progress in achieving these goals, to determine the truth or falsity of the judgments implied by Dr. Kissinger's policy statements, and to decide whether and to what extent U.S. strategic programs should be augmented or modified, the U.S. and Soviet relative nuclear capabilities must be assessed in detail and in a pertinent manner. Furthermore, one needs to illuminate the questions: how much is enough for the Soviet side to believe that a nuclear war could, for them, be an extension of policy through military means, and how much is enough for us to deny them that possibility.

There are three distinctly different ways—increasing in depth and sophistication—in which various indices, such as number of launchers (SNDVs), number of warheads, megatonnage, equivalent megatonnage, countermilitary potential against hard targets (2,000 PSI index), equivalent weapons (EW), or throw-weight can be used to measure relative capabilities and crisis stability. These three ways are:

a. That which each side has *before* a strike;

b. That surviving to the U.S. and that remaining to the Soviet side *after an initial counterforce strike* by the Soviet side;

c. That remaining to each side *after an exchange* in which the Soviet side attacks U.S. forces and the U.S. responds by reducing the Soviet side's reserved forces to the greatest useful extent.[3]

The first method involves so-called "static" indicators; it does not assess how these capabilities might react upon each other in an actual exchange; it tends not to differentiate between those capabilities useful in a counterforce role and those useful in holding the other side's population and industry hostage.

The second method, being the first step in a dynamic analysis, is more sophisticated. It reflects the counterforce capabilities of those weapons used in the initial counterforce strike, but does not, however, distinguish between the counterforce and the countervalue capabilities of the forces remaining to each side after that first step.

The third method, which carries the dynamic analysis to a second step, most clearly brings out the stability or potential instability of the relationship by making it possible to assess the relative counterforce capabilities of each side and the countervalue capabilities remaining to each side after a two-sided counterforce exchange in which all useful counterforce targets are addressed.

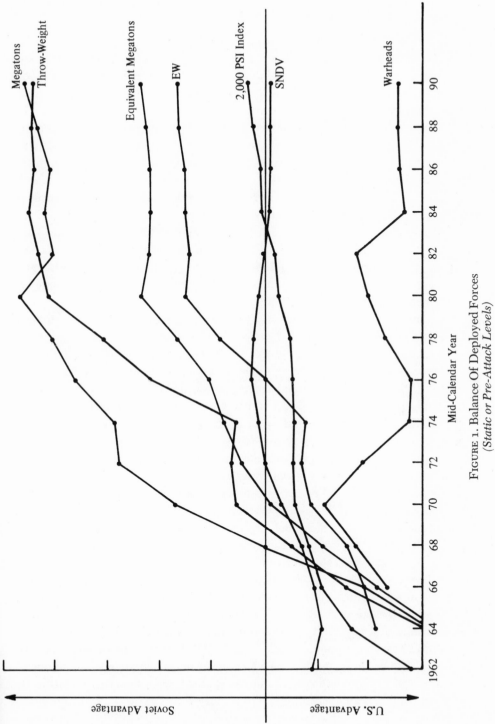

FIGURE 1. Balance Of Deployed Forces
(*Static or Pre-Attack Levels*)

Figures 1, 2, and 3 illustrate the results of one such set of analyses. Figure 1 illustrates the first method for several indices; figure 2 illustrates the second; figure 3 illustrates the third.

A word about the indices shown in these charts. In comparing the two disparate strategic forces, different indices are more significant in the different methods of analysis. I believe that in figure 1 the most useful static index is the index of equivalent weapons of a strategic force. This is perhaps the most sophisticated single index—a measure which accounts for the number and yield of the warheads, the accuracy of those warheads, and the characteristics of the targets against which they might be used. In figure 3, since at that point the counterforce targets which it was considered useful to address have been addressed, the primary indices of interest are the countervalue ones. These include throw-weight, which is the best overall measure of the countervalue potential of a strategic force,[4] total megatons, which is the best index of aggregate fallout effects, equivalent megatons, which is the best index of aggregate blast damage effects, and numbers of weapons, which is the best index of target coverage.

The calculations reflected in these charts are based on the assumption that U.S. forces would be on a normal alert status when attacked. Strategic warning generated by Soviet implementation of civil defense preparations, by an evolving crisis situation, or otherwise, would enable the U.S. to bring additional forces, primarily a portion of the nonalert bomber forces, up to an alert status. On optimistic assumptions as to the additional forces that could be brought up to alert, this could reduce the Soviet advantage after a counterforce exchange, as shown in figure 3, by 20 percent in number of warheads and 40 percent in megatonnage. This result, however, is highly dependent upon the timely deployment of the B-1 force, which has not yet been finally approved. The effect of Soviet implementation of its evacuation program and other aspects of its civil defense program, which such strategic warning would permit, could be significantly more important in limiting its potential civilian casualties.

Trends shown in these charts by all methods and in all indices move in a direction favorable to the Soviet Union from the mid–1960s through the mid–1980s. Today, after a strategic nuclear counterforce exchange under normal U.S. alert conditions, the Soviet Union would hold superiority in all indices of capability except numbers of warheads, and even that sole remaining U.S. advantage will be gone within two or three years. Neither SALT I nor the projected SALT II agreements (assumed for the analyses shown) have had—or promise—any discernible effect in arresting the trend toward an increasingly large margin of Soviet superiority. Moreover, the relationship is becoming unstable; the Soviets in coming years

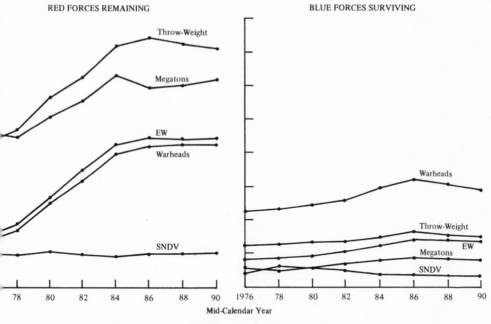

FIGURE 2. Capabilities After USSR First Strike

will be able to increase their ratio of advantage by attacking U.S. forces
(the obverse, however, is not true). This is shown in figure 4, where
methods one and three (before-any-strike, and after-the-exchange) are
compared for ratios of throw-weight. The point at which the curves cross
indicates that point at which the Soviets could, by initiating such an exchange as postulated here, increase the ratio of advantage they held at
the start of the exchange.

IV

Does any of this make any difference? Isn't it true that we could, in the
event of a Soviet counterforce attack, forego a counterforce response and
devote all of our surviving forces to an attack on Soviet population and
industry? Wouldn't such an attack satisfy Dr. Kissinger's estimate of
hundreds of millions of casualties on both sides? Isn't deterrence thereby
assured?

It is desirable that the Soviet leadership should think so. It is, moreover, possible that a U.S. president, in the absence of all other options
other than surrender, would make the decision, in the limited time which
might be available to him for decision, to launch such a countervalue
retaliatory attack. But is it desirable for a future president to be in the
position of having no other useful option? Is this the high-quality de-

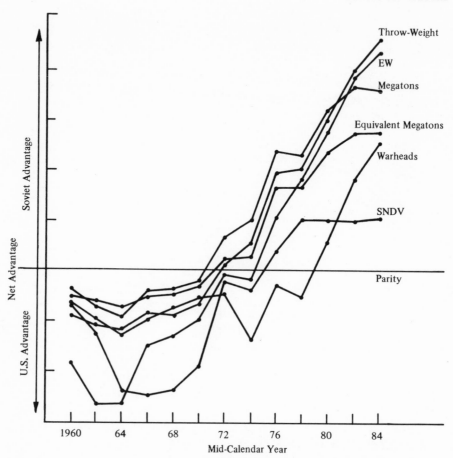

FIGURE 3. Comparison Of Alternative Indices Of Capability
(After a Counterforce Exchange)

terrence to which the United States is entitled and has striven mightily over post-World War II decades to maintain? And would the Soviet leadership think it must lose hundreds of millions of its citizens if the president were to make that decision?

I believe the answer to all these questions is negative.

Let me begin with the last question. The Soviet Union has for many years put emphasis upon the planning, organization, and training of cadres to implement a civil defense program. That program calls for the substantial evacuation of its cities and industrial plants, the sheltering of those who must stay, and the rapid construction of expedient fallout shelters by those who are evacuated and cannot otherwise be protected. In their civil defense manuals the Soviets estimate that the effective implementation of this program should hold casualties to 3 or 4 percent of their population. This would be a large number of casualties, but not

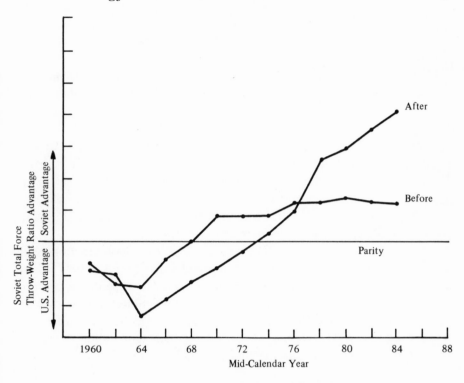

FIGURE 4. Soviet–U.S. Throw-Weight Ratios

hundreds of millions, and not a number large enough to keep their society from being able to recover with reasonable speed. This goal may not be achievable; there are many uncertainties. However, it is possible to make some gross approximations of the possible effectiveness of Soviet civil defense.

The most difficult nuclear effect for a dispersed population to defend against is fallout. Fallout is proportional to the megatonnage and the fission fraction of the weapons which are ground burst. Over the last fifteen years the U.S. has substantially reduced the megatonnage of its weapons in favor of more numerous, smaller yield, more accurate warheads.[5] Today our most survivable force is our Poseidon submarine force at sea; the aggregate megatonnage of its 2,000 or so normally alert reliable warheads is approximately 80 megatons. Because of their relatively low individual yield, it would be best to use them against point targets even in a countervalue attack, and they are most effective when fused for a height of burst optimum for blast damage effects; they would, however, then produce negligible fallout. Against such an attack the stated goal of the Soviet civil defense program might well be achieved.

Our alert bomber force is our next most survivable force. Its aggregate deliverable megatonnage could be ten times as much as that of our alert SLBM force, but the alert bombers must be launched-on-warning and a prompt decision made as to the targets which they are to hit; otherwise their survivability would be little better than that of the nonalert bombers.

Of course, the Minuteman missiles with a megatonnage roughly equal to that of the alert bomber force could be launched from under attack, but to do so allows only minutes for the decision to be made. Rough computations indicate that if all these forces were used in an all-out and immediate countervalue response to a Soviet counterforce first strike, the estimates in the Soviet civil defense manuals are somewhat over-optimistic from the Soviet viewpoint. They are not, however, wholly out of the ball park. The usual assumption that the U.S. possesses vast population overkill is, in essence, without foundation.

The crucial question is whether a future U.S. president should be left with only the option of deciding within minutes, or at most within two or three hours, to retaliate after a counterforce attack in a manner certain to result not only in military defeat for the United States but in wholly disproportionate and truly irremediable destruction to the American people. I believe not. This would be to make certain that military strategy had completely escaped from the control of policy.

V

Does any of this make any difference short of a nuclear war? The defense problems of the U.S. and the Soviet Union are quite different. The U.S. must be able to project its power over many thousands of miles to support allied defense structures on lines close to the concentrations of Soviet power. The Soviet basic defensive task is much simpler; that is, to maintain military preponderance on the exterior lines of its relatively compact landmass. Its only difficult problem is its long and narrow lines of communication to eastern Siberia. There can be little doubt that the Soviet Union has more than adequate military power for this basic defensive task.

For many years U.S. strategic nuclear preponderance has made it possible to offset Soviet military superiority at the periphery and to deter its offensive employment. It has also made it possible for the U.S. confidently to use the seas for projection of its supporting power despite the Soviet Union's always very real sea-denial capabilities.

An imbalance in favor of the Soviet Union in the strategic nuclear relationship would reverse these factors.

There is a further problem, moreover, in that the Soviet Union has in recent years been paying increasing attention to projectible power, including air mobility, longer range tactical air capabilities, intermediate range missiles, and projectible sea power. To counter such capabilities in the absence of confidence in the adequacy of our nuclear deterrent could be difficult and imprudent. Not to counter them could leave us with wholly inadequate tools of policy.

VI

What bearing does the foregoing analysis have upon the future design of our strategic forces? To my mind, the first point is that a clear distinction should be made between the two aspects of nuclear strategy: the counterforce aspect and the countervalue aspect. Neither can be ignored; both are essential to meaningful deterrence; the rquirements for each are different, distinguishable, and important.

It is my view that we have in the past failed to appreciate this distinction and have thus fallen between two stools. We have prided ourselves on our advanced technology which has given us superior accuracy, higher yield-to-weight ratios in smaller yield RVs (reentry vehicles), and leadership in developing MIRVs (multiple independently targeted reentry vehicles). For political reasons and because of the presumed destabilizing nature of a counterforce capability, we have, however, foregone the accuracy and yield combinations which would give us high single-shot kill capabilities against Soviet silos and other hardened targets. On the other hand, in order to reduce the widespread destruction which would be involved in a nuclear war if it were to occur, we have progressively reduced the megatonnage of our force. This megatonnage is now so low that it is possible for the Soviet Union to plan a civil defense program which would make a far smaller percentage of their population hostage to a U.S. countervalue attack, particularly after it has been reduced in capability by an initial Soviet counterforce attack, than our population is to a Soviet countervalue response.

The Soviet leadership appears to be fully conscious of the differing requirements for countervalue and counterforce capabilities. The question is asked why the Soviets continue to test high megatonnage single RVs on their SS–18s and SS–19s. I believe the answer is that they see the importance of deterring the deterrent; in other words, they wish to be able, after a counterforce attack, to maintain sufficient reserve megaton-nage to hold U.S. population and industry hostage in a wholly asymmetri-cal relationship. Concurrently, the accuracy and yield combinations and numbers of MIRVed RVs they are deploying promise to meet their full requirements for a highly effective counterforce capability.

The question at issue is whether we also would be well advised to make such a distinction between forces dedicated to a counterforce role and forces reserved for a countervalue role, and, if so, how much in survivable forces is enough for each of these two roles? My view is that we would be well advised to make the distinction and that it is not impossible to find reasonable criteria to determine within rough limits how much is enough for each role. I would suggest two sets of criteria. The first cri-terion would be to assure that the relationship of the yield, accuracy, survivability, and reliability of the two sides' forces is such that the Soviet side could not hope by initiating a counterforce exchange to im-prove either the absolute excess in pounds of its throw-weight over ours, or the ratio of its throw-weight to ours. To achieve this it is necessary that we deploy forces which result in bringing the throw-weight line in figure 3 closer to the parity line. This requires an increase in Minuteman sur-vivability, through development of a new multiple-aim-point basing mode; an increase in Minuteman throw-weight, through development of the MX missile; and a substantial improvement in the single-shot kill probability of U.S. RVs against hard targets, through the development and deployment of missiles and RVs with the requisite combination of accuracy, yield, and reliability to give high probability of destroying some 2,000 hard targets.

The second criterion would be to assure that the forces remaining to the U.S. after a counterforce exchange would be fully adequate to keep the Soviet population hostage to a countervalue attack in the face of the most effective civil defense programs we judge it possible for the Soviet Union to mount. It is my view that something in the order of 3,000 deliverable megatons remaining in reserve after a counterforce exchange would satisfy the second criterion.

Rough computations indicate we should be able to satisfy both criteria if we deploy 550 MX missiles in a multiple-aim-point mode, if we deploy the Trident II missile in an appropriate number of Trident submarines, if we develop the accuracy and reliability which now seem technologically feasible, and if we proceed with the planned B-1 deployments aug-mented with strategic cruise missiles. Such developments and deploy-ments will, however, take time. In the meantime, in order to retain sufficient deterrence to allow the time to restore a stable balance, urgent attention should be given to determining quick and possibly temporary fixes necessary to meet the problem as it is apt to emerge in the late 1970s and early 1980s.[6]

The objective of such short- and long-range programs would not be to give the United States a war-fighting capability; it would be to deny to the Soviet Union the possibility of a successful war-fighting capability. We would thus be acting to maintain a situation in which each side is equally and securely deterred from initiating the use of nuclear weapons against the other or the allies of the other. It is only if, and when, we persuade the Soviet side that there is no reasonable prospect that they can successfully alter that situation that we can expect them seriously to negotiate for long-term agreements assuring stable mutual deterrence at lower and equal levels of strategic nuclear capabilities.

NOTES

1. Paul H. Nitze, "Atoms, Strategy and Policy," *Foreign Affairs* 38, no. 2 (January 1956):187–98.

2. *Communist of the Armed Forces* (November 1975).

3. In Paul H. Nitze, "Assuring Nuclear Stability in an Era of Détente," *Foreign Affairs* 54, no. 2 (January 1976):207–32, this third method of analysis was the method used. This was not clear to several commentators, including Jan Lodal; see Paul H. Nitze, letter to the editor, *Foreign Affairs* 54, no. 4 (July 1976):820–23. This chapter expands upon the January 1976 article in that it deals with all three methods of analysis and concentrates on the policy issues implicit in relying on the second rather than the third method of analysis to determine force adequacy. In addition, this article attempts to get at the question of how much is enough in a quantitative way; this was dealt with only qualitatively in my 1956 *Foreign Affairs* article (see note 1).

4. "Throw-weight" is a measure of the useful weight of payload that can be propelled to intended distance. In the case of intercontinental ballistic missiles (ICBMs) and submarine-launched ballistic missiles (SLBMs), the throw-weight is a direct measure of such useful weight in terms of the potential power of the missiles' boosters. In the case of the bombers, a B-52 has been assigned an equivalent throw-weight of 10,000 lbs. and a B-1 about 19,000 lbs. through the following calculations of equivalence: The SRAM air-to-surface missile has a yield about equal to that of each of the three warheads that can be carried by a Minuteman (MM) III; hence, for every three SRAMs carried by a bomber, that bomber is given a throw-weight equivalent equal to the throw-weight of one Minuteman III. Laydown bombs are assumed to have roughly the yield of Minuteman II; hence, for each laydown bomb carried by a bomber it is given a throw-weight equivalent equal to the throw-weight of a Minuteman II.

5. See discussion on the U.S. arms history by Albert Wohlstetter in chapter 8 of this book.

6. A number of such short term quick fixes have been suggested. These include rapid development and deployment of a mobile transporter-erector-launcher and hardened capsule for MM III; a variety of simplified point defenses of the class suggested by Richard Garwin and others; provision for a potential rapid increase in bomber and SLBM alert rates; and testing of reliable and appropriate methods to launch MM from under verified large scale attack against our silos.

8

ALBERT WOHLSTETTER

Racing Forward
or Ambling Back?*

Not long ago the *Bulletin of the Atomic Scientists,* which since 1945 has kept time on the arms race, moved its famous clock ominously closer to midnight. The familiar reasoning is that American and Soviet negotiators at Geneva have failed to reach agreement on limiting strategic arms and so the race continues. The United States has forced the pace by overestimating the Soviet threat; then, to play safe, spends more resources than are needed to meet even a menace so inflated. In this way we have given the Russians no alternative than to react by spending in its own self-defense—which, in turn, we meet by still more "worst-case" analyses, increased spending, and so on and on in the deadly "action-reaction cycle." The superpowers are engaged in a mortal contest, each provoking the other into piling up arms endlessly, wasting scarce resources, increasing the indiscriminate destructiveness of weapons, lessening rather than adding to their security, and moving the world closer to nuclear holocaust.

Late in his term as secretary of state, Henry Kissinger adopted one variant of this reasoning that puts the blame on technology. He said that military technology has developed a momentum of its own, is at odds with the human capacity to comprehend it, is simply out of control or is in imminent danger of getting beyond political control. Thus we must restrain not only the number of arms but their qualitative improvement. For it seems that the very effort to design new and better techniques to protect ourselves against adversaries makes things worse for both sides and mankind.

All this is familiar, but is it true?

* I am indebted to many colleagues, but especially to David McGarvey, Steven Honda, Gregory Jones, Robert Raab, Arthur Steiner, and Zivia Wurtele.

Is it true, for example, that we chronically overestimate what the Russians will deploy and that this is the source of an "action-reaction" chain, driving the Russians and ultimately ourselves to disaster? Whatever is the case for the Soviet strategic budgets and forces, has the United States in any clear sense been racing at all? Is it true, as is claimed, that U.S. technical innovation, in particular, has spurred us to higher and higher levels of strategic spending, destructiveness, and instability?

In fact, none of this is true. Starting in the early 1960s we systematically *under*estimated how much and how rapidly the Soviets would increase their strategic offense forces. Moreover, for an even longer time, our own spending on strategic forces has been "spiraling" down rather than up. U.S. strategic program budgets ("Program I" as it is called) in real terms fell from a plateau at the end of the 1950s that was 3.5 times the present size. In fact, the peak in strategic spending occurred in fiscal year (FY) 1952 when the budget was about 4.25 times the fiscal 1976 level (in 1976 dollars the strategic program budget in FY 1952 was 32.6 billion compared to $7.7 billion in FY 1976). Finally, the net effect of major innovations in our strategic force since the 1950s was to reduce not only its cost but also its indiscriminate destructiveness, and its instability or vulnerability to attack.

These actualities seem to contrast so sharply with the standard sayings about Soviet-American competition that we need to:

1. Recall and document what the stereotypes about the strategic arms race have been.
2. Contrast the standard view that we chronically overestimate Soviet offense deployments with the facts about what Soviet offense forces we predicted in the 1960s and how these predictions turned out.
3. Contrast the theory that our strategic spending has been going up with the actual declining costs.
4. Consider briefly the concrete effects of qualitative improvements on U.S. strategic forces and budgets.

Finally, we need to ask how we could have repeated obvious untruths for so long without embarrassment. Answers to this last question must necessarily be speculative. I'll suggest some as I go along.

THE STANDARD VIEW OF THE ARMS RACE

Contemporary stereotypes about the strategic arms race resemble the arms race doctrines of Lord Grey, Bertrand Russell, Lewis Fry Richardson, and others that flourished in England between two world wars, and can be traced back at least to Cobden in the mid-nineteenth century. These doctrines suggested that each side in an arms race sees as a threat an increase in arms by the other side that is intended merely for defense. Lord Grey, who had been foreign minister when the Great War broke out, wrote:

The increase of armaments, that is intended in each nation to produce consciousness of strength, and a sense of security, does not produce these effects. On the contrary, it produces a consciousness of the strength of other nations and a sense of fear. . . . The enormous growth of armaments in Europe, the sense of insecurity and fear caused by them—it was these that made war inevitable.[1]

The Quaker physicist, Richardson, put such views into differential equations, relating the rate of increase in defense budgets on one side to the level of spending on the other, with a resulting exponential increase of budgets for both.

The doctrines of the strategic "race" that have prevailed for more than fifteen years add a few new twists to the old theory. First, they talk not simply of an exaggerated fear about the intent of an opponent in amassing armaments, but about exaggerated estimates of the size of these armaments and about plans to meet the opposing side's increase which would be overcautious (assuming the "worst case") even if the estimates of the range of possibilities were correct. Second, the British theorists between wars adopted a certain Olympian evenhandedness in describing the reciprocal fears generating the race. (Richardson talks of the mistaken fear of the "Minister of Jedesland.") But current American doctrines, like revisionist history, frequently place on America the main responsibility for the rate and scale of the arms race. Third, the current doctrines stress the instabilities brought about by technology. And fourth, they locate the source of the race especially in efforts to defend civilians and destroy offensive military forces, and see the force driving the quantitative spiral to be not merely qualitative military change, but, in particular, improved technologies for destroying not people but weapons, whether in place or already on their way to target. This perverse doctrine, widely prevalent among theorists of the arms race since Sputnik, has been summarized by a sympathizer to the view in the "frosty apothegm": "Killing people is good; killing weapons is bad." [2]

Arms race dogma about "runaway technology," "exaggerated threats," "worst-case analysis," "explosive increases," "uncapped volcanoes," "action-reaction," "treadmill to nowhere," etc., so pervades the statements on SALT and strategic interaction made by cabinet members, Congress and its staff, public interest lobbies, the academics, and the news media that selecting a few out of a mass of citations may seem redundant; it risks bruising individual sensibilities.

But as Leon Festinger, a student of apocalyptic prophesies, reminds us, prophets and their disciples often deny they meant what they said or even that they said it. So also, the apocalyptic prophets of the race to nuclear oblivion, when confronted with an empirical test and refutation of their beliefs, have responded by denying that they or anyone else hold the dogma.[3] Here then is a sample of views documenting the points challenged.

Take the exaggerated threat, "worst case" dynamic. In its more moderate form this dogma holds that our planners have a systematic bias toward exaggerating—expecting our adversary to do more than he does —and that they compound this error by designing our force to meet a force greater than we expect—a "worst plausible case." It is this minimal form I show to be in error, not only the more obviously wrong extreme that talks of "invariable overestimation" or "worst possible case."

Morton Halperin and Jeremy Stone, as if arguments can be directed only at the extreme, say the notion that "arms race analysts believe in a myth of invariable U.S. overestimation" is a "straw man." It is "obviously unlikely," they say, that "analysts believe anything is invariable." They want quotations.

For the extreme, one can introduce the flesh-and-blood Jeremy Stone to the straw Jeremy Stone, who has written, "The department invariably exaggerates the Soviet threat to obtain public and congressional support for weapons that will undermine the Soviet deterrent." [4]

And for the less or equally extreme, turn to:

Jerome Wiesner: "We always underestimate our own capabilities and overestimate those of the other fellow." [5]

Leonard Rodberg: "Even though the Soviets invariably lag far behind these predictions, our own programs go forward as if the forecasts were accurate." [6]

Herbert Scoville: "We should not again fall into the trap of perennial, compulsive reaction to timeworn, exaggerated threats." [7]

Leslie Gelb: "The common practice, as I think we all know, has been to exaggerate and overdramatize." [8]

Robert McNamara: "a strategic planner must be 'conservative' in his calculations; that is, he must prepare for the worst plausible case." [9]

Stanley Hoffmann: "The whole history of the postwar arms race is one of . . . preemptive escalation based on a worst case hypothesis which assumes the adversary's capacity and will to go ahead full speed." [10]

Paul Warnke: "in determining relative strategic balance, the other side, just as we do, must use worst case analysis. . . . They are not going to overestimate their potential and underestimate ours. If any, the error will be in the other direction." [11]

Such a belief is distinct from, but frequently associated with, a view that the United States is the catalyst for the race. Halperin and Stone observe sagely that the two views are distinct, but seem to doubt the currency of the second view as well. We might begin the next list with a characteristically temperate quote:

Jeremy Stone: "The Department of Defense has become an inventor and a merchandiser of exaggerated fears . . . an unscrupulous lobbyist to get the weapons to answer these fears. Worst of all, through the action-and-reaction phenomenon, its aggressive pursuit of the arms race has greatly undermined the security of the nation by unnecessarily stimulating Soviet efforts to keep up." [12]

Edgar Bottome: "It is my contention that with minor exceptions, the United States had led in the development of military technology and weapons production throughout the Cold war. . . . The Soviet Union has been placed in a position where all it could do was react to American initiatives in bomber or missile building programs. This American superiority, along with the highly ambitious nature of American foreign policy, has placed the United States in a position of being fundamentally responsible for every major escalation of the arms race." [13]

William Epstein: "American scientists seem to have the edge in technology and to lead the way in developing new weapons, particularly in the nuclear field, but Soviet scientists follow close behind in the action-reaction chain." [14]

Bernard Feld: "History guarantees that new American technology will certainly be followed . . . by Soviet emulation." [15]

Marshall Shulman: "This commitment . . . has led us to force the pace of the strategic arms race, and it inescapably leads to an uncontrolled military competition with the Soviet Union." [16]

John Newhouse: "America's forces apparently served as both model and catalyst for the Russians. . . . Such is the action-reaction cycle as perceived by many scientists and bureaucrats." [17]

Newhouse adds that other scientists argue, "It is the impulse of technology, not an action-reaction cycle, that drives the arms race." Most scientists in my collection see the impulse coming from us *and* technology. So, to quote Rodberg, "we have used our own superior technology to drive the arms race forward." [18] But the malign role of technology is particularly important in the dogma and deserves illustration. "Is Jerome Wiesner," Michael Nacht has demanded, choosing an evidently far-fetched case, "a modern-day Luddite?" Consider the following from a committee Wiesner headed:

It is, after all the *continuing competition to perfect and deploy new armaments* that absorbs quantities of time, energy, and resources that no static environment would demand; that exacerbates U.S. and Soviet relations with unreal considerations of strategic advantage or disadvantage; that keeps political leaders in both great powers off-balance and ill-prepared for far-reaching agreements; that fixes the attention of both sides on the most threatening aspects of the opposing posture; and, especially, that provides heightened risks of a violent *spasm of procurement—one spurring to new levels the cost, distrust, and the explosive dangers of an unending competition in arms* (italics added).[19]

The explosive dangers feared, Wiesner makes clear elsewhere, involve "an ever-increasing likelihood of war so disastrous that civilization, if not man himself, will be eradicated."[20] Anyone who holds that military innovation has a *net* bad effect (my definition of a Luddite in the military field)—let alone the effect of ultimate catastrophe—should want to impose general restraints on it. So, to quote Herbert York:

The recent small successes in controlling the quantitative side of the arms race also call for renewed efforts to control its qualitative side, to slow down the rate of weapons innovation, and hence to reduce the frequency of introduction of ever more complex and threatening weapons.[21]

Examples could be multiplied. But we need not leave Cambridge. Consider George Kistiakowsky and George Rathjens: "any understanding that slowed the rate of development and change of strategic systems would have an effect in the right direction."[22]

And take Harvey Brooks, who argues that "the most promising lines of action for controlling the qualitative arms race probably lie in mutually agreed limitations on testing," but also suggests agreements to forgo specific improvements and general declarations against destabilizing developments, even if both would be hard to interpret or verify—particularly "in closed societies."[23] Even unverifiable agreements would provide arguments in internal bureaucratic debate to those who oppose such developments—at least in open societies. Or take Paul Doty: "even better would be the adoption of a generalized set of restraints that would slow the whole development and deployment process."[24]

These would have an effect in the right direction if qualitative change has a net bias toward making strategic forces more costly, more indiscriminately destructive, more vulnerable, and harder to control. But if not, you wouldn't slow things down generally. Nor try merely to stop "unfavorable" developments (always a good idea). You would encourage the development with all deliberate speed of technologies that reduce costs, increase discriminateness, and make forces less vulnerable and easier to control.

I will present evidence that, whatever the false starts and mistakes in detail, the net effects of our major technological choices from the 1950s to the present were exactly the reverse of the Luddite stereotype. Generalized restraints would have been a bad idea.

U.S. PREDICTIONS AND SOVIET REALITIES

Systematic or even invariable overestimation need not lead to an arms spiral. If one's aim to counter a given threat is made extremely costly by expected adversary moves, because the threat is very large and the advantage is all on the other side, the game may not be worth the candle. This was in fact Secretary McNamara's chief argument against undertaking a thick antiballistic missile (ABM) defense against the Soviets. In short, the larger the threat, the more futile a response may seem. The logic that overestimating an adversary drives one to race him is not compelling. Nonetheless, it is important to ask whether the U.S. government has in fact systematically overestimated Soviet missile and bomber deployments: an assertion central to the dogma of a spiral driven by exaggerated estimates and mistaken fear.

The "missile gap," as is well known, was a U.S. overestimate, after Sputnik, of the number of intercontinental ballistic missile (ICBM) launchers that the Russians would deploy in the early 1960s. Indeed, the trauma of discovering the error formed the basis of many of Mr. McNamara's generalizations about our tendency to exaggerate and then respond to anticipated larger threats rather than to what the Soviets actually turned out to do. The missile gap has also generated a substantial confessional literature on the part of current proponents of the doctrine of an explosive arms race about their own role in creating the myth of the missile gap, and a substantial academic industry in doctoral theses and articles explaining this particular overestimate and the supposedly general and plainly evil habit of overestimating. A few comments, therefore, are in order on the missile gap before making a broader test of the habit. (Perhaps it is worth saying that I am on record, before and after Sputnik, as having steadily opposed evaluating force effectiveness on the basis of bomber or missile gaps.)

First, the "missile gap", a brief period in which the Soviets were expected to but did not deploy ICBMs more rapidly than we did, was an ICBM gap rather than a general missile gap. During the same period, in fact, we regularly and greatly underestimated the number of *intermediate and medium range* ballistic missile (IR/MRBM) launchers that the Russians would deploy at the end of the 1950s and in the early 1960s. For example, our underestimate of the number of IR and MRBM launchers that the Russians would deploy by 1963 roughly offset our overestimate of the number of ICBM launchers they would deploy. In short, we misunderstood or reversed the priorities the Russians assigned to getting capabilities against the European as distinct from the North American part of NATO. This piece of ethnocentrism on our part was characteristic. We also greatly underestimated Soviet aircraft systems directed primarily at Europe rather than ourselves.

Second, predicting the size and exact mixture of a potential adversary's weapon deployments several years hence is a hard line of work. It is intrinsically uncertain, reversible by the adversary himself between the time of prediction and the actual deployment. Moreover, an adversary may want his opponent to estimate wrongly, either up or down. In the specific case of the missile gap, Khrushchev did what he could to make the U.S. and the rest of the world believe that the Soviets had a larger initial program of ICBMs than they actually had; and he succeeded.

Whatever the source and nature of our misestimation, it helped generate the belief that we invariably expect the Russian programs to be larger than they turn out to be, that we compound this overestimate by deliberately designing our programs to meet a Russian threat that is greater even than the one we expect, and then, when the Russian threat turns out to be less rather than greater than expected, the damage is done—the overlarge U.S. force is already a reality or irreversibly committed.

It is a good idea, then, to subject to systematic test this claim of regular overestimation. It is a major element of the current dogma, repeated endlessly since 1961. In fact, the nearly universal acceptance of this belief has emerged from constant repetition of tags like "the mad momentum," "we have invariably overestimated," or "we are running a race with ourselves," etc., etc. rather than from any systematic numerical comparison with reality.[25] Figures 1 to 3 sum up the results of a search for all of the long-term predictions of Soviet strategic missile and bomber deployment that could be found in the annual presentation of programs and budgets to Congress by the secretary of defense from the start of 1962 to the start of 1972, and a comparison of these predictions with what the Russians actually deployed by mid–1972—the last date referred to in the predictions that could be checked at the time the analysis was completed.

Aside from their comparative accessibility, several reasons governed the choice of these predictions from the defense secretaries' formal statements rather than from army, navy, air force, CIA, Bureau of Intelligence Research in State, or other estimates.

First, during this extended period the secretary of defense did, regularly, every year, make predictions precise enough to be proved wrong and precise enough for measuring how much they had missed the

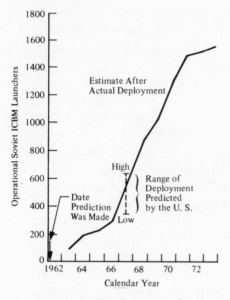

FIGURE 1a. ICBM Prediction Made in 1962

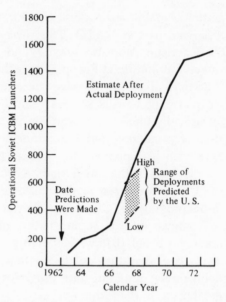

FIGURE 1b. ICBM Predictions Made in 1963

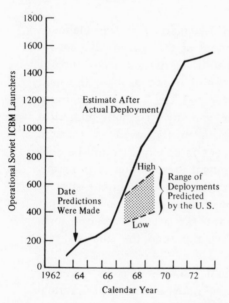

FIGURE 1c. ICBM Predictions Made in 1964

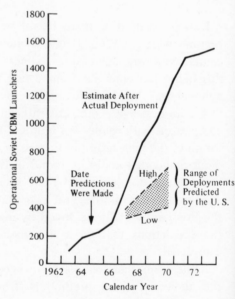

FIGURE 1d. ICBM Predictions Made in 1965

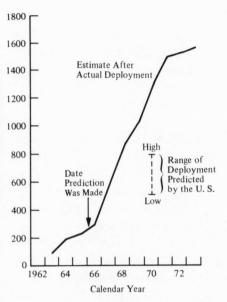

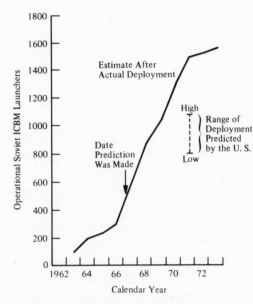

FIGURE 1e. ICBM Prediction Made in 1966

FIGURE 1f. ICBM Prediction Made in 1967

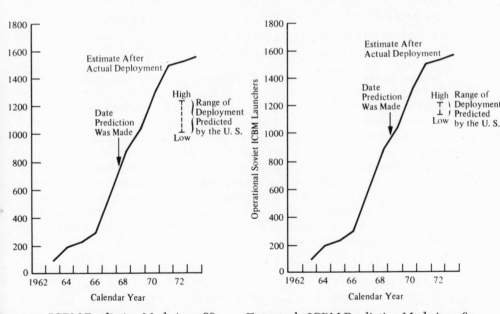

FIGURE 1g. ICBM Prediction Made in 1968

FIGURE 1h. ICBM Prediction Made in 1969

mark. The possibility of determining error here requires not only that the predictions be specific as to time and quantity, and not excessively hedged by "might" or "may conceivably," but also that the adversary realities referred to in the predictions be open to observation and highly reliable measurement by the U.S. *after the fact*. Not all objects nor all characteristics predicted nor all predictors meet these requirements. Far from it.

Second, these predictions of the secretary of defense form a well-defined, substantial population of estimates—which is not the case for intelligence predictions in general.

Third, these estimates were presented as authoritative and official.

Fourth, they were given particular prominence in the programming and budgeting process by the fact that the secretary used them directly to support his programs. And finally, these particular forecasts relate directly to the secretary's judgment and that of the Congress on the five-year defense program. They are therefore most relevant for analyzing possible relations between defense programs and defense budgets and the impetus these programs might be given by forecasts as to the future enemy force deployments. Defense systems take many years to become operational, and the forces they will confront are necessarily the subject only of long-term conjecture. In presenting these estimates the secretary emphasized this point. For example, in 1963 he testified:

Because of the long leadtimes involved in making these weapon systems operational, we must plan for our forces well in advance of the time when we will need them and, indeed, we now project our programs at least five years ahead of the current budget year. For the same reason we must also project our estimates of the enemy's forces at least five years into the future, and for some purposes, even beyond. These longer range projections of enemy capabilities are, of course, highly conjectural, particularly since they deal with a period beyond the production and deployment leadtimes of enemy weapon systems. Therefore, we are, in effect, attempting to anticipate production and deployment decisions which our opponents, themselves, may not yet have made. This fact should be borne in mind as we discuss the intelligence estimates and our own programs based on them.[26]

Figures 1a to 1h compare U.S. predictions of Soviet ICBM launchers to be deployed with the actuality as estimated after the fact. The vertical arrows indicate the date at which the prediction was made (e.g., February 1962 in figure 1a). The dashed line or lines indicate the range from high to low of what was predicted. (In figure 1a, a high of 650 and a low of 350, by mid–1967, five and a half years later.) Later projections usually included (as in figure 1b) a high and a low for more than one year. The steeply rising solid line which is the same in all the

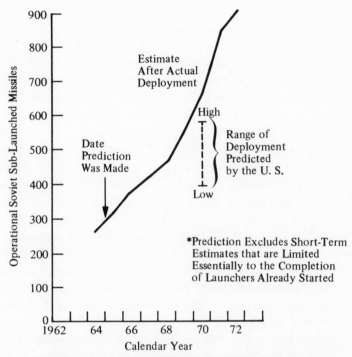

FIGURE 2. Operational Soviet Sub-launched Missiles
(*1965 U.S. Long Term Prediction Compared to the Actual Number**)

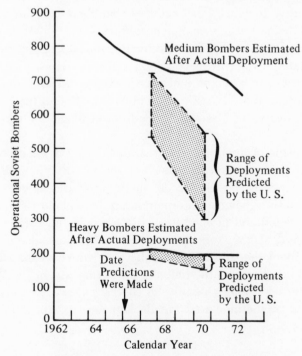

FIGURE 3. Operational Soviet Bombers
(*1966 U.S. Predictions Compared to the Actual Number*)

charts shows the number the Russians actually completed, as estimated after the fact.

Though the claim about invariable overestimation posits that at least the middle of the range between high and low always exceeds the reality, it will be apparent that even the high end of the range seldom did that, and then only at the start of the period—and even then just barely. For ICBMs the "highs" reached as high as reality only twice in eleven times. The prediction made in 1965 (figure 1d) is quite typical. Figures 2 and 3 illustrate analogously typical long-run predictions of future Soviet submarine-launched missiles (SLBM) deployed and future Soviet bomber deployments. The middle of the predicted range of the number of sublaunched missiles deployed was about three-quarters of the eventual reality. In the case of the bombers, we continued to believe that the Russians were going to phase them down and most drastically in the case of the medium bombers; but the Soviets never came down to our expectations. Tables 1 and 2 sum up some principal results. Out of fifty-one predictions, the low end of the range *never* exceeded the actual; the mean between the high and low exceeded it only twice in fifty-one times; our highs reached reality only nine times! Hardly a record of overestimation. Moreover, the ratios of projected to realized future values of the Soviet strategic force in operation display the fact that the underestimates were very substantial and that even the average of the highs was under the reality. It will be evident also that there was no systematic learning from the past as information accumulated.

In fact, since the numbers shown refer to estimates of the *cumulative* number of strategic vehicles in operation at future dates, and since the later predictions were based on much more extensive knowledge of what was already deployed or at least started in construction at the time of the prediction, the degree of bias can be made even plainer. There are several points.

First, our means of acquiring information improved greatly over the period. Second, in the later years a much larger proportion of the cumulative total in operation was already in operation at the time predictions were made. And third, we had information not only about the number of launchers completed and in operation (displayed in the rising curves of Soviet ICBM and SLBM [submarine-launched ballistic missile] launchers) but also about the substantial numbers of launchers that had been started but not completed at the time the prediction was made. We knew that ICBMs started would generally be completed, say, in about a year and a half, and submarine-based missile launchers in about two and a

TABLE 1
1962–1971 U.S. Predictions that Exceed the Actual Soviet Strategic Deployment

	ICBMs	Sub-Launched Missiles	Heavy Bombers	Medium Bombers	Total
Low predictions that exceed actual	0 of 11	0 of 15	0 of 14	0 of 11	0 of 51
Mid-range of predictions that exceed actual	0 of 11	1 of 15	1 of 14	0 of 11	2 of 51
High predictions that exceed actual	2 of 11	3 of 15	2 of 14	2 of 11	9 of 51

TABLE 2
Average Ratios of Predicted-to-Actual Cumulative Numbers
(Numbers in parentheses compare predicted to actual change)

	ICBMs (11 Estimates)	Sub-Launched Missiles (15 Estimates)	Heavy Bombers (14 Estimates)	Medium Bombers (11 Estimates)
Lower predictions	0.53 (0.16)	0.64 (0.12)	0.85	0.67
Mid-range of predictions	0.67 (0.33)	0.74 (0.47)	0.91	0.77
High predictions	0.80 (0.50)	0.84 (0.82)	0.98	0.87

NOTE: Predictions in both tables exclude short-term estimates of ICBMs and sub-launched missiles that are limited essentially to completion of launchers already started.

half years, but in any case well before the dates in our long-run predictions. In fact, estimates of the missile launchers already started that were expected to be completed by a given time were, at the midrange, only 3 percent below the actual number of ICBMs and 2 percent above it for submarine-launched missiles. If we make a rough adjustment for this fact on the one hand and on the other allow for some delay in acquiring and processing information by the date predictions were made, if we assume generously a seven-month delay, the degree of understatement will be more apparent. In effect, what was being predicted was an *increment* in the force then in operation or under construction. It is appropriate to compare that increment with the actual amount newly started and completed in the ensuing interval.

BURYING WRONG PREDICTIONS
IN THE KNOWN PAST

Our longer-term predictions about the Soviet strategic triad were under the mark for eleven years. The long term ICBM projections presented in figures 1a–1h were made during the eight years from 1962–1969. (Later ones referred to dates well after SALT I numerical limits on missiles took effect.) Did these eight years of long range ICBM predictions show systematic learning?

It would not be surprising if they did, or even if after eight years of trying, ICBM predictions finally touched reality. Programs do, in the end, level off; and the forecaster, who year after year predicts they will— sooner or later, like a stopped watch—will be right. What is surprising is that these forecasts got worse, not better.

Some analysts now grant that we underestimated, but claim that we improved with time.[27] They ignore the important difference between predicting a *cumulative* total of vehicles that will have been deployed at some future time, most of which are known to be already completed or in process at the time when the prediction is made, and predicting a *change* from this known state. This accurately known past makes up an increasing portion of the cumulative total. Nonetheless, those who detect an improvement in forecasts compare predicted with actual totals, not predicted with actual change from what was known; and so swamp unpredicted new starts in the steadily increasing total of launchers known to be started or completed.

Suppose every year a forecaster regularly predicted that during the next twelve months an adversary was going to add 10 more missile launchers; and every year, without fail, the adversary added 100. At the end of ten years, the adversary would have built up a force of 1,000 launchers. But in the beginning of the tenth year, with 900 in place, the forecaster, undaunted, might predict once more that in the *next* period the adversary would build only 10 more, so reaching a cumulative total of 910. If one used the ratio of the predicted-to-actual cumulative number deployed, it would appear that the forecaster's skill in prediction was steadily improving.[27] In the first year the predicted-to-actual ratio was 10/100, in the second year 110/200—and so on until the great success of the tenth year, when the predicted-to-actual ratio would be 910/1000. A success ratio of .91 seems a marvelous improvement over .10. However, year after year he would have been undershooting reality in the same way. The *difference* between the predicted and actual cumulative num-

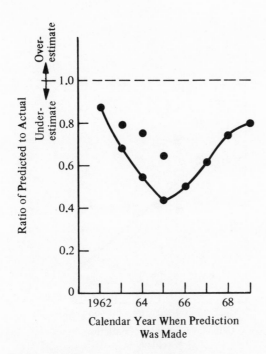

FIGURE 4a. Ratios of Predicted to Actual Cumulative Totals of Soviet ICBM Silos
(*Burying the Future in the Known Past*)*

*Midrange of Long Term Predictions.

bers would have been the same—namely 90—and the *ratio* of predicted-to-actual *increments* would have continued to be .10. The forecaster would have learned nothing about how better to anticipate the future. The cumulative ratios, as in figure 4a, miss this essential point.

Moving from hypothetical to actual history, if we exercise a little care, it is easy to see that our long-run predictions of net future change were getting no better, that if anything they were worsening. The most direct way to establish that fact is suggested by our hypothetical example, where the difference between prediction and reality remains constant while the cumulative ratios suggest an apparent improvement.

Figure 4a presents a scatter diagram that buries errors about the future in statements that are mostly about the known past. It shows ratios of predicted-to-actual cumulative totals of finished silos. The secretaries of defense made these long-term predictions during the eight-year period 1962–1968. All refer to dates no later than mid-1972. Each dot represents one such cumulative ratio calculated at the mid-range of each prediction.

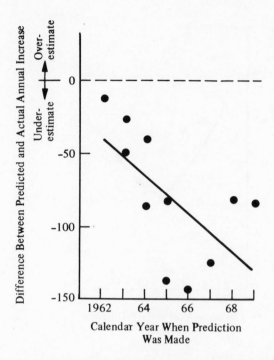

FIGURE 4b. The Average Yearly Differences Between Predicted
and Actual Numbers of Soviet ICBM Silos

In each of three of the years the secretaries made two long-range predictions. I have connected the subset of eight dots that maximize the impression that the worsening was reversed.[28]

In the more appropriate figure 4b each dot represents the mean
amount per year by which the mid-range between the high and low
of a long-term prediction missed reality. All of the dots throughout the
entire period are below zero. All undershoot reality. The average difference between predicted-and-actual silos was –80.1. Furthermore, the
dots drift downward quite steeply; that is, the underestimates tended to
get much worse year by year. A trend line fitted in the standard way to
the points representing underestimates slopes downward at the rate of
–12.59 silos per year. For the period as a whole the evidence indicates not "learning," but "unlearning." During the later subperiod starting in 1965 (the year some analysts think of as the worst) tests do not
show improvement: there is no statistically significant trend toward reducing the differences between predicted and actual. A variety of statistical tests indicates worsening.[29] Moreover, figure 4b still neglects knowledge of launchers in process. On the whole then, the evidence provided

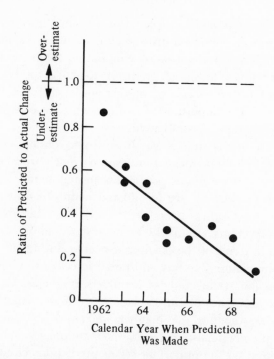

FIGURE 4c. Ratios of Predicted to Actual Increases in Soviet ICBM Silos
(Adjusted for Silos Completed or in Process When Predictions were Made)

by a study of differences between predicted and actual numbers of silos suggests both underestimation and *increasing* underestimation.

That evidence can be greatly reinforced by a closer look at ratios—provided however that one looks at ratios of predicted-to-actual *changes* from the accurately known past. At the time when predictions were being made, the forecaster had hard data not only on (a) silos completed at that time, but also on (b) those that were in process of construction. Figure 4c presents ratios adjusted both for silos completed and for those in process of construction. Since the predicted numbers were less than the actual numbers, the ratios are all less than one; all are underestimates. The predictions averaged roughly a third of the actual number. The median ratio is .34. The ratios drift downward with time, worsening at a rate of about eight percentage points a year.

In sum, the long term U.S. projections of Soviet ICBM silos were not only underestimates, but also deteriorating underestimates. The phenomenon cries out for explanation.

The distinction between predicting cumulative totals and predicting changes in these totals may explain not only recent errors in analyzing history; it may also be part of the explanation for the slowness of the forecasters themselves to recognize a drift away from reality while it was happening. For even though the use of cumulative totals of finished launchers (and especially of ratios of predicted-to-actual totals) has its hazards in an analysis of the success of predictions, such totals have an obvious current operational importance for those who are charged with planning for the contingency of combat. Adversaries must fight with the stocks they have ready at the time a war breaks out. "Orders of battle" are given in terms of such total stocks. For many current purposes, therefore, it is entirely natural to formulate predictions in such terms.

Nonetheless, when predictions are formulated mainly in this way—as they are—systematic forecasting errors will tend to be buried in the larger totals, and corrections are likely to be discovered later than if forecasts were made in terms of the changes expected during the prediction interval. Someone planning to buy additional forces or to phase some out, should focus on long-term *changes* in adversary forces. Failure to center on change is only part of the explanation. Much remains to be explained. But underestimation of bomber and missile deployments for a very long time plainly persisted. That is the main point.

So far I have focused on the important set of predictions cited by the secretaries of defense. While these plainly played a key role in the planning and budgeting process, one might well ask whether they were typical of the intelligence community. Those reluctant to give up the myth of chronic overestimation in particular ask this question, and have in mind the official consensus and, even more, the widely reported excesses of the Air Force. In fact it is familiar that during the "missile gap" Army and Navy estimates were under, and the Air Force over, the consensus. To judge how widespread underestimation became during the 1960s then, it is worth comparing Air Force long-range ICBM predictions with the official consensus starting in the fall of 1961, and comparing both with the Soviet realities counted in post-deployment estimates.

The Air Force, the Consensus, and Reality

In the first two years (Figures 5a and 5b), the Air Force did indeed exceed both the consensus and the reality. In fall 1962 the mid-range of the consensus was below the 1967 reality and the "high" barely reached it. In fall 1963, the Air Force predictions still greatly exceeded the consensus, but the two began to converge. There was some overlap between them in the early years referred to in the prediction, and in the more distant years, where the Air Force outbid the consensus, even its high dropped below reality. In fall 1964 the Air Force and official predictions came close together and overlapped for the first time in predictions about the more distant years. For these more distant years, even the Air Force highs were below reality, though the Air Force still exceeded the consensus. In fall 1965 and 1966 (Figures 5e and 5f) underestimation worsened with further convergence. Finally, in fall 1967, convergence was total. The Air Force endorsed the consensus on condition that the Soviets would deploy MRVs (Multiple Re-entry Vehicles—unlike MIRVs, *not* aimed independently), which they did. The highs of the long-term forecasts in these last years through 1967 were invariably under reality, and both the consensus and the Air Force assumed an ultimate leveling off of the Russian program well below what happened. In fall 1968 the Air Force concurred with the consensus on the assumption, now clearly conservative, that MIRVs would be deployed by mid-1978.

The steady movement toward the official forecasts suggests the power of consensus. That power is particularly impressive since final convergence occurred in fall 1967, which (McNamara observed the following January) marked a 380-silo jump from fall 1966. Deviation from the consensus on the high side went out of style just as it became objectively most plausible.

Why?

Pressures for conformity in the 1960s tended to operate against overestimating offense deployment. Overestimating rather than error had become disreputable. For example, Secretary McNamara, in January 1964, stressed that "these longer-range projections of enemy capabilities must necessarily be highly uncertain," but, "indeed the record shows that in the last several years we have consistently *over*estimated Soviet ICBM strength" (italics added). He then cited three forecasts made in 1959, 1960, and 1961, during the "missile gap," about Soviet ICBMs expected in mid–1963. All three, of course, were far above the mark. He warned, "These facts should be borne in mind as we discuss the estimates for the 1967–1969 period." But the 1964 estimate about 1967, to which he attached this caveat, turned out to be not above but way below the mark— 120 silos below at mid-range. Moreover, while in the preceding two years predictions about 1967 were also below, the 1964 prediction was worse. And the 1965 prediction about 1967 was worse still. As 1967 got closer, our aim at it sank steadily further beneath the bull's eye.

Part of the pressure to conform by underestimating was very likely a reflex overcorrecting for the "missile gap," that had publicly embarrassed the intelligence community. But this could hardly explain the extraordi-

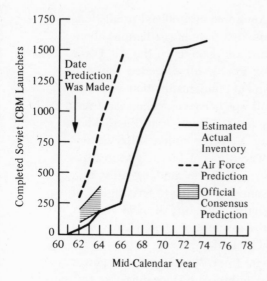

FIGURE 5a. Air Force and Official Consensus
Predictions Made in Fall 1961

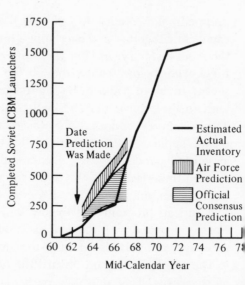

FIGURE 5b. Air Force and Official Consensus
Predictions Made in Fall 1962

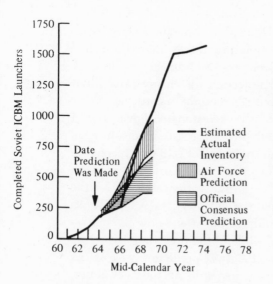

FIGURE 5c. Air Force and Official Consensus
Predictions Made in Fall 1963

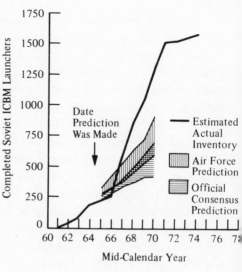

FIGURE 5d. Air Force and Official Consensus
Predictions Made in Fall 1964

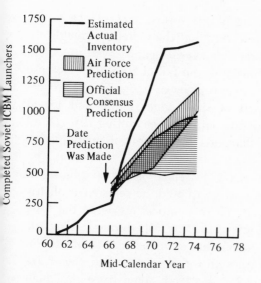

FIGURE 5e. Air Force and Official Consensus Predictions Made in Fall 1965

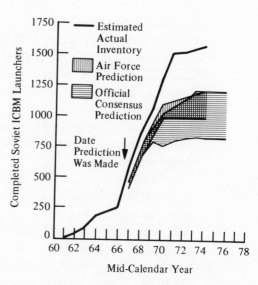

FIGURE 5f. Air Force and Official Consensus Predictions Made in Fall 1966

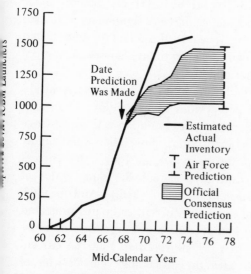

FIGURE 5g. Air Force and Official Consensus Predictions Made in Fall 1967

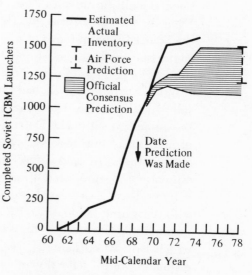

FIGURE 5h. Air Force and Official Consensus Predictions Made in Fall 1968

nary persistence and even worsening of the errors, as evidence to the contrary began to pour in. It is interesting that the secretary brought up the "missile gap" in 1964 to reinforce this caveat against overestimation. The "gap" had been given public burial in the fall of 1961. The Defense Report had not bothered to mention it in 1962 or 1963. The report revived the horrible example as part of the budget battle and issued ominous strictures against exaggeration as a way of cutting the ground from under importunate service demands based on anticipated large Soviet capabilities.

As for Soviet "capabilities," when the secretary used that phrase, or "Soviet ICBM strength," as in the passage quoted, he referred explicitly to the *number* of vehicles deployed. These numbers are what the forecasts were overwhelmingly about, just as the forecasts during the "missile gap" had been. It was only when the number of Soviet silos completed or in process came close to catching up with the ceiling we had chosen for our ICBM force that the secretary began to put some stress on "qualitative superiority." In effect, he asserted by way of comfort, the Soviets may get nearly as many missiles, but ours will be better. But his FY 1968 report insisted that especially if we counted in the SLBMs, we were still ahead even in numbers—"as of now."

"As of now, we have more than three times the number of intercontinental ballistic missiles (i.e., ICBMs and SLBMs) the Soviets have. Even by the early 1970s, we still expect to have a significant lead over the Soviet Union in terms of numbers . . . and," the secretary added, in a vague but dazzling phrase, able to comfort even today, "a very substantial superiority in terms of overall combat effectiveness."

But in 1971, the Soviets had the lead in numbers. Looking on the bright side—"quality"—may have dazzled perceptions of our failure to predict the numerical shift. The Defense Reports in fact contain a treasure trove of methods of bucking us up while blurring our view. Their very vagueness soothes. "By and large," said the secretary in 1965, "the current estimates . . . projected through mid–1970 are of the same order of magnitude as [last year's] projections through mid–1969." And in 1966, with reassuring familiarity, "By and large the current estimates projected through mid–1970 are of the same general order of magnitude as those which I discussed here last year." In 1967, he reported that the current estimates were "generally in line" with the preceding year. "Order of magnitude" is particularly mind-boggling, but strictly implied only that this year's estimates were within one-tenth to ten times as much as last year's. Which is less reassuring. In any case, the estimates were wrong and getting worse.

In 1968, after the huge 380-silo jump in one year, McNamara said, "We believe the Soviet ICBM force will continue to grow over the next few years, but at a considerably slower rate than in the recent past." But the rate specified fell far below the one later observed. In 1969, Secretary Clifford continued in the same cheery vein. The Soviet force had grown "well over threefold in a . . . little more than two years. The rate . . . has been somewhat greater than estimated a year ago. However, we believe [it] will be considerably smaller over the next two or three years." But once again the expected rate of new starts formed a small fraction of the actual. Such muffled disappointments scarcely perturbed the theory, pushed hard in 1969 and 1970, that exaggerations drove a race.

It would be wrong, I think, to conclude that the Defense Reports display a conscious effort to obscure our failure to anticipate rapid Soviet increase. More likely, wishes and policy leanings shaped—and lowered—consciousness. But much remains to be explained. Undoubtedly, various leanings—some to expand, some to cut or reallocate strategic spending—influenced estimates of contending factions. But then we need to ask not only "cui bono," but which estimates matched reality. Factions in or out of government have *some* compatible interests. Aside from a joint interest in accurate assessment for the common defense, all factions have at least an occupational self-interest in *not* making forecasts that fail disastrously.

Underestimates persisted for an extraordinarily long time after the error of the missile gap, in part because they were fortified by an American strategic view that Americans often attributed also to the Soviets. (These were "projections" in the psychoanalyst's, as well as the forecaster's sense.) That view suggested that the Soviets did not need a large expansion of forces in order to be able to destroy a few American cities and therefore did not intend to undertake it.[30]

It was common in and out of government through the mid-1960s to hold that the Soviets wanted only a minimum deterrent, a couple of hundred missiles aimed at cities (roughly the actual number of Soviet ICBMs in 1964–1965), and that they would not try to catch up.[31] We clung to this belief after they had started enough launchers to make it untenable. Then we shifted to saying they wanted *only* to catch up, just as they were passing us on the way to getting 50 percent more. "Rough parity" can be quite rough.

Action-reaction language is vague enough to rationalize events after the fact. It was a glass through which we saw darkly. It not only led us to wrong predictions about the Soviet actions, but it made inaction on our part seem reasonable. The Russians would not act to catch up, because they knew we would react to counter them, and since they would not act, we did not have to. But in fact, they acted and we did not. And sometimes the secretary argued that if we were to increase our active defense, the Russians would inevitably react by vastly increasing their offense so that in the end we would not only have wasted the money, but would end up with a net increase in the number of fatalities we might suffer. In other words, if we acted, the Russians would react; therefore, there was no point in taking action.

Unfortunately distorting and wishful myopia followed from the close polemical focus of factions in and out of government on the very latest incremental change in Soviet force dispositions and its implications for the current year's U.S. budget, as compared to that of the preceding year. Momentary pauses in Soviet construction of launchers for one missile type, perhaps because new improved systems were being readied for deployment or because of bad weather, were seized on by outside advisors and by unnamed "highly placed officials" as an indication that Soviet programs were "tapering off," "leveling off," "slowing down," "petering out," "grinding to a halt." [32] Since, characteristically, massive Soviet efforts in research, development, testing, and evaluation parallel a countercycle in deployment, and since Russian weather is notoriously intemperate, especially during their long winters when our budget debates start, there was plenty of room for confusion, ambiguity, and self-deception inside and outside the U.S. government.

As for the public view, it was only to be expected that statements about increased Soviet missile deployments would be dismissed with a kind of naive cynicism: the slickers in the Pentagon are using their annual scare tactics in support of bigger budgets. Some outside advisors protested the government's "'most outrageous' statements about the alleged buildup by Russia," whereas in fact, we were told, "the Soviet arms capability actually is tapering off." Dissonant sounds of reality were hardly audible in Establishment study groups meeting in Washington, Cambridge, and New York. The successful attempt to save the predictions and the dogma on which they were based is quite as instructive as the performance of Sabbatai Zevi's followers, a sect that managed to survive and reinterpret a public prediction that the world would end in 1648 and even to acquire new more enthusiastic adherents; or the Millerites who gathered new followers after the world failed to end as Miller had predicted by 21 March 1844.[33] Students of the subject have observed that when predictions fail, this may only increase fervor and proselytizing for the dogma that led to the prediction. After all, it is in just such adversity that a dogma needs all the recruits it can get. Editorials and articles appear with ritual regularity in the *New York Times*, the *New Republic*, the *Christian Science Monitor, Scientific American,* and elsewhere warning of the Pentagon's ritual exaggeration of the threat and presenting in full-blown form a generalized doctrine that it is just such exaggerations that accelerate the fatal spiral.

Though holders of the dogma of regular U.S. overestimation protested excessive secrecy, they were in good part protected by it. Exact quantitative comparisons of past predictions with reality take time and would have met much resistance even in private; in public a systematic long term check was impossible. However, enough has long been public to undermine the theory of regular overestimation. We have had open official statements reflecting classified estimates that the Russians would not try to get as many missiles as the U.S., that they were stopping or slowing down; and equally public figures on the actual growth of Russian strategic forces. The contrast was plain, or rather would have been plain, if only we had been taking a long hard look; or even looking. More important, the reality of understatement should have destroyed the generalized theory of overstatement, but it did not.

It would be unfortunate if we should now swing from understatement to the opposite extreme. It would be nice, though far from easy, to get it nearly right. Even if we do, the implications for our strategic budgets will by no means be simple. Sober consideration, however, will discount the threat that invariably overestimating Soviet threats drives us to exponential increases and the notion that only throwing caution to the winds can stop the "race." The threat of invariable overestimation is one that is plainly exaggerated.

Some of these policy decisions, I believe, were justified on other grounds. But prevailing doctrine offered a generalized rationale for cutting rather than expanding. That's what happened, but we didn't notice. Our perceptions of actual U.S. past declines have been as confused as our view of supposed future Soviet increases.

MYTHICAL U.S. INCREASES AND ACTUAL U.S. DECLINES

Whatever the explanation offered for the strategic race—invariably overestimating and worst case analysis, bureaucratic politics, technology out of control, etc., etc.—there is a prior question as to whether or not there has been a race. To justify the term "race," any side that is racing has at least to be rapidly increasing its strategic budgets and forces. Even if the increase does not proceed at an increasing rate, for the name "race" to make any sense at all there would have to be at the very least an increasing trend. An examination of American strategic budgets and forces since the mid-1940s suggests that on the principal relevant measures the trend is down. And an examination of the net effect of qualitative innovation in the strategic forces over the same time period equally refutes the stereotype about the net destabilizing effect of technical change. First, look at our supposed quantitative upward spiral in the total explosive energy that could be released or in its capacity for indiscriminate destruction.

A Quantitative Spiral?

Total Explosive Energy and "Overkill":   The total explosive energy that could be released by the strategic stockpile is a measure frequently used to compare U.S. and Soviet forces by conservative organizations, such as the American Security Council. It also appears in the popular vivid comparisons of the total explosive yield of all the bombs dropped in Korea (200,000 tons) or in World War II (5 million tons) with the explosive yield (measured in tons of some nonnuclear chemical explosive such as TNT) of a single nuclear warhead, several of which might be carried in one vehicle today. However, the drawbacks of such a measure are clear and most obvious in the vivid comparisons. A single bomb releasing 5 million tons of explosive energy (i.e., a five-megaton weapon) is incapable of doing anything like the damage done worldwide from Japan and Burma to West Europe and Russia by the many tens of thousands of bombs exploded in World War II, even if the total energy yield were the same. In general, one large warhead with twice the energy yield of two smaller weapons, unlike them, cannot be used to attack two very widely separated targets.

Moreover, it was understood at the dawn of the atomic age that, even though the Hiroshima bomb had roughly one thousand times the explosive yield of one of the largest World War II blockbusters, it would not do structural damage to an area one thousand times the size, but roughly one-tenth that. By comparison with the smaller bomb, some 90 percent of its energy would be "wasted" in "overhitting" or "overdestroying" or "overkilling" the nearby area.[34] For that comparison then, not 1,000, but its two-thirds power, 100, is a roughly correct approximation for determining relative structural damage. And even in comparing the destructive effect of stocks of bombs that are less varied in yield, some such adjustment is essential.

However, it is not only conservative polemic that exploits the misleading measure of gross "megatonnage" of explosive energy. Some of the crudest polemical uses are by opponents of increases in military budgets. In talking of "overkill," they usually divide the total population of the world into the aggregate explosive energy in the stockpile to arrive at some such figure as ten tons of TNT equivalent for every man, woman, and child in the world. Such a measure makes exactly the confusion that the original discussions of overhitting or overdestruction of the area near the target were designed to avoid. And it adds several other more potent confusions besides. It implies that the purpose of stocks of weapons is and should be exclusively to destroy populations, that what is wrong is not the killing of populations, but their overkilling. It is not strictly related to hypotheses about a spiraling increase in total explosive yield, or still less a spiral in the damage that might be done. However, by suggesting that the stocks are now far too large, it makes plausible the notion that there has been a steady exponential increase. In fact, nuclear

FIGURE 6. Combined U.S. Strategic Offense and Defense Megatons

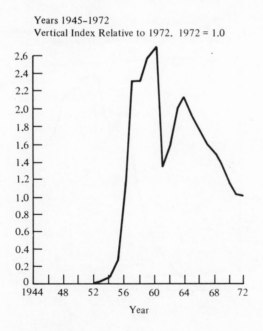

Years 1945–1972
Vertical Index Relative to 1972. 1972 = 1.0

Year

weapons are directed at any of a large variety of military targets, and there is no simple rule for deciding whether one has too many or too few. That is a problem we need not address here.[35] The question we are asking is whether on this measure there has been an exponential increase.

The answer indicated in figure 6 is "clearly not." After an initial sharp increase, the total explosive energy yield declined from a peak two-and-a-half times the 1972 figure. And 1972 was about at the level of 1955. While this aggregate includes, appropriately for contemporary arms race theories, strategic defense as well as offense warheads, the decline is about the same for the aggregate explosive yield of the offense warheads alone.

The Number of Strategic Warheads: At the opposite extreme from totting up the energy releasable by all strategic warheads is a measure that ignores the yield altogether and counts simply warheads. The smallest strategic defense warheads differ from the largest strategic offense warheads by many orders of magnitude, but even if we were to limit ourselves to strategic offense warheads, merely counting warheads while

FIGURE 7. Combined U.S. Strategic Offense and Defense Warheads

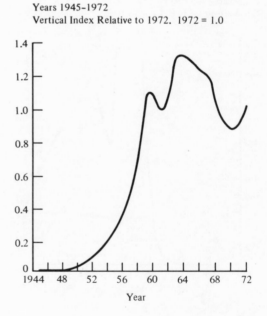

Years 1945–1972
Vertical Index Relative to 1972. 1972 = 1.0

Year

neglecting yield involves an heroic distortion. In fact, the largest offense nuclear warhead is roughly a thousand times the smallest offense nuclear warhead [36]—the same as the difference between the Hiroshima bomb and the largest nonnuclear blockbusters of World War II! Counting the largest and the smallest each as one—with evenhanded justice—would then be exactly like dismissing the first two nuclear weapons as of negligible importance since they increased the stocks of "blockbusters" by only a fraction of a percent.

While there is no adequate single common measure for so heterogeneous a collection of vehicles and weapons, clearly something better is possible than a simple count of warheads.[37] That the latter is used so uncritically is one of the intellectual scandals of the current debate on SALT. Nonetheless one may ask whether the number of strategic offense and defense warheads has spiraled. And as figure 7 shows, for this disparate aggregate the answer is that it has not. It peaked in 1964 at roughly 30 percent higher than in 1972, which was about the 1960 level.[38]

The sense of post-Sputnik arms race doctrine, with its central strictures against all weapons aimed at weapons and therefore against active defense as particularly destabilizing, plainly calls for including the Spartan, Sprint, Nike-Hercules, Falcon, and all other defense warheads in the total. However, given the opportunism of the current debate, it is hardly surprising that, when convenient, the distortion involved in counting warheads is compounded by excluding the supposedly most destabilizing —the defense warheads. In fact, one great oddity is that in spite of all the fire leveled at active defense, the debaters hardly notice that U.S. defense warheads, interceptor aircraft, surface-to-air, and air-to-air missiles have decreased drastically. The number of offense warheads has increased over time, but their average yield has decreased even more. From 1958–1960 to 1972 they increased roughly by half. But their average yield was divided by four-and-one-half (figure 8). It is essential then to consider some measure in between counting megatons and counting warheads. We turn now to a measurement widely used for that purpose in the defense and arms control technical community.

Measures of Relative Destructive Area (EMT): No single number adequately measures the destructive power of military weapons, still less other important attributes of military forces—their susceptibility to attack, their safety from "accidental" or mistaken or unauthorized use, their political controllability, their capability for discriminating between non-

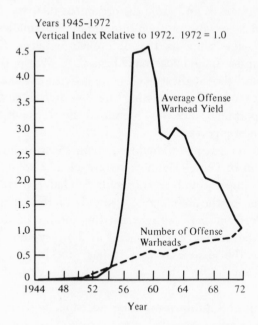

Years 1945-1972
Vertical Index Relative to 1972. 1972 = 1.0

FIGURE 8. Average U.S. Strategic Offense Warhead Yield

military and military targets, and between friend and foe, their flexibility in a variety of political-military contingencies, etc. Nonetheless, as we have said, it is not hard to do better than counting warheads or counting megatons, and for comparing highly varied stocks of weapons at two different times or in two different countries, an index known (misleadingly) as "equivalent megatonnage" (EMT) has come into widespread technical use. It counts the number of weapons and their yields but makes a rough adjustment for the relative waste of explosive energy by the larger weapons through overconcentration near the target. Taking a one-megaton weapon as standard, it measures any given stock in terms of the number of such one-megaton weapons that under a variety of relevant conditions would do structural damage over an equal area.[39]

EMT, like all other indexes, has its limitations, but it captures some essentials missed in simply adding unadjusted megatons or warheads. Figure 9 shows a dramatic decrease since 1960 in the relative destructiveness, so measured, of the U.S. strategic force. At its peak it was nearly double the 1972 figure; and 1972 was roughly at the 1956 level! In any case, no spiral. This measure is relevant among other things to test the

Years 1945–1972
Vertical Index Relative to 1972. 1972 = 1.0

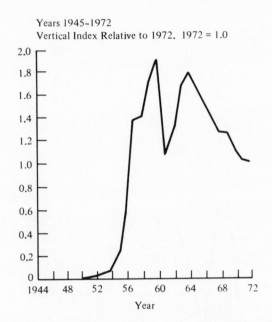

FIGURE 9. U.S. Strategic Offense Equivalent Megatonnage

arms race argument that the uncontrolled destructiveness of U.S. strategic forces has increased. It has not. The area that might sustain structural damage has been halved and there has been a similar decline in potential fallout.

Offense and Defense Budgets

I could reinforce these results using curves on further physical measures. Instead I turn now to measures of the resources used in deploying a strategic force. Since these resources must be diverted from important alternative civilian uses, such measures are properly at the heart of the defense debate. In any case, they are central to arms race doctrines. Expenditures on strategic forces are most frequently identified as the variable that is supposed to be accelerating.

Figure 10 shows the total strategic budget as measured in the Defense Department Program I,[40] extending back in time to World War II. The top curve shows that the strategic budget in 1976 dollars declined from a peak of $32.6 billion in FY 1952 to $7.7 billion in FY 1976. Strategic ex-

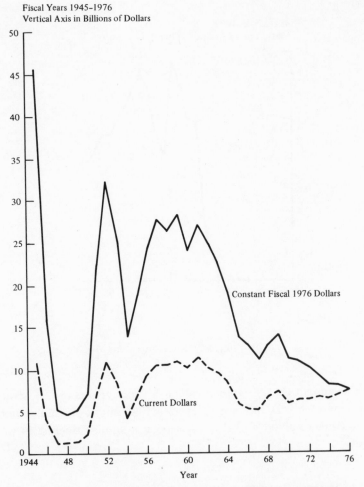

Fiscal Years 1945–1976
Vertical Axis in Billions of Dollars

FIGURE 10. Combined U.S. Strategic Offense and Defense Obligational Authority

penditures have fluctuated, with a brief sharp decline and recovery after Korea, to very high levels varying between $24 and $28 billion in the seven years beginning in 1956; and then a more or less steady drastic decline to the recent low levels. In short, in real terms the strategic budget was well over four times higher during the Korean War and about three times as high at the end of the Eisenhower administration as in 1976. This scarcely looks like an exponential increase in strategic budgets. Rather more like an exponential decrease.[41] For the twenty-four years from 1952 to 1976, the average rate of decline was about 5 percent. For the fifteen years from fiscal 1961 to 1976, there was a decline averaging

8 percent per year. I want to stress that this long-term decline is not simply in percent of GNP but in real terms. It is an absolute decline. Since real GNP was rising while strategic budgets in real terms were declining, strategic spending declined even more in percentage of GNP. In percent of GNP it was nearly seven times higher in the early 1950s and about five times higher in the late 1950s than in FY 1976 (3.2 percent and about 2.5 percent compared with .48 percent).

How is it possible for the constantly expanding literature on ever accelerating strategic budgets to ignore this increasing divergence between doctrine and reality?

First, exponents using the doctrine as a weapon in budget battles handle rather carelessly the familiar distinction between real and inflated dollar costs. This can hide somewhat the drastic extent of the decline, but not the decline itself. Even in current, depreciating dollars the budget dropped from generally high levels in the 1950s and a peak of $12.1 billion in 1961 to $7.7 billion in 1976.[42]

Second, the curves show minor local peaks and dips. Men concentrating on the immediate budget fight may easily take an ant's eye view. Looking forward from the bottom of a shallow local dip, the future looks all uphill. This opportune but myopic focus has tended to obscure the very trends that any arms race doctrine would have to confront. Such doctrines after all do not pretend to be concerned only with the brief rise, say, from 1960 to 1961. An intense focus on the current year's budget battle also leads to a related confusion: comparing the new budget request not with last year's request, but with the actual amount approved by Congress in the prior year—which can be considerably less. For example, for the defense budget as a whole, the total obligational authority approved in 1973 was $3.6 billion less, and in 1972, $4.1 billion less than the amount requested. For the FY 1974 strategic program the net difference between the requested and total obligational authority appeared, as of summer 1974, to be about $0.5 billion. (In the most recent defense budgets, requests may have been more nearly fulfilled.)

Third, the drastic fall in strategic budgets measured in Program I may be partially obscured by adding in a rising but quite arbitrary "overhead" figure.[43] The program budgets for strategic or for general purpose forces aim to include all the costs of equipment, matériel, and personnel that can be directly attributed to the program mission, including all support costs that "follow directly from the number of combat units."[44] Overhead allocations, whatever their accounting uses, are by definition arbitrary, and those now current have little or no causal relation to past or future reductions in the number of strategic combat vehicles. These arbitrarily allocated costs have tended to remain the same or to rise even though the strategic forces and their direct costs have been greatly reduced.

The formula that the Brookings Institution uses when dealing with past or current budgets would assign to the strategic forces an amount of overhead equal to less than half their direct costs during the 1950s, and over one-and-a-half times their direct costs in 1974.[45] Meanwhile, direct costs of general purpose forces have varied in size from less than one-and-two-thirds to nearly five times the direct costs of the strategic forces, and the formula, year after year, splits the intelligence and communications budgets evenly between them. Of course, it has always been clear that some of these "overhead" costs may vary inversely with direct costs. Take intelligence for example. Large SALT (or unilateral) reductions might call for greatly increased national means of monitoring variations in adversary forces, since marginal absolute changes make a larger proportional difference in small forces. (Dr. Wiesner in the past has suggested that inspection might have to double if the forces were halved, and so on linearly.) But then one should expect future cuts in the direct costs of strategic forces to be partly offset by increases in intelligence costs.

If one considers not merely what causes changes in "overhead," but also what the effects are of increases in overhead on an adversary, it is hard to see how these programs, many of which could well be classified under human resources or social welfare, would strike terror in the heart of an enemy. For example, CHAMPUS (Civilian Health and Medical Program of the Uniformed Services) includes such items as medical care for retirees, their dependents, and survivors. A drastic cut in the number of strategic combat vehicles would hardly decrease these costs and their increase should hardly seem menacing to the Soviet Union.

Nonetheless, even if these arbitrary costs are added on, they can only partially obscure the drastic decline. Using the formula Brookings applies to past budgets, the FY 1962 budget was nearly double that in FY 1976 (this is displayed in the dotted line in figure 11). The method Brookings applies to future projected budgets is less reducible to formula and involves more subjective judgment and even larger uncertainties.[46] If that method were applied to determine past trends, however, the decrease would be more drastic. Still other allocation methods, all necessarily arbitrary, show declines from a peak more than double the present budget. For example, a method used by the Department of Defense shows a decline in FY 1976 dollars of over $2 billion in the late 1950s from a peak 2.5 times as high as the FY 1976 budget including overhead. With recently improved deflators the decline would be even larger.[47] Overhead allocations have their uses, but they are limited. All of them distribute some unallocable costs. When added to program costs without any breakdown, they obscure more than they illuminate change. Nonetheless, overhead allocation with which I am familiar can hide the sharp declines in strategic budgets. Whether the decline is from a peak over four or two-and-a-half or twice recent levels, it should be fatal to the dogma about "ever-accelerating spending."

Nonetheless that dogma does die hard. Paul Warnke, for example, has agreed that some facts do damage the arms race figures of speech. But he talks of our continuing "to spend these steadily increasing billions" and of our "formula for endless escalation in defense costs." Indeed, Warnke is so seized by the idea that the U.S. strategic budget and the defense budget as a whole have been steadily climbing that he can read a long document devoted to showing that both budgets have been sinking for years, with plunging graphs to illustrate, and not notice their trend.[48] He did not, for example, notice the point of the article which painstakingly evidenced the drastic fall in the strategic program budget in real terms over the preceding fourteen years. (The defense budget as a whole had been declining for a shorter time—since 1968.) He understands it to be saying that the United States and the Soviet Union have both been increasing strategic spending, but at different rates. Running at different speeds, he thinks, might still be a race. However, we have been moving not only at different speeds, but in opposite directions. If that doesn't do lethal damage to the arms race metaphor, nothing will.[49]

Fourth, in spite of the fact that arms race theorists take strategic defense along with counterforce as the villain in the piece and the principal force driving the race, they sometimes look for exponential increases in strategic budgets that cover only offense and allow for no compensating decreases in strategic defense. However, Figure 12 shows that in 1962 the budget for offense taken alone was over three times its 1974 level.[50]

Fifth, I suspect the major reason for failure to observe the decline is that public debate usually concentrates intensely on the initial decision to buy and deploy a new system; much less on the operation and maintenance of the system once in; and hardly at all on its phasing out. In particular, the present exponents of arms race doctrines have had their gaze focused on the introduction of new systems—in line with their dominant preoccupation with innovation. As advocates they have been very

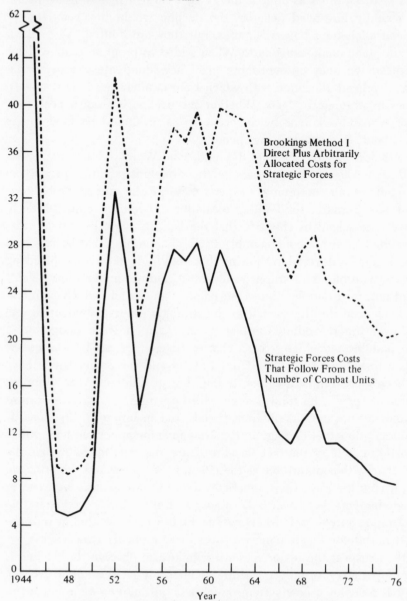

Fiscal Year 1945–1976
Vertical Axis in Billions of FY 76 Dollars

Brookings Method I
Direct Plus Arbitrarily
Allocated Costs for
Strategic Forces

Strategic Forces Costs
That Follow From the
Number of Combat Units

Year

FIGURE 11. Strategic Costs That Follow From the Number
of Combat Units With and Without Indirect
Costs as Allocated by Brookings Method I

Fiscal Years 1958–1974
Vertical Axis in Billions of Dollars

Constant Fiscal 1976 Dollars

Current Dollars

Year

FIGURE 12. U.S. Strategic Offense Obligational Authority

much in on the beginnings, in favor of the new systems in the 1950s and generally against them in the 1960s. But the phasing out seems to escape their attention.

Systems starting from zero or near it are likely to grow very rapidly in the initial phases; they can scarcely go down. It is easy apparently to slip into the belief that there has been an "across-the-board growth of our own strategic forces." [51] However, an examination of the components of the strategic budget and an analysis of the entry into the force and the exit of various combat vehicles suggests the broad solution to the puzzle as to how this popular impressionistic doctrine can fit the facts so poorly.

U.S. strategic forces have not grown "across the board." On the contrary, as new systems were brought in, many others, including some very expensive ones, were taken out. At the end of FY 1956, for example, the strategic force included nearly 1,500 B–47 and RB–47 medium bombers, some 270 B–36 and RB–36 heavy bombers, a remnant of the B–50s and B–29s, and nearly 850 KC–97 and KC–29 tanker aircraft, all of which have since made their exit, along with or preceded by a drastic reduction in overseas strategic operating bases and a multibillion-dollar cut in overseas stocks for strategic forces. Between 1956 and the late 1960s the B–58 supersonic bomber, the Snark intercontinental cruise missile, the Atlas ICBM, and the Titan I ICBM have come and gone. So also has the Bomarc area defense missile, and most of the Nike-Hercules and fighter interceptors. In fact, air defense vehicles, promoted so vigorously in the 1950s by many who oppose them today as destabilizing, show an exponential decline from a peak of over 8,000 in 1959 to a force less than one-seventh as large in 1972; and to less than that now.

The terms of the public debate have been scandalously loose and they have received very little critical attention from the media. SALT rhetoric and headlines linking new strategic programs to RECORD DEFENSE SPENDING help foster the impression that strategic budgets especially must be out of control, since they are spotted as the main culprit in the general increase. In real terms, however, there had been no general increase in defense spending from FY 68 through FY 75. Witness figure 13. Picking on the strategic budget as the guilty party in the nonexistent general increase in the defense budget as a whole seems particularly absurd, since the strategic decline has been larger, more consistent, and more durable. But guilt by association has its effect, because the smaller decline in total defense budgets is more easily obscured by neglecting inflation.

It is hard to fault the media when academics and politicians who

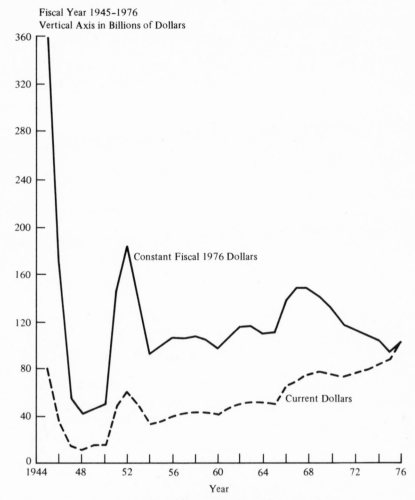

FIGURE 13. Total Defense Obligational Authority
(Sum of DoD Programs 1-X)

specialize in defense and arms control matters make such blunders themselves, but even so, the media handling of the defense budget in recent
years needs some comment. Take the distinction between real and inflated changes in dollar amounts. Although there are some sophisticated
questions about methods of allowing for inflation, the gross sense of the
distinction is not at all arcane. Newsmen handle it all the time without
stumbling. When in a recession year, 1970, the American gross national
product neared $1 trillion ($970.1 billion) by comparison with $930.3
billion the preceding year, no headline greeted the news by announcing
a record advance in production. On the contrary, the press observed that

FIGURE 14.

LOS ANGELES TIMES   FEBRUARY 5, 1974

Record Defense Spending Plan Includes New Nuclear Systems

BY RUDY ABRAMSON
Times Staff Writer

WASHINGTON—President Nixon Monday sent Congress a defense budget surpassing the peak spending period of World War II and laying the foundation for a new generation of nuclear weapons as insurance against the failure of strategic arms talks with the Soviet Union.

"If negotiations fail and the Soviet Union seeks military advantage," Mr. Nixon said in his budget message, "the United States must be prepared to increase its forces quickly and effectively."

"Because the time required for development and deployment of major weapons systems is long, decisions made today will shape the ability of the United States to maintain its strength 5 to 10 years from now."

In asking a record defense outlay of $87.7 billion in the year beginning next July 1. the Administration proposed an $8.4 billion Pentagon research and development program plus more than $1 billion for the Atomic Energy Commission's nuclear weapons and propulsion projects.

Besides continuing work on the new B-1 strategic bomber and the giant Trident missile-firing submarine, the Defense Department asked Congress for $249 million for research and development on:

—Larger warheads for intercontinental ballistic missiles.

—Improved accuracy for ICBMs.

—A new missile-firing submarine smaller than those in the current Polaris-Poseidon fleet.

—Mobile ICBMs, which would be

Please Turn to Page 21, Col. 1

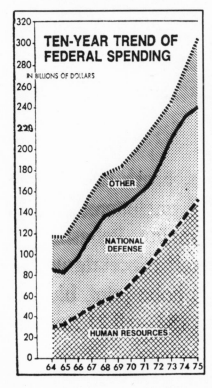

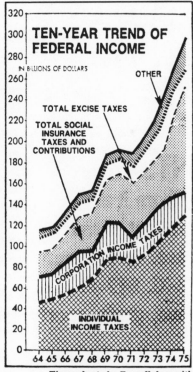

Times charts by Russell Arasmith

the GNP in 1970 was lower in real terms than it had been the year before. But year after year of defense department requests for budgets
lower in "real" terms than the 1968 peak have been announced as "record
budgets," apparently because in this case the media regard the distinction as unreal. And a press that with some justice prides itself on its
energetic factual investigations is considerably weaker on analysis and
reflection about even moderately complex matters. There predisposition
is more likely to hold sway.

The sloppiness is suggested in the largely unconscious predispositions
implicit in the way the data are described or pictured. One can find
examples among good journalists and excellent newspapers. Take the
case of the Los Angeles *Times* announcing the new defense budget request in February 1974 (see figure 14). The article headlines "record
defense spending" and suggests the primary cause for the increase in
new strategic nuclear weapons of the kind that SALT is supposed to
limit. Thus the lead paragraph states "a defense budget surpassing the
peak spending period of World War II and laying the foundation for
a new generation of nuclear weapons." Only later in the article is it
acknowledged that inflation might have something to do with the budget
increases, and even then in wording that suggests this may just be a
Pentagon claim—"While the research on new nuclear weapons systems
could portend massive new spending several years hence, the $6.3 bil-
lion increase in the Pentagon's new budget largely was attributed to pay
increases and in higher costs across the board for hardware and supplies."

The graph, "Ten-Year Trend of Federal Spending," accompanying the
article, not only reinforces the impression that national defense expenditures have been steadily climbing; it also suggests to the casual reader
that they are the primary reason for the growth in the total federal budget. This effect results from piling the "National Defense" expenditures
on top of those for "Human Resources."

Figure 15 is a redrawing of this chart for clarity, and figure 16 shows
exactly the same data as figure 15 at exactly the same scale.[52] The only
change is that "National Defense" rather than "Human Resources" is now
presented on the bottom. The resulting chart gives quite a different and
more accurate impression than that in the article. It shows that the major source of the increase in federal spending has been due to increases
in human resources, not national defense.

But even figure 16 is misleading, since it is in current dollars and
hence ignores the effects of inflation. Figure 17 presents the data of
figure 16 adjusted to inflation, i.e., in dollars of constant purchasing

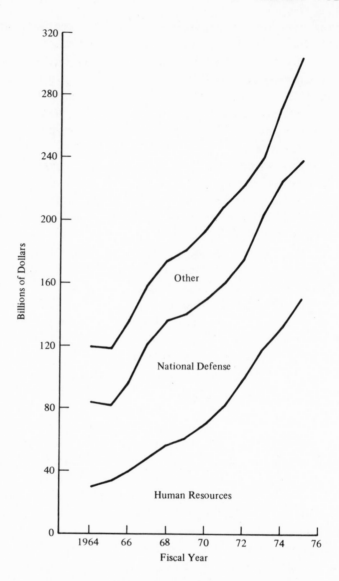

FIGURE 15. Ten-year Trend of Federal Spending

Source: Los Angeles Times Chart February 5, 1974.

power. We now see a *downward* trend in national defense spending that is more than overcome by an *upward* trend in spending for human resources. (In fact, more authoritative results indicate a sharper downward trend for national defense expenditures than is shown in figure 16. The

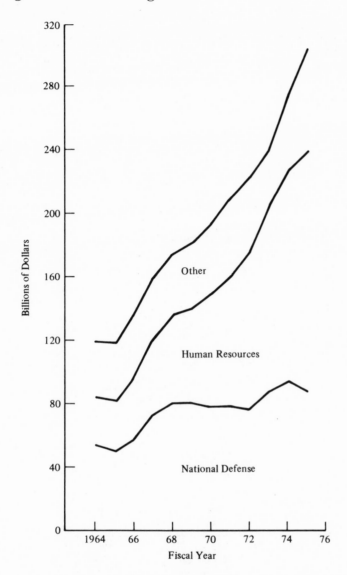

FIGURE 16. Ten-year Trend of Federal Spending—With National
Defense Rather Than Human Resources on Bottom

Source: Los Angeles Times Chart February 5, 1974.

data in the original article contain some anomalies. Retirement pay seems
to have been included in the national defense category, and this would
help to explain the slower decline shown.)

Belief in an exploding arms race is so ingrained by now in the way the

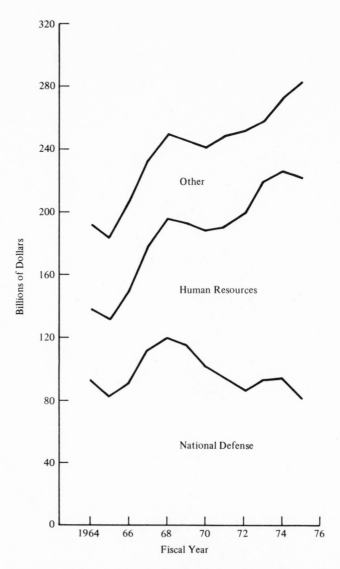

FIGURE 17. Ten-year Trend of Federal Spending—Adjusted for Inflation
(Constant FY 1974 Dollars)

Source: Los Angeles Times Chart February 5, 1974.

media look at things that it seems even the chartmakers and layout men
make their own *trompe l'oeil* contribution to its existence. However,
the regular annual alarms in the press about an upward trend in the strategic budget can often point to economic projections *for several future*

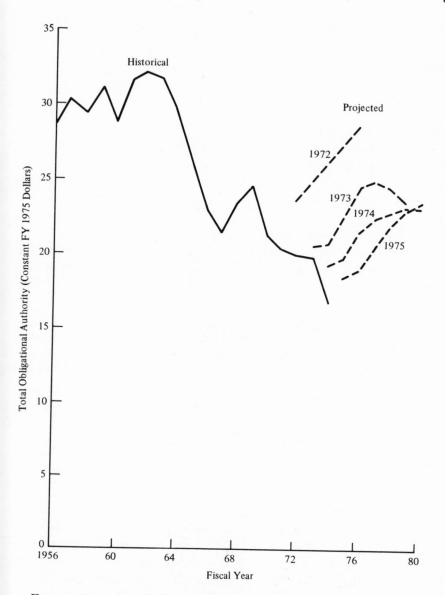

FIGURE 18. Brookings' Historical Versus Brookings' Projected Strategic Costs
(Including "Overhead")

years, based on gleanings from testimony before Congress on defense department and service plans. Such indications of plans can mislead in the same way as comparing this year's budget request with the last enacted budget, but even more so, since the long-term plans are even more tentative and subject to attrition than requests formally submitted to Congress. They must run a recurring gauntlet through many stages of bargaining and review within defense, budget, the White House, and Congress. It is appropriate to study the uncertain long term costs implicit in various defense plans, but not to treat them as if they reflected the likely course of defense spending. Brookings says as much: "A note of warning must be emphasized. The projections should not be taken as predictions of future defense budgets." [53] As with drugs and cigarettes, however, users may ignore the warning label. (Even Brookings, normally more careful than its readers, sometimes forgets its own warning.) In any case, figure 18 shows vividly that year after year the Brookings projections of strategic cost have sloped steeply upward, as year after year the actual budgets have continued to decline.[53a] This perpetual picture of a strategic budget on the point of exploding—so useful in budget battles—sticks in our mind, rather than any glimpse of actual history.

There is an amusing paradox, intelligible only in political debating terms, about the one-eyed vision displayed by exponents of arms race doctrines. On the one hand they fail to observe the increasingly obvious fact that in spite of their theory of invariable American overestimation of the size of Russian strategic forces, these forces have for many years systematically exceeded our expectation. Their one good eye in this case is focused on any momentary pause in the continuing deployment and expansion of existing strategic weapons systems. They turn a blind eye when the Russians start new systems. They see the Russians stopping, seldom starting. On the other hand, when it comes to U.S. strategic forces, they can barely preserve their belief that the American strategic budget is rising at an accelerating rate by fixing their gaze narrowly on the phasing in of new systems or their continuance and by neglecting the phasing out of the old. For the Americans, it seems, they notice the starts, not the stops. If they cannot find a trend of increase in the plunging figures of the last twenty-four years, they find it in rosy service visions of the future, undampened by executive or congressional budget considerations.

However one explains the failure of arms race theorists to note the deviation of reality from their theory, it is quite plain that reality has diverged massively. Not only in the facts of *under*estimation that destroy a principal element of the supposed dynamics of the arms race, but also in the plain fact that the United States has not been running a quantitative strategic race.

It would be possible to present similar results for many other measures:

for example, while strategic defense vehicles have declined for a decade and a half from a peak more than *seven* times their present number, offense vehicles have remained roughly the same for many years. The total of strategic vehicles therefore has gone down. The point should be very clear. There is no serious evidence of a quantitative strategic spiral.

That's quite a different point from saying that as a result of these declines, we are uniformly worse off. While I have differed with many specific development and deployment decisions, on the whole my view is that the sum effect of changes over this long period, from the mid–1950s through the 1960s to the present time, has been an improvement in our force in key respects. *My view is indeed the opposite of the commonplace about the exponential arms race, which has it that as we have spent more and more on our strategic forces, our security has steadily declined.* To evaluate the commonplace we need to consider the nature of the major qualitative innovations in strategic force and their net effect.

THE NET EFFECT OF QUALITATIVE CHANGE

Theories of the quantitative strategic race are an extraordinary muddle of errors and self-deceptions. Yet notions about "qualitative races" may even be worse off. In fact Secretary Kissinger recently expressed a longing for a "conceptual breakthrough" that would bring our understanding of qualitative races up to the present standard on the quantitative strategy race. Heaven forfend! The modesty of the desire, however, may measure the current confusion about qualitative competition.

Though discussion is far from rigorous, the kinds of changes usually thought of as "qualitative" are alterations in some relevant unit performance characteristic. The most obvious historic example is the thousand-fold increase in the average unit explosive yield accomplished by the first A-bombs. A second almost equally famous example is the introduction of the H-bomb in the 1950s which, as originally envisaged, was expected to multiply the yield of a single A-bomb again a thousand-fold. Another equally crucial case is the increase in the average speed of a strategic vehicle from about 500 to 13,000 miles per hour, made possible by the development of intercontinental rockets. Other unit performance

characteristics affected by innovation have been mentioned earlier—
blast resistance, concealability, accuracy, reliability and controllability,
and resistance to "accidental" or unauthorized use.

Some technical changes, it seems obvious, might worsen the position
of everybody. Indeed, many now think that not rare but typical even of
civilian technology, which is increasingly assigned all the hyperbolic
traits recently attributed by the secretary of state to military technology:
it has "developed a momentum of its own," is "at odds with the human
capacity to comprehend it," is, in brief, "out of control." Shades of
Friedrich Juenger. Or Jacques Ellul, who holds: "Technique itself . . .
selects among the means to be employed. The human being is no longer
in any sense the agent of choice," and "everything which is technique is
necessarily used as soon as it is available, without distinction of good or
evil. This is the principal law of our age." [54] The use of the A-bomb for
Ellul only illustrates this law and is a symbol of "technical evolution"
in general. Such symbols recall the cloudy determinism of Oswald
Spengler's portentous "that which is a possibility is a necessity."

For environmentalists today, as for Juenger, a civilian technology out
of control is the source more typically for polluting than humanizing
the environment. We owe the environmental movement a debt for stress-
ing that it is important in choosing among technologies to take into careful account the indirect, long term, and public costs as well as the direct,
immediate, and private costs of technical change. It has unfortunately
also encouraged the revival of a more general Luddite view of technology as a threat to us all. The Luddite view, moreover, is particularly
tempting when it comes to military technology. Most of us have little
affection for weapons; and weapons improvements are likely to arouse
a good deal less enthusiasm than technical advances in general. It is
easy to believe that such "improvements" might make things worse all
around.

However, just as in the civilian case one can only choose *among*
technologies and it is highly unlikely that existing technologies are ideal,
so also in the military case it is extremely implausible that current technologies are optimal, that they fit our political purposes beyond any
possibility of improvement. We have to choose and we do. But the conditions of thoughtful choice are only obscured by the immoderate rhetoric, characteristic of Ellul, and also typical of the arms debate in the
post-Sputnik era. So Lipton and Rodberg talk of the "mystique of
technological progress within the defense establishment, where feasibility
is equated with obligation, where if we can build it, we must." [55] A
purple passage of that sort is expressive. But what is its meaning? It has

no plain application to the real world in which a very long list of development projects were cancelled after much spending, but before deployment.[56] And many more development ideas were stillborn before any substantial money had been spent in their pursuit.

Moreover, it is clear that qualitative changes need not affect both sides badly. Some changes might benefit one side primarily (as radar favored the British more than the Germans in World War II). Still others might conceivably help both, since the two sides have some objectives in common. So, for example, fail-safe techniques that prevent a war from starting by mistake through a failure of communication or a false alarm, or Permissive Action Links that prevent local arming of weapons without a release from a remote responsible command center, and modes of protection that make it possible to ride out an attack and depend less on hair-trigger response. Neither side would like to see a nuclear war start by "accident" or through some unauthorized act.

The problem of judging the effect of a specific qualitative change in key performance parameters is complicated by the fact that it may be ambiguous. It may serve the interests of just one adversary in some particular respect and in another respect the interests of both. For example, improvements in reconnaissance may permit more precise location and destruction of a target, but also may reduce collateral damage and serve as a key national means of verifying that alterations in an adversary's force are no more menacing than is permitted by an arms treaty. The SALT agreements would be infeasible without precise national means of surveillance other than ground inspection. No case-by-case analysis of qualitative changes since the mid–1950s can be given. However, it is unnecessary for the purpose of evaluating the Luddite stereotype in the contemporary debate. According to that stereotype, major innovations (1) lead to new and higher levels of strategic expenditure, (2) make strategic forces more destructive, (3) make them less secure, and (4) make them harder to control politically. To test this familiar view, it is important to look broadly at the net outcome of such major technological innovations as the development of fusion weapons and strategic rocketry.

Before forming some judgment on this subject, it may provide perspective to observe that the view of innovation as generating an unstable arms race, though widespread in recent times, is by no means universal. One of the few serious studies of arms races, that by Samuel P. Huntington, held that military innovation was fundamentally benign, among other reasons because it enabled the redeployment rather than the increase of arms budgets.[57] Moreover, since it did not increase the share of national resources devoted to defense, it did not produce the strains leading to war, but in fact made war less likely.

Huntington's hypothesis about the effect of technological change, though it runs counter to the present fashion, is by no means implausible. A qualitative improvement has to do with some relevant performance characteristics of a weapon. Painting bombs blue, for example, would not generally qualify as an improvement. Increasing the explosive yield for a given weight or the accuracy of delivery would. Such changes mean that effectiveness per unit or per dollar is increased and this implies in turn that a given task might be done with fewer units or at less expense.

To meet an adverse change in a potential enemy's force, then, a government has the alternative, through qualitative change, to redeploy resources, just as Huntington asserts, rather than simply to multiply them. He also points out that a self-imposed or a treaty constraint on improving qualitative performance may impel a simple multiplication of units—that is, it may generate a quantitative race. Moreover, though it is possible that opposing governments may blindly introduce changes that worsen the position of both sides, and though it is surely true that governments make a lot of bad choices, they have plenty of incentives for looking beyond the immediate consequences of a procurement decision. And not all of their choices have been grossly wrong. It is not hard to dig up governmental analyses, good and bad, that look well beyond the next immediate step.

Conventional arms race theory presupposes a totally mechanical or instinctual behavior, that reacts only to the immediate move, never looking forward. But it is by no means clear that governments are as fatally concentrated on the immediate as arms race theorists debating the current budget. Both the U.S. and the Russians introduced (in good part independently) the revolutionary technologies of rocketry and fusion weapons. But we made adaptations in our force that exploited these technologies precisely to avoid the kind of deterioration the dogma suggests is automatic.

The main methods worked out in the early 1950s for protecting the strategic force based in the United States for the rest of the decade depended on tactical warning and a rapid, safely repeatable response by our force that did not commit it to war on the basis of substantially uncertain warning. These methods could work reasonably well, so long as the speed of attacking vehicles was that typical of manned aircraft. But it soon became clear that strategic rockets were likely to be a feasible operational component of strategic forces in the 1960s.

Rockets, because of their speed, might, in current jargon, have been described as "intrinsically destabilizing." However, no single performance characteristic taken in isolation, whether speed or accuracy or whatever, can be so established. If one had believed that speed was intrinsically destabilizing, one might conceivably have tried to get an agreement banning rockets altogether; or tried to increase their travel time by getting agreements to use extreme lofted trajectories; or—still more far-fetched—an agreement to orbit them several times before landing; or (as in the 1958 Surprise Attack Conference) to construct an elaborate international warning system shared with adversaries in order to preserve the possibility of timely, secure response. Instead of trying simply to stop or slow down technology, the tack taken to maintain an improved second strike capability was to make unilateral adaptations that exploited both the initial limitations of the new rockets, specifically their great inaccuracy, and also their substantial advantages for defense penetration and for developing new, cheaper, and better modes of protection against attack, including mobility. Useful adaptations of the new techniques were feasible, even though our understanding of them was only partial and uncertain. Our adjustments to them did not have to be made all at once. They were made incrementally as various pitfalls and opportunities presented by these techniques became plainer.

In short, in spite of the recent as well as the age-old romantic antagonism to technology and the belief expressed by such critics of technology as Jacques Ellul, we are not slaves to technique. We can and do make technical choices, and in doing so sometimes improve matters. The alternative is an indiscriminate hostility to innovation per se, but that rests on the implicit assumption that the point at which we have arrived cannot possibly be improved—a rather odd view for the critics of technology to hold, who otherwise stress the arbitrary and irrational process by which past decisions on development have been made. In effect, an antagonism to all innovation amounts to a sentimental attachment to older technology rather than a hostility to technique in general.

A study of the major changes in technologies from the 1950s to the present and their effects on the strategic force supports the view that whatever the false starts and mistakes in detail, on the whole the outcome was exactly the reverse of the stereotype in the four respects listed on page 159.

Much of this is implicit in the analysis of quantitative changes already offered. So I can be brief. First, strategic spending did not rise to new levels. From the late 1950s it fell almost by two-thirds. Second, the relative destructiveness of our strategic forces as measured by EMT declined. Moreover, in precise contradiction to the standard view, this decline responded in good part to the increased size and effectiveness of actual and anticipated Soviet active defenses. On the whole, the shifts in the American force from gravity bombs to air-to-surface missiles carried on strategic aircraft and to ICBMs and SLBMs themselves were in the first instance basically a response to the formidable growth of Russian air defenses. But these as well as later developments meant a drastic reduction in total and average explosive yield and in EMT. Third, through such devices as placing rockets on submarines moving continuously underwater or in highly blast-resistant complex silos, the strategic forces became less vulnerable than they had been in the 1950s—with a resultant increase in stability. In the mid–1950s our strategic forces were concentrated at a few points, were soft, slow to respond, inadequately warned, and inadequately protected by active defense.[58] The Soviet forces were even more vulnerable, and remained so much longer, but greatly improved in this respect in the mid–1960s. Fourth, the controllability of the force was improved by the very methods of protection adopted, which made hair-trigger response unnecessary; also by a variety of fail-safe devices and arrangements permitting positive control, and by improving the protection of the command and control arrangements themselves.

Finally, many of the measures that so improved the strategic force were adopted self-consciously as alternatives to simply multiplying the force and increasing budgets. They did not undertake the hopeless task of stopping qualitative change. Rather, they adapted qualitative change roughly to our purposes, not all of which are incompatible with those of potential adversaries.

The combination of fusion weapons and missilery that enabled us to choose cheaper, safer, less destructive, and better controlled strategic forces were some of the very technologies that were thought at the time inevitably to have the opposite effects. Fusion warheads and the vastly increased speed of strategic rockets in particular made obsolete existing methods of protecting strategic forces, but they opened up new opportunities to increase the stability of the force. The principal effect of fusion technology was not so much to make weapons higher in yield, but to make low- and medium-yield weapons smaller, lighter, and cheaper. This in turn made it possible to put them in rockets more easily protected by blast shelters or in constantly moving submarines. An attempt simply to stop or slow this technology would have reduced the survivability of deterrent forces and therefore diminished international stability.

INCREASING THE CHOICES

Perverse current dogmas center most of all on an attempt to stop or slow technologies of discriminateness and control. However, the remarkable improvements in accuracy and control in prospect will permit nonnuclear weapons to replace nuclear ones in a wide range of contingencies. Moreover, such improvements will permit new forms of mobility for strategic forces, making it easier for deterrent forces to survive. More important, they will also increase the range of choice to include more discriminate, less brutal, less suicidal responses to attack—responses that are more believable. And only a politically believable response will deter.

Some technologies reduce the range of political choice; some increase it. If our concern about technology getting beyond political control is genuine rather than rhetorical, then we should actively encourage the development of techniques that increase the possibilities of political control. There will be a continuing need for the exercise of thought to make strategic forces secure and discriminatingly responsive to our aims, and to do this as economically as we can. Agreements with adversaries can play a useful role, but they cannot replace national choice. And neither the agreements nor the national choices are aided by the sort of hysteria implicit in theories of a strategic race always on the point of exploding.

Political language—and with variations this is true of all political parties, from Conservatives to Anarchists—is designed to make lies sound truthful and murder respectable, and to give an appearance of solidity to pure wind.

Orwell, who said that, prescribed never using a metaphor you are used to seeing in print as his very first rule for reducing the decay. That would cut the vast clutter of images about racing and uncapped volcanoes that we use to hide from ourselves what has been happening and what the issues are. In the chaotic "debate" about Vladivostok, the proponents claimed it would put a "cap" or "lid" on the explosive increase. Opponents, from Senator Jackson on to the Left, said it wouldn't: like SALT I, it would only force continuing the spiral in strategic spending. But before and after SALT I, the spiral was pure wind; and it will be wind in the present political circumstance with or without SALT II. For the United States, one might conceivably talk about a "shoe" or a "floor," but hardly a "cap." Vladivostok also illustrates the absurdity of the exaggerated threat, "worst case" dynamic. Here, overblown estimates of future Russian programs may lend a specious urgency to rapid agreement—another "miracle" for the secretary of state.

And when Secretary Kissinger asks, "What in the name of God is strategic superiority . . . at these levels?" he seems to be saying it doesn't make any difference how many more missiles the Russians have than we—in which case it's hard to see any urgency in agreement. He sometimes explicitly means that it makes no difference, because each side now can—in the stereotype—kill every man, woman, and child several times over. But that is an example of exactly the use of language Orwell had in mind. For it implies in fine moral tones that we should measure the adequacy of our weapons in terms of the number of civilians they can kill. The secretary, however, doesn't believe that. He has also said that attacks on population are a "political impossibility, not to say a moral impossibility." I am all for probing the premises of thought on arms and arms control which the secretary is said to want. But that can only start when we face up to evasions making "murder respectable" in such chaste phrases as "countervalue attacks" and in all the unreflective vocabulary of the arms race. This is an important part of rethinking policy about our relations with allies and adversaries, long overdue and essential for reducing the present chaos.

NOTES

1. Sir Edward Grey, *Twenty-Five Years, 1892–1916*, vol. 1 (New York: Frederick A. Stokes Co., 1925):89–90.

2. John Newhouse, *Cold Dawn: The Story of SALT* (New York: Holt, Rinehart, and Winston, 1973), p. 176.

3. See, for example, Morton H. Halperin and Jeremy J. Stone, "Rivals but No Race: Comment," *Foreign Policy* 16 (Fall 1974):88; see also the views represented in Michael L. Nacht, "The Delicate Balance of Error," *Foreign Policy* 19 (Summer 1975):163–77.

4. Jeremy J. Stone, in *American Miltarism 1970*, edited by Erwin Knoll and Judith Nies McFadden (New York: The Viking Press, 1969), p. 71.

5. Jerome Wiesner, *Anti-Ballistic Missile: Yes or No?* (New York: Hill and Wang, 1969), pp. 13–14.

6. Nancy Lipton and Leonard S. Rodberg, "The Missile Race—The Contest with Ourselves," in *The Pentagon Watchers*, edited by Leonard S. Rodberg and Derek Shearer (New York: Doubleday and Co., Inc., 1970), p. 303.

7. U.S. Congress, Senate, Committee on Armed Services, *Fiscal Year 1972 Authorization for Military Procurement: Hearings*, Part 2 (3 May 1971), 92d Congress, 1st Session, p. 1767.

8. *National Security Policy and Changing World Power Alignment*, Hearing-Symposium before the Subcommittee on National Security Policy and Scientific Developments of the Committee on Foreign Affairs, House of Representatives, 92d Congress, 2d Session, 31 May 1972, p. 98.

9. Robert S. McNamara, speech, 18 September 1967, "The Dynamics of Nuclear Strategy," *Department of State Bulletin* 57, no. 1476 (9 October 1967):445.

10. U.S. Congress, Senate, Committee on Foreign Relations, *Strategic Arms Limitation Agreement: Hearings* (28 June 1972), 92d Congress, 2d Session, p. 193.

11. *Arms Control Implications of Current Defense Budget,* Hearings before the Subcommittee on Arms Control and International Organizations, U.S. Senate Committee on Foreign Relations, 13 July 1971, pp. 205–6.

12. Knoll and McFadden, *American Militarism 1970,* p. 68.

13. Edgar M. Bottome, *The Balance of Terror: A Guide to the Arms Race* (Boston: Beacon Press, 1972), pp. xv–xvi.

14. William Epstein, "Will the Russians Play 'American Roulette'?" *Saturday Review World* 1 (29 June 1974):7–8. Epstein is a former director of the UN Secretariat, Disarmament Division.

15. Bernard T. Feld, "The Sorry History of Arms Control," *Bulletin of the Atomic Scientists* 26 (September 1970):26.

16. U.S. Congress, Senate, Committee on Foreign Relations, *Strategic Arms Limitation Agreement: Hearings* (26 June 1972), 92d Congress, 2d Session, p. 139.

17. Newhouse, *Cold Dawn,* p. 13.

18. Lipton and Rodberg, "The Missile Race," p. 303.

19. National Citizen's Commission, Report of the Committee on Arms Control and Disarmament, White House Conference on International Cooperation, 28 November–1 December 1965.

20. Jerome Wiesner, Foreword, in *Arms Control, Disarmament and National Security,* edited by Donald G. Brennan (New York: George Braziller, 1961), p. 14.

21. Herbert York, "Controlling the Qualitative Arms Race," *Bulletin of the Atomic Scientists* 29 (March 1973):4.

22. George Kistiakowsky and George Rathjens in *Scientific American* 222, no. 1 (January 1970):27.

23. Harvey Brooks, "The Military Innovation System and the Qualitative Arms Race," draft (rev.) distributed at Aspen Conference on Arms Control, August 1974.

24. *Détente,* Hearings before the U.S. Senate Committee on Foreign Relations on Relations with Communist Countries, 93d Congress, 2d Session, 12 September 1974, p. 195.

25. See, for example, Lipton and Rodberg, "The Missile Race," p. 303; Dr. Jerome B. Wiesner, *ABM: Yes or No?* (Santa Barbara, Cal.: Center for the Study of Democratic Institutions, 1969), p. 18; Dr. W. K. H. Panofsky, "Roots of the Strategic Arms Race: Ambiguity and Ignorance," *Bulletin of the Atomic Scientists* 27 (June 1971):15.

26. U.S. Congress, House, Armed Services Committee, *Statement of Secretary of Defense Robert S. McNamara on the Fiscal Year 1964–68 Defense Program and 1964 Defense Budget,* 88th Congress, 1st Session (Washington, D.C.: Office of the Secretary of Defense, January 1963).

27. See, for example, Nacht, "The Delicate Balance of Error."

28. In this we follow ibid.

29. Impressions from even a relevant picture, such as figure 4b, can stand supplementing by the computation of a few statistics and the summary of the results of a variety of statistical tests on the differences between predicted and actual silos: (a) The mean understanding of –80.1 silos per year is significant (using the Student's t-test) at the .001 level using the more rigorous "two-sided" criterion; that is, assuming appropriately that predictions can exceed as well as understate the reality. (b) The least squares trend lines has an r^2 equal to .40, but its slope, –12.59, is significant at the .05 level. (c) There is no significant trend up or down at the .05 level for the subperiod (1965–1969). (d) The worsening displayed is confirmed by the Student's t-test for the difference between sample means for 1962–1964 compared with 1965–1969. (The difference between predicted and actual is worse for the second sample at the .01 level.) (e) And finally, the Wilcoxon two-sample test, a robust "distribution-free" test, using only rank orders, also shows the later sample to be worse than the earlier at the .05 significance level. All of the above tests are two-sided.

30. Such a view was never consistently adopted by Mr. McNamara. He came to use action-reaction language, and often talked as if the adequacy of strategic forces could be measured solely in terms of their use to destroy cities. However, he brilliantly attacked the overkill theory and continued through his last Posture Statement to insist that we keep the objective of limiting damage in case deterrence failed.

31. See, for example, "Interview with Robert S. McNamara, Defense Secretary," *U.S. News and World Report* (12 April 1965), p. 52: "The Soviets . . . are not seeking to engage us in . . . the quantitative race. . . . There is no indication that the Soviets are seeking to develop a strategic nuclear force as large as ours." Compare this statement to that in *Military Balance, 1962–1963* (London: International Institute of Strategic Studies), p. 2, which often reflects the views of the British intelligence community: "The Soviet Union thus appears committed to a policy of 'minimum' or counter-city deterrence in relation to the United States, though the large medium range missile force it has now developed and deployed against targets in Europe and Japan may serve as both." This view was held by men with little else in common—Hedley Bull, *The Control of the Arms Race*, 2d ed. (New York: Frederick A. Praeger, 1965), p. xxii: "The Soviet Union did not embark upon the massive programme of intercontinental missile construction that had been anticipated, but seemed to settle for the sort of capability that in the United States is associated with the policy of 'minimum deterrence'"; Richard J. Barnet and Marcus G. Raskin, *After Twenty Years: Alternatives to the Cold War in Europe* (New York: Random House, 1965), p. 4: "Where we once believed that the Soviets were bent on surpassing the U.S. in military power, it now appears that . . . they are quite willing to put up with a missile gap: Indeed, we have been running much of the arms race with ourselves."

32. For this focus on the momentary or partial pauses, see, for example, the *New York Times*, 27 April 1969; the *Chicago Sun Times*, 22 April 1970; the *Milwaukee Journal*, 26 April 1970; *SIPRI Yearbook of World Armaments and Disarmament, 1969–1970* (New York: Humanities Press, 1970), p. 53; the *Wall Street Journal*, 17 December 1970; the *Manchester Guardian*, 7 November 1971; *Survival* (September/October 1972).

33. These two cases of failed predictions are described by Leon Festinger, *When Prophecy Fails* (New York: Harper Torch Book, 1964); idem, *Theory of Cognitive Dissonance* (Stanford, Cal.: Stanford University Press, 1967). Festinger's model of cognitive dissonance fits the history of the theory of systematic overestimation rather well.

34. For an early appreciation of this point, see, for example, P. M. S. Blackett, *The Political and Military Consequences of Atomic Energy* (London: Turnstile Press, 1948).

35. I address the problem briefly in *Pacem in Terris III*, vol. 2, *The Military Dimensions of Foreign Policy*, edited by Fred Warner Neal and Mary Kersey Harvey (Santa Barbara, Cal.: Fund for the Republic, Inc., 1974). I favor a U.S.–Soviet reduction to equal lower totals. That is quite independent of the question as to whether the U.S. totals have increased exponentially or at all.

36. Even this fact (and not merely its implications for the incomparability of the elements in the aggregate of offense warheads) is not always recognized. It is sometimes said that U.S. strategic warheads in general are in the megaton range. See, for example, *Arms Control: Readings from Scientific American* (San Francisco: W. H. Freeman and Co., 1973), p. 179.

37. One argument for simply counting warheads is the notion that the dangers of an accidental detonation increase linearly with that number. However, this is plainly false. The probability of an accidental, unauthorized detonation depends among other things on arrangements for weapons safety and for the centralization of control and command over these weapons.

38. The curves on numbers of warheads (see figure 7 and bottom of figure 8) are smoothed in order to approximate the calculated data points, but closely enough so that deviations from the trends discussed are not significant.

39. The EMT of a weapon is computed by raising its yield, expressed in megatons,

to the two-thirds power. See, for example, George Rathjens, "The Dynamics of the Arms Race."

40. "Program I" refers to Strategic Forces; "Program II" refers to General Purpose Forces. We have used unpublished computer tabulations dated July 24, 1975, available from the Office of the Assistant Secretary of Defense, Comptroller (Programs and Budget) of Total Obligational Authority by Program. These data have been extended back beyond FY 1956 only recently.

41. The decreasing exponential fit is rather good. The r^2 for the period 1952 is .75 and the r^2 for the period FY 1961–1976 is .88.

42. Recent Department of Defense computer tabulations have revised upward the 1961 current dollar estimate from its earlier reported level of $11.5 billion.

43. For example, see the discussion in the program "The Advocates," WETA–TV, Washington, D.C., 14 February 1974. Transcript available from WGBH–TV, Boston, Massachusetts.

44. Martin Binkin, "Support Costs in the Defense Budget," Brookings Institution Staff Paper (Washington, D.C., 1972), pp. 45–46.

45. The Brookings Institution uses a different method, which we call "Method II," when estimating the effects on overhead of future reductions in the strategic combat forces. For a description of Method I, see B. M. Blechman, E. M. Gramlich, and R. W. Hartman, *Setting National Priorities: The 1975 Budget* (Washington, D.C.: The Brookings Institution, 1974), p. 72 in the notes to Table 4–3. Method II projects total direct and arbitrarily allocated overhead costs in a manner that does not involve a separate computation of the direct costs. For a partial description of Method II, see Ibid., p. 91, Table 4–8, including the notes to the Table. Similar descriptions can be found in other editions of the *Setting National Priorities* series.

46. If I were to suggest changes to Brookings, one would be to display separately, in past and future budgets, the overhead fraction. This would help especially for future budgets. It is easy to expect greater overhead savings from direct program cuts than are likely: total overhead and the direct program budgets have moved in opposite directions. Yet the Brookings overhead formula for past budgets, like most such allocations, assumes overhead costs vary in a straight line with direct or operating costs without any time lag. And it loads an increasing proportion of total overhead onto the strategic budget. For such reasons I present figures on the strategic budget *with and without* Brookings overhead allocation.

47. Recent improvements in deflators for Total Obligational Authority take into account the fact that a substantial fraction of the funds authorized in a given year are spent in later years.

48. Paul C. Warnke, "Apes on a Treadmill," *Foreign Policy* 18 (Spring 1975): 12–29.

49. Maybe nothing will. As an even more striking example of how hard the dogma dies, consider the following statement by Bernard Brodie ("On Clarifying Objectives of Arms Control," ACIS Working Paper No. 1 [University of California at Los Angeles, Program in Arms Control and International Security, April 1976], p. 22), written after I had assured Mr. Warnke that I was indeed saying that the total cost of our strategic force has gone down, not up: "We should note here Albert Wohlstetter's denial that there is an arms race between the two superpowers, though he concedes there is an arms competition which raises costs on both sides." Mr. Brodie cites not only my original paper which documented the decline in U.S. strategic costs, but also a reply to Mr. Warnke in which I said again that U.S. strategic costs had not "escalated" but had gone down.

50. Computed by adding up separately cost estimates for all programs in Package I that were identifiably offensive and those that were identifiably defensive. Data for this breakdown were available only through FY 1974. The resulting offense and defense costs were then adjusted so that their total equaled the total used for Figure 10, while preserving the offense-to-defense cost ratio. Arms race theorists, faced recently with the divergence of strategic budgets from their theory of how they should behave, have suggested that the decline in the total strategic budget since it includes defensive forces merely displays the benefit of SALT I, which limited

ABMs. But the May 1972 agreements could hardly have affected anything before FY 1973, and the strategic defenses declined drastically many years before that; cf., "The Advocates," WETA–TV telecast cited above.

51. Lipton and Rodberg, "The Missile Race," p. 301.

52. Figures 15 and 16 were drawn by first reading the data points on the graphs in the original article as carefully as possible, using a ruler and right triangle. I do not know the source of the data used or kinds of budget monies employed (e.g., obligational authority, expenditures, or other), or what definitions were used for the three categories displayed, and I have made no attempt to justify the data or explain the anomalies in it. In particular, I am at a loss to explain why national defense expenditures show a decline from 1974 to 1975, even though the article talks about a $6.3 billion increase.

53. B. M. Blechman, E. M. Gramlich, R. W. Hartman, Setting National Priorities: The 1975 Budget (Washington, D.C.: Brookings Institution, 1974), p. 306.

53a. The historical curve is based on unpublished computer tabulations available from the Office of the Assistant Secretary of Defense, Comptroller (Programs and Budget) of Total Obligational Authority by Program, April 1974. For the historical curve, we have followed Brookings' practice of using their Method I for computing arbitrarily allocated overhead from similar Defense Department computer runs. By intention, the computer tabulation and inflation rates used are the same as used by Brookings for Fiscal Years 1964 and 1968 in Blechman, Gramlich, and Hartman, Setting National Priorities: The 1975 Budget, p. 72; and hence this curve agrees with that edition's calculations for those years. More recent data from the Comptroller's office has been used for Fiscal Year 1974 and Fiscal Year 1975.

Sources for the projected costs are the editions of Setting National Priorities for the indicated budget years. Projections in the editions for 1972 and 1973 include retirement pay which we have subtracted. Each edition's projections were constant dollars for that budget year. We have converted these to Fiscal Year 1975 dollars.

54. Jacques Ellul, The Technological Society (New York: Vintage Books, 1964), pp. 80, 99; cf. Friedrich Juenger, The Failure of Technology (Chicago: Gateway Editions, Inc., Henry Regnery Co., 1956), pp. 163–64.

55. Lipton and Rodberg, "The Missile Race," p. 302; cf. Richard Barnet, "The National Security Bureaucracy and Military Intervention," paper delivered at Adlai Stevenson Institute, 3 June 1968, p. 27.

56. Nuclear propelled aircraft, started in 1951 and cancelled ten years later; the XB–70 bomber started in 1958 and cancelled in 1967; the Hard Rock Silo project, started in 1968 and cancelled in 1970; the SCAD Armed Decoys begun in 1968 and cancelled in 1973; the Navajo ramjet intercontinental missile begun in 1954, cancelled in 1957; the Rascal, the Skybolt, the mobile medium range ballistic missile, Regulus II, the Manned Orbiting Lab, and so on.

57. Samuel P. Huntington, "Arms Races: Prerequisites and Results," Public Policy, vol. 8, edited by Carl J. Friedrich and Seymour E. Harris (Cambridge: Harvard University Press, 1958), pp. 41–86.

58. For a contemporary analysis of the vulnerability of strategic forces in 1956, see, for example, Albert J. Wohlstetter, F. S. Hoffman, H. S. Rowen, Protecting U.S. Power to Strike Back in the 1950's and 1960's, R–290 (Santa Monica, Cal.: RAND, September 1956), pp. 30, 41; for earlier analyses by the same authors published by RAND, see The Selection of Strategic Bases, R–244S (April 1953), and The Selection and Use of Strategic Air Base Systems, R–266 (March 1954).

9

EDWARD N. LUTTWAK

European Insecurity
and American Policy

I

Ever since the defeat of Hitler's Germany, Western Europe has been the major arena and chief prize of the struggle between the Soviet Union and the United States. It has always been understood that all the confrontations in the Middle East, the variegated crises in Africa, and even the shooting wars in Asia have been peripheral: so long as the nations of Western Europe remain free of Soviet control, no extension of Russian power beyond the borders of the USSR can be fully secure; so long as the power of the Soviet Union continues to threaten the independence of Western Europe, the very survival of Western civilization will remain in question. Hence the absolute centrality of Europe in the struggle pursued since 1945 by every instrumentality of policy, except for war itself.

Each side has registered great achievements and great failures. On the Western side, the success of the postwar policy of reconstruction foreclosed most avenues of subversion; but it was never within the scope of American policy to cure the deep political maladies of the Latin societies, in which the decay of Catholic authoritarianism has left behind a natural following for the authoritarians of the hour—the Communist parties of Italy, France, and Spain. Now that the regime sustained by Franco has entered an uncertain path towards democracy, all three countries are vulnerable to their domestic Communist parties at each general election. Nor could American policy resist the obscure processes which have caused Britain to decline so relentlessly: once a valid ally for the United States in much of the world, Britain is now scarcely able to sustain its modest role in European defense. Equally, the successful creation of NATO as the operational instrument of collective security for the North Atlantic alliance has been diminished by the defection of France and by the wasteful diversity of the armed forces of its members.

On the Russian side, the great achievement has been the successful maintenance of imperial rule over the peoples of Eastern Europe, in spite of their greater advancement in all spheres of civil life. The equally great failure has been the inability of the Soviet Union to convert the brittle structures of overt domination into a more resilient, if looser, predominance with which the autonomy of the peoples of Eastern Europe could coexist. The refusal of the Russians to tolerate any genuine democratization means that any move toward internal freedom must become an immediate challenge to Soviet hegemony. Thus Soviet soldiers must secure through their direct physical presence an obedience which a more subtle policy could perhaps have obtained by consent.

Whether Russian conduct merely incorporates the traditions of Asiatic oppression, or whether it is a conscious and rational manifestation of the imperatives of repression *within* the USSR, the result is the same: so long as national cultures and ethnic identities survive in East Germany, Poland, Hungary, and Czechoslovakia, Soviet hegemony can only be sustained by the direct pressure of armed force and shall always remain vulnerable to internal upheaval. Only in Bulgaria does the Soviet Union have a willing client, and only in Romania does a nationalist and self-reliantly repressive regime offer a limited obedience not imposed by the latent force of the Soviet army.

It is upon the delicate fabric of European politics, and upon the still more delicate web of relations between the United States and the free nations of Europe, that the impact of the post–1972 détente policy has been felt most severely. And it is in Europe that the costs of détente have been highest and its benefits least. The most significant *potential* benefit of détente was the reduction of the probability of conflict, and this could only be of small value in Europe, because in Europe—and only Europe—there is an alliance structure which precisely demarcates East and West, and which can therefore harness the full force of the balance of terror to avert war. For this reason, the avoidance of armed conflict in Europe has been an absolute imperative of Soviet policy for more than two decades.

By contrast, the most evident cost of détente, the unilateral suspension of the ideological struggle, has been at its highest in Europe, for it remains the central theater of the struggle of ideas. Elsewhere in the world men are still preoccupied by the more brutish exigencies of food and shelter, and both count for more than ideas; or, as in the Middle East and parts of Africa, it is religious fanaticism and racial hatred that dominate men's minds. In Europe, by contrast, there is a mass of humanity sufficiently progressed to be influenced by ideas and ideals.

So long as the tone and content of American policy provided a clear and powerful alternative to the authoritarian appeal of Communism; so long as the Soviet Union was held at arms' length by the United States in its diplomacy, so long as the voice of the West could be heard to challenge the pretensions of the East, there remained in Western Europe a dominant majority which would keep domestic communism at bay and would support NATO. Equally, in Eastern Europe there remained a silent majority which was ready perhaps to endure the present, but which looked to the West for its major hopes and ultimate aspirations.

When it became apparent that the leaders of the United States were primarily interested in developing a web of relations with the Soviet Union, all restraints to the separate pursuit of purely national diplomacies with Moscow were abandoned. The West German *Ostpolitik*, which featured in large part the exchange of tangible concessions by Bonn for promises by Moscow and which was motivated by the unique predicament of a Germany divided, was adopted as a model by the rest. If the *American* secretary of state and the *American* president took the lead in conviviality and diplomacy with the Russians, why should not the others follow?

When it became apparent that the leaders of the United States saw a reliable and acceptable partner in the Soviet regime, it no longer seemed compulsory to reject the participation of domestic communism in political life. How could there be an objection to the cooperation of Socialist parties with the Communists of France, Italy, or Spain when the *Americans* were so keen to cooperate with the Communists in Moscow?

When it became apparent that the leaders of the United States were willing to build "structures of peace" in partnership with their oppressors, how could the peoples of Eastern Europe retain hope of an eventual independence? It only remained for the then Senator Fulbright to argue with sinister innocence that the free radios should be shut down "since the cold war is over"; and then, quite recently, for a senior State Department official to explain in a closed assembly of American ambassadors that the strivings for independence in Eastern Europe were a threat to peace.

On this side of the Atlantic, men may perhaps delude themselves that it is the higher interests of peace that impose such actions. In Eastern Europe, on the other hand, living as they do much closer to a harsher reality, men undestand that only fear or greed can induce the free to welcome intimate understandings with their oppressors.

Nor could the greater fear of the Soviet Union be invoked to control the ancestral hostility of Greeks and Turks (as it had been successfully invoked in all the previous Cyprus crises), when the United States itself had done so much to diminish the saliency of the Russian threat. Even while the number of Soviet troops in Europe was being increased, even while a similar but more rapid growth was taking place in the Soviet air forces deployed against Western Europe, the declaratory policy of the United States proclaimed the new benevolence of the Soviet regime and the solidity of the newly assured peace. In the resulting climate of European opinion, all the restraints and all the sacrifices that imminent danger could impose were inevitably diminished. Thus the final breakdown in Greco-Turkish relations, and thus the new and stronger pressure to reduce defense budgets already inadequate.

It is of course deeply ironical that even though the processes of détente have worked to the disadvantage of the West, they have nevertheless been possible only because some adequate balance of military power has been maintained between the forces of NATO and those controlled by the Soviet Union. Were it not for this, the Soviet Union might have been tempted to take directly what it has instead so patiently pursued by the slower processes of détente. And were it not for this, the Soviet Union would certainly have obtained by diplomatic coercion what it now pursues by a gentler diplomacy of enticement.

The forces of NATO have always had a triple function: to deter attack, to defend in the wake of a failure in deterrence; and—by far the most important—to counter the armed suasion which the threat of Soviet military power would otherwise have exercised in the diplomatic arena. With the possibility of any major conflagration made very unlikely by the linkage of European security to strategic-nuclear deterrence and with the opportunities for minor attacks or swift territorial seizures denied by the clear demarcation of the NATO territories, it is primarily the political shadow cast by Soviet power which the alliance has had to oppose. It is for this reason that the underlying military balance remains the critical variable of East-West relations, even while the prospect of war has tended to remain exceedingly remote. And the measure of this balance has always been the expected outcome of an armed confrontation.

II

What impinges on the minds of the political leaders who must decide whether to conciliate Soviet demands or firmly resist them—what influences the attitudes of public opinion—is precisely the expected-outcome view of the military balance. In the light of their own notions of the shape of future war, observers try to construe the probabilities of victory, defeat, or—more likely—mass destruction on the basis of their perceptions of each side's combat capabilities. The Italians, who cannot visualize Soviet forces ever reaching Italy in an offensive (a reason for opposing defense expenditures), the Danes, who cannot conceive of any effective defense against a Soviet land-sea assault (an opposite reason to reduce defense expenditures), and the West Germans, who accept both the possibility of war and the feasibility of an effective defense, are all constructing their own scenarios and comparing the expected combat capabilities of the two sides in that specific setting. This way of thinking about the military balance is more natural and far more meaningful than the comparative lists of manpower and matériel *inputs*, which are usually offered in print under the rubric of the "military balance." It is after all the combat *outputs* that matter and not the inputs, which measure only the *cost* of military forces and not their capabilities.

It is, of course, very difficult to evaluate expected combat capabilities in a war scenario; moreover, the result will be very sensitive to the specific assumptions made in each scenario. On the other hand, the more familiar "input" comparisons are of general applicability, and have a simplicity that many find irresistible. The most common assessments of NATO and Warsaw Pact "capabilities" compound the distortion common to all input comparisons by using divisions as the unit of measurement (see table 1).

It is by now notorious that such divisional counts are grossly misleading since the "divisions" thus counted are not all uniform. Units in the non-armored category comprise both divisions of 10,000 lightly armed Italians and divisions of 16,300 heavily armed Americans, and the term may

TABLE 1

Divisions and Division Equivalents, mid–1976

Sectors of Deployment	AFNORTH–AFCENT *	AFSOUTH †
NATO forces	27	39
NATO + France	29	39
Of which armored	12	6
Warsaw Pact	68	31
Of which Soviet	40	8
Of which armored	31	7

SOURCE: *Military Balance 1975–1976* (London: International Institute of Strategic Studies [IISS]), p. 95.
* AFNORTH: Norway, Denmark, Schleswig-Holstein, and W. German Baltic coast; AFCENT: Belgium, the Netherlands, and W. Germany.
† AFSOUTH: Italy, Greece, and Turkey.

describe indifferently formations of 10,500 Romanian light-infantry or Soviet divisions of 12,000 men equipped with 266 battle tanks and several hundred combat carriers, each fitted with both a gun and missiles. Nor is the distinction between armored and other divisions very useful now-adays: in modern armies "armored"—or in Soviet usage, "tank"—divisions will merely have more tanks than "mechanized infantry" divisions, but the latter are in fact armored formations also, as with the Soviet mecha-nized division itemized above. (The Soviet tank division has 9,500 men and 325 tanks at full strength, only 59 tanks more than the "mechanized infantry" division.)

The obvious defects of division counts have prompted analysts to develop across-the-board comparisons of combat manpower, as illus-trated in table 2.

While somewhat less misleading, the combat manpower comparison is still quite inadequate as a guide to effective capabilities, *even in the abstract.* For one thing, the figures thus heroically aggregated count as

TABLE 2

Combat and Direct-Support Troops, mid–1976

Sectors of Deployment	AFNORTH–AFCENT	AFSOUTH
NATO	625,000	575,000
NATO + France	657,000	575,000
Warsaw Pact	895,000	345,000
Of which Soviet	595,000	115,000

SOURCE: *Military Balance 1975–1976* (IISS), p. 96.

equals the Turkish soldier armed with a bolt-action rifle of 1898 design vintage and the West German soldier who might go to war in a well-protected combat carrier fitted with a 20mm gun; the figures also aggregate forces of unequal capability, such as the Bulgarian infantry with East German tank crews. Clearly the manpower figures should be weighted by a weaponry factor, since equipment differences remain extreme both within and between the two camps. The one hardware count that is normally introduced as a corrective to the manpower figures applies to tanks, and more particularly to "battle" (medium and heavy) tanks (see table 3).

TABLE 3
Deployed Battle Tanks in Operational Units, mid–1976

Sectors of Deployment	AFNORTH–AFCENT	AFSOUTH
NATO	7,000	3,500
Warsaw Pact	19,000	7,250

SOURCE: *Military Balance 1975–1976* (IISS), p. 99.

Once again, extreme qualitative differences invalidate the purely numerical comparison: a "tank" may be a *T–34/85* in Hungarian service built perhaps thirty years ago or a British *Chieftain* built last year, fitted with a 120mm gun several times as effective as the old 85mm on the *T–34* and provided with armor perhaps three times as protective; similarly, modern Soviet *T–62s* are equated to decrepit *Centurions* in Canadian service, still powered by the original gasoline engine, grossly inadequate even thirty years ago. Such quality differences are critical and the numbers mislead.

Moreover, it is not at all clear that tank numbers are worth comparing in isolation, merely because the figures are easily available. NATO and Warsaw Pact armies vary in their styles of deployment (with much sharper differences among the former than among the latter), but all modern ground forces have long since copied the German innovation of the mixed combat team. Hence, if the hardware is to be evaluated, the comparison should include in a balanced fashion the artillery, troop, and combat carriers, engineer equipment, and communications gear *as well as* the battle tanks, light tanks, and armored scout vehicles. If NATO and Warsaw Pact armies accorded an equal emphasis on the tank element within them, then the simple tank count could indeed serve as a very convenient equipment index on its own. But in fact the most significant difference between NATO and Warsaw Pact ground forces is precisely the much higher priority given to tanks within the latter. In fact, until quite recently the Soviet army had no self-propelled artillery at all (except for small numbers of SP antitank guns in airborne divisions) and not all that many tracked troop carriers either, while it has always fielded more tanks than all the other armies in the world combined. In contrast to this tank-heavy deployment, NATO armies have tended to distribute their resources much more evenly between the combat branches: taken together, the artillery and infantry have more than twice as many tracked, armored vehicles than the tank units. In the Warsaw Pact the ratio is one-to-one. Hence the tank figures are very poor equipment indices.

This difference between NATO and Warsaw Pact force-structures reflects in part the fundamental strategic asymmetry between the essentially defensive nature of the Western alliance and the markedly offensive character of the Warsaw Pact. There is no need to engage in political analysis in search of a difference of intent: the deployment structures of the two sides are eloquent. NATO forces are organized in divisional and corps clusters deployed in depth, equipped and trained to execute defensive operations. By contrast, the Warsaw Pact armies, especially the Soviet, present the classic profile of mobile striking-forces designed to carry out swift offensives on a continental scale.

It follows that any valid assessment must begin by comparing the *offensive* capabilities of the Warsaw Pact with the *defensive* potential of NATO. If the number of men and weapons is to be counted, if the quality of training, morale, cohesion, and leadership is to be evaluated (as it must, because the importance of such intangibles *ordinarily* outweighs the material factors), then all must be done in the offense-defense context and not in the abstract, as a parallel assessment. Thus, for example, Warsaw Pact tank forces should be compared to overall NATO *anti*tank capabilities. The parallel count of the tanks deployed on each side can tell us little.

Another fundamental asymmetry is found in the logistic tail-to-combat teeth ratio of the two sides. Soviet and East European ground forces stress ready combat power at the expense of endurance, while NATO aims at a sixty- to ninety-day endurance and accepts a corresponding reduction in ready combat manpower. Organized into relatively small divisions with much armor and artillery fielded with skimpy logistic support, Warsaw Pact forces are intended to advance rapidly over ground in a battle of continuous penetration and limited duration. On the other hand, NATO forces are better able to maintain and resupply their forces, albeit at the price of a diminished level of ready striking power. It is

TABLE 4

NATO and Warsaw Pact Manpower in Ground Forces, mid–1976

NATO		Warsaw Pact	
Belgium	62,700	Bulgaria	120,000
Britain	174,900	Czechoslovakia	155,000
Canada	28,000	East Germany	98,000
Denmark	21,500	Hungary	90,000
France	331,500	Poland	210,000
West Germany	345,000	Romania	141,000
Greece	121,000	Soviet Union	
Italy	306,500	Army	1,825,000
Netherlands	75,000	Border Troops	200,000 [b]
Norway	18,000		
Portugal	179,000		
Turkey	365,000		
United States			
Army	785,000		
Marine Corps	108,000 [a]		
TOTAL	2,921,100	TOTAL	2,839,000

SOURCE: *Military Balance 1975–1976* (IISS), passim.
NOTE: The figures in this table cannot be used as capability indices since much of the manpower could not be usefully employed in a European war under *any* circumstances; see *Military Balance 1975–1976* (IISS), pp. 5–26.
[a] This figure is arbitrary. The MC total including air elements is 197,000.
[b] The KGB (Soviet State Security Committee) border troops are more heavily armed than either Warsaw Pact or NATO troops, on average.

for this reason that the larger NATO manpower totals translate into lower "combat and direct support" troop levels (see table 4).

The endurance imbalance between the Warsaw Pact and NATO makes it likely that it will be Soviet strategy to fight any future war "in one long breath." The Soviet aim would be to achieve decisive results before unit supplies are exhausted, and before too many fighting vehicles fall out in need of repairs which the field forces cannot accomplish. By contrast, it must be NATO strategy to prolong the struggle until the endurance advantage can be brought to bear. In any event, the defense would have to fight a holding battle while its troops are prepared and deployed for combat. In some cases, NATO forces are stationed in peacetime quite far from their assigned wartime sectors: for example, troops would have to be sent into northern Norway to hold the Finnmark, critical territory in which adequate peacetime deployments are not practical; more important, U.S. forces that are still stationed at their 1945 terminus in southern Germany, would have to be redeployed northwards.

Much would depend on the feasibility of such moves in a wartime environment, and that in turn would heavily depend on the course of the war in the air: if NATO can establish an adequate degree of air superiority, *and* if the weather conditions allow air power to be used with some effect, the ground forces are much more likely to survive the initial shock of the attack and accomplish the forward moves they must make. If, on the other hand, NATO air power cannot be used "positively" to slow down the offense—or worse still, if the Soviet air force can significantly disrupt ground movements—then an effective NATO defense becomes virtually impossible.

Historically NATO has enjoyed a clear advantage in the air, in spite of numerical inferiorities (see table 5).

TABLE 5

Deployed Tactical Aircraft in Operational Units, mid–1976

	AFNORTH–AFCENT		AFSOUTH	
Sectors of deployment [a]	NATO	Warsaw Pact	NATO	Warsaw Pact
Fighter—interceptors	350	2,000	275	625
Fighter—reconnaissance	300	475	125	75
Fighter—ground strike	1,250	1,325	450	200
TOTAL	1,900	3,800	850	900

SOURCE: *Military Balance 1975–1976* (IISS), p. 100.
[a] Includes some out-of-area aircraft on both sides. These figures are only roughly indicative. Each side could deploy many more aircraft into the area.

Until quite recently, the numerical superiority of the Warsaw Pact air forces was more than compensated by the much higher quality, and greater mission-suitability, of NATO air power. Soviet tactical aircraft —the *only* combat aircraft deployed by the pact except for some Czech armed trainers—were primarily lightweight fighters suitable for air combat but not for ground attack; *MiG–17s, MiG–19s,* various versions of the *MiG–21,* and *Su–7s.* Only the latter were configured as fighter-bombers, and even these (as also the strike versions of the *MiG–21*) were simply too small to offer adequate payloads, given the efficiencies of Soviet air technology. The *Il–28* light bomber did have a payload comparable to that of Western fighter-bombers (4,500 pounds) but its subsonic speed and very primitive avionics undercut its utility in European conditions.

The shortcomings of Warsaw Pact tactical aircraft in the ground-attack role were of particular significance because they unbalanced the overall deployment: while the ground forces were poised to carry out a *Blitz-krieg*, the air forces were primarily suited for short-range, defensive, air-to-air combat over friendly territory. It is true that advancing armor would need air cover, but they would also require close air support in order to maintain momentum in the face of resistance, and this the Warsaw Pact air forces could not effectively provide.

It is true that the Soviet "long-range" (strategic) air force included several hundred *Tu–16* medium bombers with substantial payloads (10,000 pounds or more); but the actual combat value of these aircraft in a tactical role was much reduced by the inability of the subsonic, medium altitude *Tu–16s* to survive in a hostile air space. Besides, it is not clear to what extent the *Tu–16s* could be spared from their prime mission of nuclear delivery.

The broader deficiency of Warsaw Pact air power applied to all missions, even air defense, for which the aircraft themselves were well suited as air vehicles. The inferior quality of Soviet radar technology, the poor performance of Soviet air-to-air missiles, the low rate of fire of their aircraft guns, and the inferior quality of their ground-attack ordnance (unguided rockets and gravity bombs) undercut the effectiveness of the aircraft.

No other aspect of the overall decline in the relative strength of NATO is as serious as the slow but accelerating change in the air balance. The introduction of the *Su–17/20* (*Fitter C*)—a variable-geometry conversion of the old *Su–7*—the replacement of the old *MiG–17* with the altogether more capable *MiG–23*, and the deployment of the *Su–19 Fencer*—the first deep interdiction aircraft in Soviet service—are providing the Warsaw Pact with delivery-capacity increases of 2–400 percent for each air unit thus reequipped. At the same time, the crucial quality gap in air weapons and electronics is perceptibly decreasing. Since new aircraft are replacing the old at a much more rapid rate in the Warsaw Pact than in NATO, the real, *average quality*, gap is closing quite rapidly.

It is important to realize that the adverse change in the air power balance has a more-than-proportionate impact: in the wake of an attack, NATO would be critically dependent on secure internal lines in order to muster its forces and deploy them where they would be needed. The disruption of lines of communications by air interdiction could deprive NATO of its one advantage: its superior reinforcement capability. The maximum number of additional combat troops which the Soviet Union could deploy in a European war within a 90–120-day period could not exceed 300,000 or so, organized in thirty divisions. This would be an increment of less than 50 percent on the peacetime deployment. By contrast, the United States could double its combat troops in the European area within a 90-day period, with a steady flow of additional troops becoming available thereafter. Similarly, the reinforcement potential of the allies in Europe in the event of a major war would exceed that of the East Europeans if, that is, France chooses to participate.

The United States maintains less than one-fifth of its active ground forces and tactical air power in Europe, hence the reinforcement potential. But the use of sea transport would be indispensable to bring munitions and heavy weapons from the United States, even if all the troops were sent by air. Except for the three division-equivalents whose heavy equipment is already stored in Europe, all other reinforcements could only be usefully employed if Western shipping could cross the Atlantic safely.

The heavy investment made by the United States in its antisubmarine forces reflects the assumption that a protracted war is indeed possible in Europe. What remains uncertain is the *net* potential of a wartime NATO sealift in face of the growing strength of the Soviet navy. It is not necessary to take into account the uncertain capabilities of the Soviet surface fleet in order to resolve the question: the decisive factor would be the effectiveness of the Soviet submarine force. If it is assumed that a Soviet offensive would be prepared in advance, the prior positioning of Soviet submarines in the North Atlantic must be assumed also. Even if a good many boats remained in the Pacific, Western antisubmarine warfare forces might have to contend with fifty or more nuclear boats operational and on station, another fifty or so modern diesel boats, and fifty older diesel boats (the latter could not expect to survive for long but they might be expended profitably). What reveals the magnitude of the threat is that even at its peak the German U-boat force of the Second World War never numbered more than fifty operational boats on station. It is true that since 1945 the techniques of antisubmarine warfare have made great progress, but it is also generally accepted that the submarine has made greater progress still.

During the first weeks of a conflict, the transfer of supplies from American stocks would be of critical importance. Unless the fighting lasts for very much longer than it seems reasonable to expect, current production would be of small significance. Hence the great significance of American inventories, which now include ca. 9,000 tanks of all types (viz. 40,000 for the Soviet Union), 22,000 armored carriers (viz. 35,000) and 6,000 artillery pieces (viz. 15,000). Less than a third of this equipment is already in Europe, and the rest would be needed there with extreme urgency. Any losses at sea would be irreplaceable for all practical purposes. Thus the submarines of the Soviet navy would have a much higher value target than the U-boats ever had: instead of having to attack the Western *stock of shipping*, they could accomplish their task by merely sinking a high proportion of the early shipments.

III

The great weakness of NATO is that it is a voluntary multinational alliance: its forces are equipped with a wide variety of weapons which are neither standardized nor interoperable, its troops are trained to execute divergent national tactics, and above all, its operational commands are vulnerable to the tensions that attend the common warfare of dissimilar allies. By contrast, the great weakness of the Warsaw Pact is that it is *not* a voluntary alliance. While the forces of the pact enjoy the benefits of an imposed commonality, being fully standardized on Russian equipment and Russian tactics, the Soviet high command must contend with the great unknown of an always latent disaffection. Depending on the particular circumstances attending the outbreak of war, East European troops may fight hard, they may desert, or they may even turn against the Russians. Familiar techniques of control ("sandwich" formations, retention of dominant weapons, etc.) may provide some reassurance to the Russians, but no techniques and no procedures can ensure the loyalty of the unwilling.

This political uncertainty may well interact with the great contingency of any European war: the use of nuclear weapons. Both sides have deemed it worthwhile to pay the high costs of maintaining large *non*-nuclear forces. They did so even when official doctrines and published strategies called for the prompt and extensive use of nuclear weapons in a European war. It is obvious that political leaders on both sides did not accept the logical implications of the declared strategy of their soldiers: had they done so, NATO forces could have been reduced to a mere border guard, and Soviet forces to an imperial gendarmerie. At present, each side deploys several thousand theater nuclear devices in the shape of gravity bombs, artillery shells, demolition charges, surface-to-air missiles, bombardment rockets, and surface-to-surface missiles.

It seems *logical* to expect that if either side were to appear to be losing, it would appeal the verdict of conventional war in the higher court of nuclear warfare. Even in a stalemate, if the fighting were extensive and prolonged, and the destruction of civil life progressed accordingly, America's allies might well demand the use of nuclear weapons, if only on a small scale, and if only to inflict a "negotiating shock" designed to prompt an agreed cease-fire. On the other side of the fence, *any* war which is not immediately successful might engender the fatal disaffection of Eastern Europe, and this might well trigger a Soviet resort to nuclear war. And then there are those who argue that the notion of a large-scale but nonnuclear war in Europe is wholly unrealistic, that in the chaos and panic of the very first days of war the use of nuclear weapons would be imposed by circumstances! Certainly it would be unrealistic to assume that the conduct of NATO would truly be bound by its formal strategy, including the 1967 decision in favor of a "flexible-response" strategy, which relegates nuclear weapons to the role of a last resort.

IV

In the early debates on the West German *Ostpolitik* and the American détente policy, opponents argued that the main effect would be to undermine the political foundations of Western defense. Specifically, it was said that the atmospherics of détente would release irresistible pressures for reduction of the defense budgets and terms of conscription for the na-

TABLE 6

Terms of Conscription in NATO, and Active Manpower Totals

	1971		1975	
NATO	Manpower	Term (months)	Manpower	Term (months)
Belgium	96,500	12	87,000	10–12
Britain	380,900	—	345,100	—
Canada	85,000	—	77,000	—
Denmark	40,500	12	34,400	9
France	501,500	12	502,500	12
West Germany	467,000	18	495,000	15
Greece	159,000	24	161,200	24
Italy	414,000	15–24	421,000	12–18
Netherlands	116,500	16–21	112,500	16–21
Norway	35,900	12–15	35,000	12–15
Turkey	508,500	20	453,000	20

SOURCE: *Military Balance 1971–1972, 1975–1976* (IISS).

tional-service armies of Western Europe. At the same time, it was argued that the Soviet Union would exploit but not emulate any "relaxation of tensions," and indeed that it would continue to increase the strength of the Soviet armed forces. Now that some years have passed, interim returns are in, and they suggest that the critics were right (see table 6).

No NATO army has increased its term of conscription; four have reduced it. By contrast, terms of service in the Warsaw Pact have not changed at all, and all the armies have increased in size. Soviet armed forces numbered 3.4 million men in 1971, pre-détente, while their number exceeded the 4-million mark by 1975. Over the same time period U.S. forces have declined from 2.7 million men to 2.1 million. Such aggregate trends are of course wholly unrelated to the impact of détente in Europe. But the trend in the level of *Soviet* troops and equipments deployed against Western Europe is very definitely related, and the trend suggests that the critics of the détente policy were right in their predictions (see table 7). Moreover, there has been a striking increase in unit capabilities: during these years of détente, the Soviet leaders evidently have deemed it wise to increase gross numbers while at the same time adding much new equipment of drastically enhanced effectiveness. Whatever their understanding of the processes of détente, it is evident that the resultant "relaxation of tensions" was to be strictly one-sided.

In view of this, the fate of the MBFR talks on bilateral force reductions, the most explicit manifestation of the U.S. détente policy in Europe, can hardly be surprising. A bare chronology suffices to illustrate the attitudes on both sides, and the respective willingness of each to "reduce tensions":

June 1968   The NATO Council of Foreign Ministers calls for negotiations on *the mutual and balanced* reduction of forces in Europe (MBFR) with "undiminished security" for both sides.
May 1970   Secretary L. Brezhnev speaking in Tiflis suggests the possibility of negotiations.

TABLE 7
Soviet Combat and Direct Support Troops and Deployed Tanks

Sectors of Deployment	AFNORTH–AFCENT		AFSOUTH	
	1971	1975	1971	1975
Troop level	588,000	595,000	90,000	115,000
Number of battle tanks (equipment index)	10,000	11,500	1,600	2,250

SOURCE: *Military Balance 1971–1972*, pp. 77–78; ibid. *1975–1976*, pp. 96–99 (IISS).

January 1973	Preparatory consultations in Vienna.
May 1973	The Soviet delegation refuses to include the term "balanced" in the title of the negotiations.
June 1973	Membership and status definition. The Soviets insist that Hungary be excluded from full status (i.e., from Central Europe). MBFR talks officially named "MURFAAMCE" (Mutual Reduction of Forces and Armaments and Associated Measures in Central Europe), the United States having pressed its allies to accept the Soviet demand that the adjective "balanced" be eliminated from the title.
November 1973	Soviet proposal: a 20,000-man across-the-board reduction alliance-wide in 1975; a proportionate (5 percent) reduction in 1976; a further 10 percent reduction in 1977.

Effect

	Base Force	Phase I	Phase II	Phase III
NATO	1,010,000	990,000	940,500	846,450
WP	1,103,000	1,083,000	974,700	877,230
WP Advantage	93,000	93,000	34,200	30,780

NATO proposal: a proportionate reduction of 15 percent for U.S. and Soviet forces in Phase 1 and progress towards a negotiated ceiling of 700,000 ground troops for each side. Many other associated proposals for verification, tension-reducing measures, etc.

| July 1974 | Adjournment. |
| October 1974 | Soviet proposal: reductions of 10,000 troops by the U.S. and the Soviet Union, and phased reductions of 5,000 by others thereafter. |

Effect

	Base Force	Phase I	Phase II	Phase III
NATO	1,010,000	1,000,000	995,000	990,000
WP	1,103,000	1,093,000	1,088,000	1,083,000
WP Advantage	93,000	93,000	93,000	93,000

Since the presentation of the second Soviet proposal, which envisaged the maintenance of a *fixed numerical superiority* on a *diminishing base*, and which was thus a less desirable proposal than the first one, there have been other proposals and other suggestions. But no progress has been made.

Originally invented as a device with which to oppose senatorial demands for unilateral reductions in U.S. troop levels in Europe, later mobilized as a vehicle of détente diplomacy, and as such the scene of un-requited concessions by the United States in 1973–1974, the MBFR (or rather MURFAAMCE) talks should now be given a decent burial. Just as the Soviet Union uses "Polish" proposals as *ballons d'essai* for its diplomacy, the valiant diplomats of Luxembourg may perhaps be called upon to issue an ultimatum: balanced reductions or nothing.

It was, in fact, always unwarranted to regard the Soviet forces in Central Europe as in any way symmetrical to those of NATO. The first mission of the Soviet forces is to secure the unwilling obedience of the peoples of Eastern Europe; the second is to project military power into Western Europe, in order to obtain a degree of diplomatic leverage which neither their provincial culture, nor their unattractive society, nor their primitive economy can secure for them; and it is only their third mission to defend the Soviet Union in the exceedingly remote possi-bility that a NATO military threat might materialize. By contrast, U.S. and NATO forces are deployed for a purely military—and purely nega-tive—defensive purpose in the face of a threat which remains disturb-ingly vivid. Western troops have no functions of internal control, and none of the NATO forces generate any perceptible diplomatic leverage. Thus, if the forces of each side are to be reduced "with undiminished security," Soviet forces must be reduced *more* than proportionately: their offensive potential confronts a defense already inadequate, which would become still more so as the base strengths decline since the de-fense must cover a fixed geographic frontage which does not diminish with reciprocal force reductions. Moreover, since any American forces reduced would be transferred across the insecure Atlantic while Soviet forces would remain at the other end of rail lines leading directly to the front, only measures of actual demobilization can provide "undi-minished security."

V

Its evident neglect of the alliance relationship under the aegis of the détente policy has been justified by the State Department on the grounds that European conduct allowed no other possibility: the West Germans actually preceded the American course in their *Ostpolitik;* the French as usual, pursued short-sighted policies which they thought were profit-able merely because they were so overtly selfish; as for the milk-fed carnivores of British diplomacy, their conduct was no better for being presented in good English prose. Of the Italians in perpetual crisis, the Belgians deeply divided, and the Danes—who are willing to do anything for NATO except pay for it—the less said the better. The Dutch and the Norwegians could be trusted, but Holland ceased to be a Great Power in the seventeenth century and Norway has not been one since the days of the Vikings.

All this is true, if undiplomatic. But also true is that the irresolute, divided, and sometimes overtly self-seeking Europeans are still the one body of humanity whose welfare and security is inextricably bound with our own. Our economic prosperity, our cultural vitality, our moral economy require a secure, prosperous, creative, and stable Europe. For all its defects, the Europe that exists is the only Europe we have, and it is time that it be made the central concern of our policy.

10

NORMAN POLMAR

The U.S.–Soviet Naval Balance

The most surprising international development since World War II has been the development of the Soviet naval and maritime fleets. While other postwar Soviet advances such as producing nuclear and thermo-nuclear weapons and establishing satellites in Eastern Europe could be predicted, history, geography, defense requirements, and other factors suggested that the USSR would not develop major maritime forces.

HISTORICAL PERSPECTIVE

Russia—under tsars and then commissars—has been primarily a land power. With brief exceptions, such as when Peter I established a fleet in the Baltic or when the Russians enjoyed successes in the Black Sea and Mediterranean against the Turks, Russian efforts at sea generally have been failures. In both world wars Soviet successes at sea were few and far between, even in the Baltic and Black Seas where the Russians had numerical superiority.

When NATO was established in 1949 it was primarily as a counter to the massive Soviet ground forces in Europe. At sea the threat was from the Soviet submarine force only. The word "only" can be used for two reasons: First, the Soviet surface fleet was virtually nonexistent. Although still operating a number of U.S. and British warships transferred during the war, plus a few German, Italian, and Japanese prizes, the capability of this surface fleet even in Soviet coastal waters was essentially nil. Stalin initiated a major ship-construction program immediately after the war, but it was traditional and archaic in concept, and the program died in 1953 along with the dictator.

Second, even the Soviet submarine threat was itself marginal. Not until 1949 did the first submarines of postwar design emerge from Soviet shipyards. These new submarines were based on the highly capable German Type XXI, and several shipyards were turning out these advanced undersea craft. Still, the Soviet yards failed to produce anywhere near the 1,200 submarines that were being predicted in the West during the 1950s, and those that went to sea rarely ventured far from Red ports.

Although the Soviet submarine force reached a peak of some 475 undersea craft in the early 1960s, their operational capabilities were limited: they could snorkel only with difficulty, engineering problems forced several boats to be towed back to the USSR, and the U.S. navy made all six Soviet submarines in the Caribbean region surface during the 1962 missile crisis. Further, most of the Soviet fleet was based in the Baltic, where NATO forces could easily block it from exiting through the narrow and twisting Danish straits.

These conditions, coupled with Soviet traditions, interests, economic relationships, and geography, made it unlikely that the nation would emerge as a major sea power in the decades following World War II. On the other hand, the rejuvenation of the U.S. fleet during the Korean war (1950–1953) insured that America would be predominant at sea for the next two or three decades.

But several occurrences in the 1950s altered that which had been tradition and that which would be future. The end of the massive Soviet shipbuilding effort in 1953 with Stalin's death provided the opportunity for radical change. Nikita Khrushchev's assumption of leadership soon afterward brought about an emphasis on advanced weapon technologies (popularly described in the West as "more bang for the buck") and on commercial trade with the West. Another major factor was the dismissal of Admiral N. G. Kuznetsov as head of the navy and his replacement by a young admiral (barely forty-six years old) named S. G. Gorshkov.[1]

The new naval commander-in-chief had neither ocean nor submarine experience. His war service, during which he was promoted to rear admiral at age thirty-one, had been mainly in the Black Sea and Sea of Azov. There he had mostly commanded shallow-water forces, often working with the army and dealing with General Andrei Grechko, probably with political commissar Nikita Khrushchev, and possibly with political officer Leonid Brezhnev.[2]

The events of the 1950s led to fundamental changes in Soviet maritime development. In lieu of Stalin's planned battle cruisers and aircraft carriers, after less than a decade of design and construction in the 1960s the Soviets began to put to sea several new classes of cruisers, destroyers, and submarines intended primarily to defend the Soviet homeland against U.S. aircraft carriers and (later) against Polaris missile submarines. They also built large numbers of coastal missile craft.

Stalin's efforts did provide the basis for a large, modern shipbuilding industry. This capability, supplemented with additional major yards established for *merchant* ship construction under Khrushchev and periodically updated through modernization programs, today produces large, sophisticated warships and support ships for the Soviet navy. Shipbuilding strength is a key element of the ability of the USSR to send a modern fleet to sea and sustain it, and is a factor often overlooked in correlating a nation's ability to produce a navy.

As noted above, the large numbers of surface warships and submarines were intended to defend the Soviet Union against attack from the sea by Western aircraft carriers and missile submarines. Other missions of this naval force were to interdict the sea lines of communication between the United States and Western Europe, and to support Soviet ground operations in the coastal regions of Europe and Asia.

Although developed for these missions, events outside of the Soviet Union provided new opportunities for warships flying the hammer-and-sickle ensign. By the late 1960s the Soviet Union had achieved "parity" or "rough equality" with the United States in strategic weapon arsenals. This strategic parity meant that no longer could U.S. leaders threaten—directly or indirectly—to use strategic weapons to intimidate or coerce the Soviet Union. Gone was the nuclear "umbrella" under which lower-level U.S.-Soviet confrontations could be resolved invariably in favor of the United States because of the specter of escalation.

VIETNAM AND AFTERMATH

The effects of the Vietnam war on the U.S. navy were equally significant. The Vietnam war simply wore out the U.S. fleet. The hectic pace of naval operations off Korea and later off Vietnam hastened the demise of large numbers of ships that had been built during World War II.

Furthermore, the urgencies of war repairs during the Vietnam war, especially repairs required by several carriers that had suffered operational disasters, delayed routine overhauls and maintenance and wore down the older ships even more. Finally, new ship procurement was deferred as defense-funding priorities went to war-fighting opportunities.

In this situation, the U.S. Chief of Naval Operations at the end of the Vietnam War, Admiral Elmo R. Zumwalt, decommissioned and scrapped most of the surviving World War II–built warships as they reached the end of their nominal twenty-five- to thirty-year lives in order to save their high operating, maintenance, and overhaul costs. Admiral Zumwalt proposed to apply the funds thus saved to constructing a number of new ship designs, among them the sea control ship (SCS), a small carrier for helicopters and vertical/short take-off and landing (VSTOL) aircraft; patrol frigates (PF) for ocean escort, and small hydrofoil missile ships (PHM).

However, in 1974, with the U.S. policy of replacing military service chiefs every four years, Zumwalt retired. His successor, Admiral James L. Holloway, III, had different views of naval policy and many of Zumwalt's programs were halted in favor of others. Simultaneously, the nation's high inflation rate caused ship construction costs to soar upward, while debates over the question of nuclear propulsion for surface ships imposed still another set of constraints on U.S. naval programs.

The number of ships in the U.S. fleet declined rapidly (see figure 1). By 1975 the fleet was half the size it had been only five years earlier and much smaller even than before the Vietnam buildup. True, many new ships entering the fleet were much more capable than their predecessors, but with the U.S. overseas commitments remaining at essentially the same level as before Vietnam (except higher with respect to interests in the Indian Ocean region), the loss of numbers was keenly felt. Also, by 1975 many questions were being asked about the quality of U.S. warships vis-à-vis new Soviet designs. Chief of Naval Operations Admiral Holloway, stated:

The surface combatant force is, at this time [1975], greatly in need of modernization in AAW [antiair warfare], ASW [antisubmarine warfare], and offensive capabilities. New ships are entering the fleet, but the majority of them are particularly limited in the capability to attrite a preemptive anti-ship missile attack, and they are generally outranged by our potential opponents in anti-ship weaponry.[3]

This valid description of the U.S. fleet in the mid–1970s was made when most of the aircraft carriers (ten of thirteen) and the cruisers (twenty-three of twenty-seven), and all of the frigates, submarines, and amphibious ships were of post–World War II design and construction.

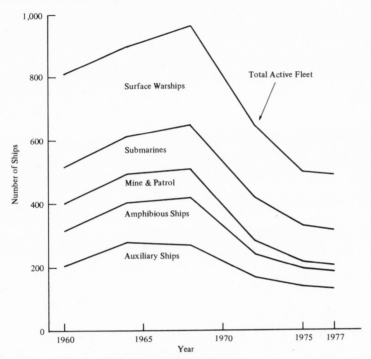

FIGURE 1. U.S. Navy Force Levels
(1960–1977)

There was thus the paradox of a relatively modern and, in some respects, large U.S. fleet unable to cope with its potential opponent at
sea in certain war scenarios.

This situation arose because of the nature of U.S. naval development
since the Second World War. The fleet that evolved after VJ-Day, and
which performed so superbly in Korea, the Cuban missile crisis, Vietnam,
and a score of other cold war actions and near-actions, had been primarily a "projection" fleet. That is, it was configured to project U.S.
military power overseas—to carry and land marines on hostile beaches,
to attack targets at sea and ashore with aircraft launched from carriers,
and (with the development of intercontinental missiles) to strike land
targets with submarine-launched nuclear weapons.

In its ability to project power into remote areas, the U.S. navy is
unequaled. The assault at Inchon in 1950, which changed the direction
of the Korean war, the putting of troops ashore in Lebanon in 1958 to
stabilize that nation's political situation, the "almost" landing in the
Cuban missile crisis, carrier air strikes in Korea and Vietnam, and various
evacuations of U.S. nationals from troubled areas have conclusively
demonstrated the navy's conventional force projection capabilities.
"Strategic" force projection, residing from about 1951 onward in the

nuclear strike capabilities of aircraft carriers, later supplemented and then superseded by missile-armed submarines, has not been demonstrated. Nevertheless, today the U.S. navy's forty-one nuclear-propelled submarines armed with Polaris and Poseidon missiles are considered the nation's most survivable and, in many respects, most effective strategic deterrent weapon. These forty-one submarines now provide almost one-third of the launch vehicles (bombers and missiles) and just over one-half of the separate warheads in the U.S. strategic arsenal.

The principal components of the navy's power projection forces are thus large aircraft carriers, amphibious ships, and strategic missile submarines, supplemented by large, high-speed (thirty-plus knots) cruisers and destroyers armed with antiaircraft and antisubmarine weapons to defend the carriers and amphibious forces.

The postwar fleet has developed around a second mission also, that of sea control. This mission is more difficult to describe because of the ambiguity of the term "sea control." Although some authorities argue that control of the sea implies the ability of the fleet to go anywhere at any time, a more realistic definition would speak in terms of assuring the flow of ships—warships, merchant, amphibious—between the United States and specific overseas areas with only acceptable (or no) losses. The U.S. need for sea control should be obvious to anyone who looks at a globe; the United States is essentially an island, separated by seas from its foreign resources, marketplaces, cultural ties, allies, and (hopefully) battlefields.

As the Soviet submarine threat began to emerge in the early 1950s, the U.S. navy initiated a number of antisubmarine programs, among them a continuous effort of building escort ships or frigates—essentially slow (twenty-five to twenty-seven knots) ships with sensors and weapons to fight submarines, but little capability against surface ships or aircraft. Similarly, U.S. submarines were soon optimized to fight other submarines: the U.S. attack (ASW) submarines emphasize quiet running, large sonars to detect other submarines, and advanced torpedoes and rockets for attacking enemy submarines. Submarine speed and weapons for use against surface ships were not stressed because of the lack of a Soviet naval or merchant fleet at the time.

Sea-control forces also include highly advanced land-based and carrier-based aircraft for seeking out submarines, seafloor acoustic detection systems, and other ASW-related systems. When not performing in the projection or sea-control missions—that is, most of the time—these same forces become most useful for political "presence." The United States is a world power and the greatest trading nation. The presence of a U.S. warship to demonstrate American interests and, to some extent, capabilities in a region is important to our political and economic activities. In the post-1945 "cold war" for men's minds, their markets, and their resources, the presence of military forces in overseas areas has become of major importance to both Western nations and the Soviet Union.

In the mid–1970s, the U.S. navy is optimized for the missions of force projection and sea control in the antisubmarine context. Interestingly, the principal conventional force projection weapon, the large aircraft carrier, is also probably the best sea-control platform for use against hostile surface ships and aircraft over the ocean. But the phenomenally high construction costs of these ships (now over $2 *billion*) and the costs of their 100-plane air wings have led to a severe reduction in this type of ship as the older, war-era ships have worn out without replacement. Whereas in 1965 the U.S. navy had twenty-four "flattops," today there are only thirteen.

To compensate for the loss of carriers and in response to the modern Soviet surface and merchant fleets, the U.S. navy belatedly is developing antiship missiles and plans to construct smaller (less expensive) carriers to operate only helicopters and VSTOL aircraft. Although the latter cannot equal the performance of conventional carrier planes, they have the advantage of not requiring large flight decks with catapults and arresting wires.

This is the U.S. navy of the 1970s: smaller in ship numbers than at any time since the late 1930s; largely of modern construction (now averaging a few months *younger* than the Soviet navy); and optimized for force projection and ASW. Unfortunately, on the basis of many criteria the current U.S. fleet is too small to carry out all of the nation's current and potential requirements, especially when one considers the increasing capabilities of the Soviet navy and the extensive Soviet use of merchant and fishing fleets to carry out military-related and political activities for which the United States employs naval units. In the 1970s— for the first time since 1942—there is a naval force at sea which could effectively contest U.S. use of the world's oceans.

CUBAN AFTERMATH

In the fall of 1962—almost simultaneously with the Soviet backdown in the Cuban missile crisis—there emerged from Soviet shipyards the first of a series of advanced-technology warships. The Kynda-class cruisers were the world's first major warships designed and built with ship-to-ship missiles, while the Kashin-class missile destroyers were the world's first gas-turbine warships. (Gas turbines provide an excellent weight-to-horsepower ratio and make the Kashins the world's fastest ocean-going warships at thirty-five to possibly thirty-eight knots.)

These were the first major Soviet surface ships of the "Gorshkov era," whose designs were completed and whose construction started after Admiral Gorshkov took command of the Red navy in early 1956. His ships were dictated by Khrushchev, who demanded that the "metal-eating" shipbuilders cease constructing the battle cruisers and other big ships of the Stalin era and concentrate instead on defensive naval forces and on trade-building merchant ships.

Gorshkov, as directed, scrapped the remaining Soviet battleships and most of the older cruisers, but kept fourteen new Sverdlov-class, six-inch-gun cruisers, as well as the lesser surface warships. This was a triumph after Khrushchev's boast to scrap all the cruisers which, he said, were suitable only for carrying admirals on port visits. Similarly, submarine programs were continued (they were considered "defensive"), while small missile craft and missile-carrying bombers were built to better defend the USSR against U.S. carrier and amphibious attack. Within a few years, when Gorshkov's position was sufficiently secure and the world situation sufficiently insecure (the Suez crisis and war of 1956, Lebanon in 1958, and Cuba in 1962), he began to construct an ocean-going fleet for the Soviet Union.

The Kynda-class cruisers were followed by the larger Kresta I, Kresta II, and Kara designs, each more capable than the previous class, although there is disagreement among intelligence experts as to whether their main battery is antiship or ASW missiles. Also built were the two Polaris-hunting helicopter carriers of the Moskva class; probably additional ships were planned but canceled because of greater-than-expected ranges of U.S. submarine missiles. More, improved destroyers were built, as were large numbers of submarines, frigates, patrol and missile craft, minesweepers, and the many other ship types that characterize a major navy.

Especially significant, under Gorshkov the Soviet navy gained almost 300 missile-armed Badger jet bombers, plus other Badgers for reconnaissance, tanker, and electronic jamming roles. These now are being supplemented by about one-half of the Backfire swing-wing bombers being produced (probably attesting to their nonstrategic role). Also, under Gorshkov the Soviet naval infantry or marine corps has been reinstituted; several battalions eventually will be assigned to each of the four Red fleets for a total strength in the mid–1970s of some 15,000 men.[4]

These troops are carried by large numbers of new-construction landing ships. While not as large or far-ranging as the U.S. navy's amphibious vessels, these Polish-built landing ships can carry Soviet marines as far as a thousand miles to assault beaches along the seas that border the Soviet Union. They can thus seize strategic straits or islands. Or they can carry Soviet military equipment to foreign lands. These long-range lifts are supplemented by the several new classes of "commercial" vehicle-carrying ships now being produced for the Soviet merchant marine, some of which already have carried tanks and other weapons to Black Africa and the Middle East with record unloading times. Related to potential Soviet amphibious assault capabilities, there are indications of planning for joint airborne-naval landings in Soviet writings. Interestingly, the head of Soviet airborne forces, General of the Army V. F. Margelov, is a former naval infantry officer.[5] Also, several Soviet army divisions are reported to have undergone amphibious training.

Under Admiral Gorshkov, the Soviet navy's number of ships has actually declined slightly; however, there has been extensive modernization with several new technologies introduced. An official U.S. navy evaluation of U.S. and Soviet areas of naval leadership listed: [6]

United States Navy	Soviet Navy
Carrier aviation	Antiship missiles
Amphibious assault	Submarines [7]
Submarine detection	Small combat craft
Submarine quieting	Tactical coordination of submarines/aircraft/ships
Underway replenishment	Ocean surveillance
Nuclear surface ships	New technology application
	Shipbuilding initiative
	Military/naval education
	Integration of maritime resources

Perhaps more important than Admiral Gorshkov's guidance, leading to the quality and quantity of the current fleet, is the fact that he has pushed the Red navy out of the Baltic and onto the world's oceans. Before Gorshkov, most of the major Soviet ships and submarines were based in the Baltic, where there access to the Atlantic through the narrow Danish Straits could be easily blocked. Today the Soviet navy's oceangoing forces—all of the nuclear and strategic missile submarines, most of the new cruisers, and the long-range reconnaissance planes—are based in the Northern and Pacific Fleets where they have more direct access to the oceans. The Baltic Fleet—now with mostly coastal craft—apparently has missions only inside the Baltic: support of and cooperation with the Soviet army, harassing NATO forces, trials, and training. The Black Sea Fleet exists primarily to maintain a rotation of warships and support ships in the Mediterranean. It includes the two helicopter carriers of the *Moskva* class and the new *Kiev*-class VSTOL carrier, as well as an impressive array of missile-armed cruisers, destroyers, and other ships. The submarines for the Mediterrranean deploy from the Northern Fleet because of treaty limitations on their passage from the Black Sea. Soviet ships and aircraft now regularly operate from bases in Cuba, Guinea, Syria, Iraq, Aden, and Somalia. Admiral Gorshkov has thus partly overcome the geographic limitations with which the Soviet navy had long been burdened.

In addition, the Soviet navy's at-sea time has increased dramatically under his leadership. There was no sustained Soviet naval presence outside of coastal area waters until the early 1960s; today the Soviet navy has about as many "ship days" out-of-area as does the U.S. navy. This sending of ships to sea has been a personal triumph for Gorshkov, who has stated that Soviet naval units now visit more foreign ports than do U.S. ships. At sea, these ships have begun to provide the Soviets with a limited capability for sea projection as well as a political presence. The latest major addition to the Soviet fleet, the VSTOL carrier *Kiev*, will increase both of these capabilities. The *Kiev*—with at least two sister carriers under construction—will enable the Soviet navy to put tactical aircraft over task forces and beaches far from their air bases. Displacing almost 40,000 tons and heavily laden with guns, missiles, and electronic equipment, the *Kiev* presents an impressive "presence."

The Soviet navy has been ably supported and supplemented in out-of-area operations by the world's largest merchant fleet (measured in number of hulls), largest fishing fleet, largest ocean-research fleet, and largest space-event support fleet, all flying the Soviet flag. For example, the merchant fleet provides about 70 percent of the fuel transferred to Red warships on the high seas, while the other components of Soviet sea power can undertake communication relay, intelligence, research and surveying, political presence, and other assignments. There appears to be an extremely high degree of coordination and cooperation among these maritime activities that is far beyond that possible (or even understood?) in the economics-oriented West.

ON BALANCE

Comparisons of the two superpower navies are both difficult and misleading. As Admiral Zumwalt has remarked, "The question of which navy
is first or second is meaningless. The question is: which navy does the
job it was designed to do better?"

TABLE 1

U.S.–Soviet Naval Balance

(Active mid-1976)

	United States	Soviet Union
Submarines—nuclear-propelled		
Ballistic missile submarines		
(12/16 missiles)	41+	45+
Ballistic missile submarines		
(3 missiles)	0	8
Cruise missile submarines	0	40+
Torpedo attack submarines	65+	40+
Submarines—diesel-propelled		
Ballistic missile submarines		
(3 missiles)	0	20
Cruise missile submarines	0	25
Torpedo attack submarines	8 [a]	150+
Aircraft carriers	13+	0
Aircraft carriers (VSTOL)	0	1+
Helicopter carriers (ASW-missile)	0	2
Helicopter carriers (amphibious)	8+	0
Cruisers		
Guided missile cruisers	27+	21+
Gun-armed cruisers	0	10 [d]
Destroyers		
Guided missile destroyers	39	64+
Gun-armed destroyers	60+ [b]	35
Frigates		
Guided missile frigates	6+	0
Gun-armed frigates	59	110+
Small combatant craft		
Missile craft	1+	130+
Patrol/ASW/torpedo craft	30 [b]	450+
Minesweepers	25 [b]	270+
Amphibious ships (over 200 feet)	58 [b]	95+
Land-based ASW/patrol aircraft	380+ [c]	150+
Land-based missile-strike aircraft	0	290+

+ additional ships/aircraft under construction.

[a] Plus 3 transport and research submarines.

[b] Includes 30 destroyers, 22 patrol craft, 22 minesweepers, and 3 amphibious ships manned
mostly by reservists.

[c] Plus reserve ASW/patrol aircraft.

[d] Includes 2 command ships.

Still, even simple numerical comparisons are instructive (see table 1). In numbers of surface warships, submarines, and small craft, the Soviet navy is by far the larger. In tonnage, the U.S. navy is larger. Interestingly, if one subtracts the tonnage of the U.S. navy's thirteen aircraft carriers, the Red fleet has more tonnage. Other—and possibly more valid—comparisons include numbers of missile launchers, gun barrels, reloads, endurance, shipboard and land-based aircraft, and a score of other considerations. Also significant is geography. An action in the Eastern Mediterranean would be within easy range of Soviet air bases in the Crimea and the Middle East; on the other hand, in the Western Mediterranean U.S. ships could receive support from U.S. navy and air force planes based in Spain. Another factor is that the Mediterranean is thousands of miles from Norfolk and hundreds of miles from Sevastopol.

NATO and Warsaw Pact naval forces could play important roles—politics aside—in specific areas. Norway, for example, has fifteen coastal submarines that could influence a battle along its coastline, but could not operate in the Atlantic or Mediterranean. Similarly, Polish and East German naval (and air) forces could insure Soviet Bloc control of the Baltic, but could not be counted on to influence operations in the Mediterranean.

If the current Soviet-U.S. naval balance is difficult to fathom, the course that the U.S. navy should steer in the future is even more difficult to decide. Seeking to rebuild the fleet after its post-Vietnam nadir, the navy's current leadership, under Secretary J. William Middendorf II and Admiral Holloway, had long sought a balanced fleet of some 600 ships. "Balance" here means a proper mix of warships—cruisers, carriers, destroyers, frigates, submarines, et al—as well as amphibious ships and auxiliary ships.

Congress, seeking to carry out its Constitutional duty "to provide and maintain a Navy," has put forth concepts at variance with the navy's views. The House Armed Services and Appropriations Committees, under Melvin Price and George Mahon respectively, have favored mostly large nuclear ships—carriers, cruisers, and submarines. These are highly capable but expensive, and can be bought only in small numbers. At the same time, the Senate Armed Services Committee under John Stennis, but especially pushed on by Robert Taft, seeks to emphasize smaller submarines and advanced-technology programs such as the VSTOL carriers, hydrofoils, and surface-effect ships.[8]

Still other voices can be heard. For example, Representative Les Aspin, a regular critic of the defense establishment, in mid–1976 accused the navy of lying about Soviet attack-submarine construction in order to justify higher U.S. building programs. This rather odd accusation was made in a year when the Soviets operated more submarines than the U.S. navy (some 335 to our 118), had more nuclear submarines (about 135 to our 106), and were expected to complete ten nuclear submarines compared to *two* in U.S. shipyards.

U.S. nuclear submarine deliveries will increase during the late 1970s, probably peaking at seven per year in 1980. However, current Department of Defense planning provides for only three or four submarines per year during the 1980s. There is no reason to expect Soviet deliveries, now at about ten per year, to decline, and they may well increase during the 1980s as the USSR reaches its SALT limit of sixty-two modern strategic missile submarines (the U.S. limit is forty-four) and turns to producing more of the smaller nuclear attack submarines for antishipping and ASW operations. Soviet nuclear submarine building capacity is now estimated at twenty to twenty-four units per year in peacetime; U.S. capacity is given at seven. In addition, the Soviets still construct conventional (diesel-electric) combat submarines while the United States does not. Other categories of warship construction are more difficult to compare. In general, the Soviet Union builds many more naval ships than the United States, but most of the U.S. ships are larger.

More balanced and more meaningful criticisms than Aspin's attacks on U.S. naval programs have come from others. Many members of Congress have criticized specific navy ships or schedules, but have recognized the obvious: that the United States must have the ability to use the sea, control portions of it, and be able to strike from the sea if it is to remain a viable, twentieth-century political and economic power.

Present congressional interest in the naval balance is intensive and perhaps more searching than ever before. It occurs at a time when naval warfare is unquestionably more sophisticated and more complex than ever before. Gone are the simple criteria of the early part of this century when one simply counted up the number of dreadnoughts and the weight and range of their broadsides. Admiral Gorshkov has noted: "We have had to cease comparing the number of warships of one type or another and their total displacement (or the number of guns in a salvo or the weight of this salvo), and turn to a more complex, but also more correct, appraisal of the striking and defensive power of ships, based on a mathematical analysis of their capabilities and qualitative characteristics." [9] And, it should be noted, one must undertake such analyses in the context of the different U.S. and Soviet roles and missions at sea.

The debate probably will continue for the next few years: how large should the U.S. navy be and what should be its composition? Unfortunately, most participants in the debate will look at the Soviet navy and seek to match up numbers rather than consider roles and missions. Also, simplistic comparisons do not take into account that submarines do fight other submarines, but so do surface ships and aircraft—ASW sensors can also be provided in moored seafloor systems and possibly even satellites. Similarly, "commercial" merchant ships can effectively carry troops or tanks for force projection, or can provide underway replenishment of warships. Further, how does one measure or compare Command-Control-Communications (C^3), Chemical-Biological-Radiological (CBR), and Electro-Magnetic Pulse (EMP) defense capabilities, all of which are important in modern naval warfare?

Most important, many of those engaged in the debate will draw up comparisons of specific fleet strengths and capabilities at a specific time, failing to seek out trends. But trends are absolutely crucial to any meaningful understanding of the U.S.-Soviet naval balance. Ten or fifteen years ago the question of "who is number one" would not have been seriously raised. Yet today, highly competent authorities are debating the issue, with some authorities being less than optimistic about most outcomes of U.S.-Soviet war-at-sea scenarios.

If the trend continues, what will be the U.S.-Soviet naval balance in five years? Or in ten or fifteen years? Admiral Zumwalt, U.S. Chief of Naval Operations 1970–1974, believes the probability of a U.S. victory over the Soviets in a conventional war at sea is less than "50:50", Dr. Malcolm Currie, U.S. Director of Defense Research and Engineering, has made the sobering observation that "a simple continuation of present trends could lead to dominance by the Soviet Union in deployed military technology in a decade." Finally, it is important to remember that this debate over the naval balance occurs when the United States is more dependent upon use of the sea for political, economic, and military reasons than ever before in the nation's 200-year history.

NOTES

1. Admiral Kuznetsov served as head of the Soviet navy from April 1939 to January 1947, and again from July 1951 to January 1956. Admiral Gorshkov became commander-in-chief of the Soviet navy and a deputy minister of defense in January 1956; he continues to serve in those positions at this writing.

2. Brezhnev, now first secretary of the Communist party, served as a political officer with Black Sea naval forces in World War II; in the early 1950s he was the chief political officer of the Soviet navy.

3. Admiral James L. Holloway, III, U.S. Navy Department of Defense Appropriations for Fiscal Year 1976. Hearings before a subcommittee of the Committee on Appropriations, 94th Congress, 1st Session, Senate, Part 3—Department of the Navy (1975, GPO, Washington, D.C.), p. 81.

4. Northern Fleet (headquartered at Severodvinsk), Baltic Fleet (Baltiisk/Pillau), Black Sea Fleet (Sevastopol), and Pacific Fleet (Vladivostok). There also is a flotilla on the Caspian Sea.

5. The Soviet Union maintains at least seven airborne divisions. The U.S. army has one on active duty.

6. Norman Polmar from public data.

7. Based on quantity, number of classes introduced in the past few years, antiship weapons, speed, etc.

8. A contribution in this area has been Senator Robert Taft, "White Paper on Defense" (March 1976, mimeo, Senator Taft's office) a 164-page treatise released in March 1976 that seeks to explore "a fundamental restructuring of our armed forces and rethinking of our strategy [which] might provide even better defense that would not entail greater cost to the taxpayers." The paper then calls for "a new defense plan based on sea power."

9. Statement to the troops at Minsk, 14 March 1970.

III

Human Rights and Freedoms

11

ROBERT CONQUEST

The Human Rights Issue

"Human rights" constitute the central crux of the whole relationship between ourselves and the Soviet Union. The suppression of undesirable political, economic, or religious ideas; the persecution of those who express them, by imprisonment, pseudo-psychiatric incarceration, and expulsion from the country; the refusal to allow the circulation of foreign books and periodicals; the banning from their homelands of the million-odd Crimean Tatars, Meskhetians, and Volga Germans; the harassing of the Jews. All this is profoundly distasteful to those who cherish the principles of the Western culture.

There are areas of the world in which tyranny, however distasteful, is not a direct threat to the West; others where the hostile regime lacks any power to harm us, or—itself under threat—might arguably help us. Areas, in fact, where the matter is purely, or almost purely, a moral one. Human rights in the USSR, however, do not concern us simply on principle, but also—and overwhelmingly—as regards our interests. I shall here be less concerned with the humanitarian aspect than with its profound significance—even on the most cold-blooded calculation—for Western foreign policy.

First, the Soviets' conduct on human rights gives us the clearest understanding of the essentials of their political attitude; and without such understanding our own foreign policy must lack its necessary foundation. Misunderstanding of the nature—and even the existence—of the differences between the essentially divergent political cultures which divide our planet is the central problem of politics today. We are all prone to inappropriate and parochial presumptions about other political cultures and about their deepest motivations. It requires a constant effort of the intellect—and not only of the intellect but of the imagination too—to keep us free from the habit of making these unconscious assumptions about the present thoughts and future actions of the Soviet leaders.

Apart from anything else, the concept of détente seems based on the assumption that those leaders have the same "natural" interest as the West in lessening tension. Western policymakers have thus failed to grasp the basic differences, not so much of opinion as of motivation. Political Man is seen as a sort of android robot, programmed with one or another "opinion"; if the opinion is removed and another substituted by demonstration and argument, his total behavior will change. It is thought that we may thus "rationalize" political conduct by applying criteria of reason and reasonableness which seem natural to our own culture but are quite alien to others. In reality Political Man in different systems is not just basically the same creature holding different theoretical opinions, but rather a life form which has evolved into radically different phyla, each with deep-set attitudes historically determined over long periods—and subject to natural selection as between different temperamental groups. In the USSR the present Marxist-Leninist ruling elements are actually unable to see the world in terms other than their own.

We may conveniently make a basic distinction between the "civic" and the "despotic" cultures. In the former, the policy is articulated and decisions are made in accord—in principle at least—with a balance of interests and views, through consultation with and acceptance by various sections of the community. In the "despotic" culture decisions are made by a single man or group regarded as uniquely qualified, and the population is merely a passive element.

The despotic form of culture divides naturally into two general types. In the traditional "imperial" system it is assumed that the true form of the state has already been achieved; the messianic revolutionary type seeks by an act of will to bring history to an eschatologically predetermined conclusion. The two varieties have much more in common with each other than they do with the Western culture. But above all, the present Soviet regime amounts to a fusion of the two.

HUMAN RIGHTS AND THE RUSSIAN STATE TRADITION

In the Russian tradition, since Mongol times, the state claimed absolute control over society as a matter of principle. The revolutionary countertradition which developed in it was equally total in outlook: the elect, with their perfect doctrine, would seize power with an absolute claim to rule over the population. Even before the revolution, the Polish revolutionary Rosa Luxemburg had noted how the idea of the infallible Bolshevik Central Committee was no more than a mirror image of tsarist autocracy. It is true that from about 1860 there had been the rise of a Europeanized civic attitude, with courts, juries, eventually a fairly free press, and a duma; but this development was crushed between the millstones of traditionalist and messianic despotism. In fact, the main achievement of the October revolution may be seen as the destruction of the fruit of two generations of precarious civic development.

Not all traditional despotisms had been expansionist. But tsarism, as Marx noted, carried a tendency to universal expansion; while communism was explicitly a world-idea, and Lenin and his successors ruled that only the soviet model would serve. Similarly, both traditions held the same view of the unofficial thinker; and Brezhnev's Russia resembles the Russia of Nicholas I far more closely than, for example, Britain resembles the Britain of 1830.

This is to say that the Soviet rulers are the product of a long tradition, a deep-seated political psychology. They are not to be converted to new ideas by argument; hardly by experience. Though some of them are also deeply involved in the exegesis of ideology, that is not the point. The others, who may not spend their time reciting or studying the texts of Marxism-Leninism, are nevertheless soaked in that tradition and determined by it. And this background is likely to weigh more heavily with them than the syllogisms of Western statesmen.

The important thing is not so much the wickedness or otherwise of their culture as its strangeness, from our point of view. We can see this, for example, in the agricultural problem, which is a gross and inefficient burden on the economy. They are unable to change it, for reasons of doctrinal habit alone. They are similarly unable to grant the legitimacy of any non-Soviet regime—even a Communist regime, as we saw in Czechoslovakia in 1968. They are unable to abandon the world claims intrinsic to their whole psychology.

The Soviet attitude to mere truth would make them very uneasy company among the nations. It will be remembered that one of the great issues between the Brezhnevite repression and the dissenters was not merely that the latter were expressing intolerable opinions, but that they were also trying to discover and publish the true facts about Soviet history. We are used to the nature of the regime, for otherwise it would— as it should—strike us as quite fantastic that no account, true or false, is now available about the Stalin terror, which was the vastest and most determining event to have moulded the country in modern times. The political struggle, the great trials, the enormous death roll, the archipelago of camps, have simply disappeared from the public prints. The period is filled instead with industrial construction. The only explanation for this is that the leaders are psychologically unable to countenance truth, or to abandon the idea that the past is freely to be manipulated at their behest. And, of course, these overweening rights extend also to the present and the future.

Thus, when it comes to human rights, their refusal of free opinions or free movement of their subjects is no mere accidental or temporary willfulness on the part of the Soviet rulers. On the contrary, it is something that characterizes the essence of their political attitudes. For them society, and members of society, have no rights against the state. And all other attitudes on the part of individuals or foreign states are not merely mistaken, but wholly damnable and subject to extirpation as a simple duty, wherever and whenever tactically possible.

The single issue of human rights tells us the essential nature of the Soviet political culture and its attitude to aberrant nations as well as individuals. And therefore the human rights issue is the crucial test when it comes to establishing peace in a durable sense. Human rights is the one demand—the only essential demand—we can make; and the degree of its fulfullment is the one true criterion of progress to peace.

THE HELSINKI AGREEMENT, 1975

This understanding, particularly on the part of certain Northern European leaders, led to the inclusion of Basket Three in the 1975 Helsinki Agreement. Its formulation was, of course, in terms of the free movement of people and ideas—which, expressed in concepts suitable to international relations, emphasized the liberty of the subject and freedom of thought.

Of the two, the first, though of vital importance, does not have the scope of the second. Although it is a pity that the principle of free movement has become reduced in many Western minds to the free emigration of Jews (who are of course not specified in either the Helsinki Agreement or the Jackson amendment), that principle is an indispensable last sanction by the oppressed against the claims of the state, and once secured, even in part, would be an enormous first step to civilizing Russia. But the free movement of ideas goes to the heart of the matter. When Milton wrote "Give me liberty to know, to utter, and to argue freely according to conscience, above all liberties," he implied the truth that while freedom of thought does not contain all the other things we would list as human rights, it contains their potentiality, and they cannot be realized or sustained without it.

Moreover, the free movement of ideas is not some parochial fad of the Western culture. It is what distinguishes a society with the possibility of change and progress, even of peaceful progress, from one without it. It is what distinguishes an articulated social order, with its compromises and consensuses, from a barracks or a prison. It is what distinguishes a country able to live in a world with various state forms and ideas, from one based on the principle of the imposition everywhere of received truth. It constitutes, in fact, all that can be meant by political civilization; and it provides the criterion of an essentially peaceable, as against an essentially aggressive, state.

The Soviet interpretation of détente places the emphasis elsewhere. The Soviet leadership are frank in their public speeches in describing détente —or "peaceful coexistence," as they have till very recently preferred to call it—as itself a form of struggle; and in emphasizing that the "ideological" struggle continues, that the "class struggle" on a world scale cannot be stopped. But just as class struggle on the world stage does not mean supporting the aims of genuine proletariats but merely of any political forces whatever who serve Soviet interests, so ideological struggle does not consist—as some Westerners seem to interpret it—of a harmless campaign of honest argument about ideas, with the best man winning. On the contrary, its main components are: a) a stepping-up of anti-Western propaganda by pro-Soviet groupings in the West and Soviet radio broadcasts abroad; b) an intensification of anti-Western "vigilance" and militarist propaganda in the USSR; c) the suppression of pro-Western (and indeed pro-Maoist, pro-Islamic, pro–non-Soviet) voices wherever possible; d) a soft-spoken, weasel-word "dialogue" with any Western elements—Christian, trade union, or whatever—who may have failed to notice a), b) and c) and in spite of everything still present pathic targets to the surprised and delighted Marxist-Leninist. Thus for the Kremlin, détente is simply a matter of tactics comparable to that adopted by the Sun in Aesop's fable: when the Wind's attempt to make the Traveller shed his coat by violent blasts has failed, and the tactic of friendly warmth proves more successful.

DISTINGUISHING TWO ASPECTS OF NEGOTIATION

At this point it will be appropriate to disentangle the two different aspects of negotiation with the Soviet Union which have been lumped together under the détente label. First, the consultations for mutual reductions in and control of armament, and for arrangements on "crisis management." Even if the two blocs remain in principle in a state of complete hostility, it is still sensible to seek arms reduction, both for economic reasons and to lessen the purely military danger. While it may be argued that these considerations will prove inadequate in the long run without some measure of goodwill, at least it cannot be denied that some progress might be made. The Soviets maintain, of course, that such progress cannot be made unless we accept their intransigence on human rights and other matters; and they have had some success among shortsighted Westerners. But in fact, it is plain enough that, regardless of other issues, they will not come to any agreement on armaments unless they conceive it in their interests to do so—in which case they will.

Such agreements could somewhat reduce immediate risks, but they could not destroy long-term dangers, a solution to which must be sought by other means. Moreover, the disarmament problem itself is affected directly and in detail, as well as in basic principle, by the Soviet stand on state control of the movement of people and ideas. For the refusal of adequate *in situ* inspection is a product of their hostile siege mentality. Moreover, arms control becomes in principle more difficult if there is a well founded general distrust of the bona fides of one of the negotiators. At the same time, crisis management becomes more refractory if crises are continually provoked on the principle that, in Brezhnev's words, détente does not apply to "class and liberation struggles in the capitalist countries and the colonies."

It is sometimes urged that the denied goodwill and mutual tolerance, the "mellowing" of the Soviet system, are in fact gradually being achieved as by-products of piecemeal trade, cultural, diplomatic, and other bonds—somewhat as the Lilliputians sought to bind Gulliver with a thousand weak threads, each strengthening the last. In this way, it is hoped, direct confrontation on the human rights issue can be avoided, since *apparatchik* resistance will eventually be outflanked in a painless manner.

Cultural exchange, it is true, clearly has some minimal effect in eroding the rigor of monopolistic party conviction in a limited circle of Soviet citizens; and it even implies, in fact, a very small contribution to greater movement of people. The Kremlin has indeed made this small payment under fairly careful conditions, and partly motivated by the necessities of scientific progress. Still, the controls are definite, and even if it does produce a certain increase in alienation on the part of some intellectuals, that alienation is already present in the USSR—the whole *raison d'être* of the dictatorship is the containment and suppression of the alienated. The state and party machine built by Stalin and his successors is a mechanism for that purpose. And the central question is precisely to ensure that that state and party, rather than suspect subjects, develop a tolerance of the outside world. Naturally, in the long run, one must rely in part on social and intellectual pressures within the USSR to secure the evolution or elimination of the regime. But as dissidents so often tell us, these pressures are impotent without active Western encouragement and support, in the sense of firm pressure on our part too.

Many people believe that the import of technology itself implies the import of ideas. No doubt, again, a certain penumbra of unorthodox thought may penetrate with the technological trading. But, again, it seems untenable that this peripheral seepage has any tangible effect on— or that it presents any but the slightest and most readily containable threat to—the ruling apparat.

There is nothing new in this. Russia's rulers have always aimed to import Western technology for the purpose of strengthening the old system —especially in the military field. Such was the principle and practice of Peter the Great, Catherine the Great, and Stalin the (in his own way) equally Great. On each occasion the influx of Western technique, though inseparable from a minor drift of ideas, was accompanied by an intensification of serfdom and a general tightening of despotism.

Moreover, when it comes to trade, and indeed other aspects of negotiation—if we omit in this context the military aspects of détente— it is clear that on the face of it the Soviets have virtually nothing we want. While the Kremlin is fully conscious of its need for Western computers and, on occasion, for Western wheat, it has very little, economically speaking, to give in exchange.

The same argument applies to the questions of legitimation of the Eastern European status quo, and other problems discussed at Helsinki.

And while it is true we would wish for some measure of liberty in Eastern Europe, it is clear that our statesmen will not press for it with the same militancy the USSR uses to extend its own system. Détenters tell us we should not cause trouble in the area. But, again, the liberties of Eastern Europe are primarily part of the human rights issue, which remains our only substantial demand and bargaining counter in negotiation.

THE NEED FOR "PSYCHOLOGICAL DISARMAMENT"

Thirty years ago, in an article published in the *New York Times* magazine (10 March 1946) and in the London left wing *Tribune*, Arthur Koestler argued that world peace must remain precarious without "psychological disarmament." He had no objection to

criticism directed by one country against another. This democratic right is as vital on the international as on the national scale. . . . But it becomes poisonous if the country attacked is deprived of the right of defense—as the Western countries are at present. . . . A country which builds a Maginot line of censorship from which it fires its propaganda salvoes is committing psychological aggression. Since the end of the War the USSR has raised certain claims. . . . The Western Powers, who have no territorial counterclaims to make, should table instead a demand for psychological disarmament, including: free access of foreign newspapers . . . to the USSR; such modifications of the Russian censorship . . . as to permit the free circulation of information about the outside world throughout Soviet territory; . . . the abolishing of restrictions on travel for foreigners in Soviet territory, and Soviet citizens abroad. . . . No one in his senses will expect the Soviet leaders to agree to this easily. Hence the suggestion that psychological disarmament should be made a bargaining object in all future negotiations, and given high priority on the political agenda. The demand for the free circulation of ideas across frontiers, for restoring the arrested bloodstream of the world, should be raised at every meeting of . . . the Security Council, the Committees and Assembly of the United Nations; it should be made the precondition of concessions in the geographical, economic and scientific field. To get it accepted, the use of all levers of pressure, political and economic, would for once be morally justified.

The crises of the 1940s were solved by military strength and a staunch political will, now alas lacking. But since the root of the problem was not after all dealt with, it has continued over the decades to bear the bitter fruits of psychological aggression. The danger of war has remained in being.

HELSINKI AND THE BETRAYAL OF HUMAN RIGHTS

At Helsinki some effort was made to come to grips with the essential. But the Soviet Union has in effect welshed on this one part of the Helsinki accord—the issue of human rights—from which the West and the world really stood to gain. No serious attempt has been made to secure Soviet compliance. The few token gestures they made on the issue—usually concerning individuals only—have been tacitly accepted. Which is to say that the Western détentists have effectively welshed on Helsinki too.

Soviet inaction has been justified by the theory that the rights granted at Helsinki should be implemented only to the degree that they do not contradict "national sovereignty," which in this case signifies the Soviet right to treat their subjects as they wish, regardless of their international undertakings. Of course, the visits of Suslov and Ponomarev to the congresses of Western Communist parties devoted to the Sovietization of Western society do not, on this view, constitute interference in the affairs of other states. Nor does the often virulent output of Radio Moscow on international channels—unlike the generally factual or serious output of the Western international broadcasts. But, to take an even closer parallel, the appeal to national sovereignty is incompatible with, for example, United Nations and Soviet-supported campaigns against apartheid in sovereign South Africa, which is precisely a violation of human rights in the same sense as the Soviet violations they now declare sacrosanct.

In any case, on this reading, in merely obtaining Soviet signatures to international documents on human rights the West has obtained nothing. The problem remains that of enforcement. Indeed, a default on a signed guarantee—on the grounds that treaties only apply when the USSR finds it convenient—may seem to prove the total unreliability of the Soviet signature to any document whatever. (It is certainly true that Soviet guarantees of the independence of the Baltic States and—in the peace treaties and at Potsdam—of the freedom of operation of all antifascist parties in the Balkan countries and East Germany meant and mean nothing.) Yet our negotiators probably did not insist on the provisos of Basket Three being made watertight because they thought the USSR would not then sign; and they had some vague hope that the evadable phraseology might nevertheless produce some miniscule result in exchange for the substantial Western concessions on other issues. Now that we know this sort of bargain to be pretty well worthless, perhaps future negotiators will insist on some element of genuine substance—or alternatively, refuse the Russians a *quid pro nihil* and abandon the appeasement.

For here, as ever, one is driven to the position that the Soviets will do nothing unless they are refused the benefits they seek under other items of the various agreements they have obtained. The advantage of the Jackson amendment is that it insisted, with safeguards against non-fulfillment, on the human rights *quid pro quo*. It did not grant benefits without a mechanism for checking on Soviet performance of their own side of the bargain. In these cases, if the Russians comply, well and good. If not, we have avoided giving something for nothing, and the inducement to—or pressure for—more civilized and peaceable conduct remains. Russia never had a tradition that trade or negotiation can lead to mutual benefit: the first true merchant bank in the country was only founded in the 1860s. The Communist contribution to this outlook was Lenin's basic principle *"Kto kove?"* ("Who—whom?"): the idea that every act is part of a struggle in which one side loses and the other wins. The Soviets will not make any concession unless it is made absolutely clear that they can gain no benefit by defaulting.

We should note, moreover, that the attempts to secure an improvement in the Soviet attitude have not been—as one might gather from some critics—anything like an all-or-none, bullheaded demand for instant total compliance. On the contrary, it was mere minima which were at issue. Just as Koestler speaks not of the abolition of censorship but only its relaxation, so the Helsinki Agreement is in terms of "gradually to simplify and to administer flexibly the procedures for exit and entry," "to ease regulations," "gradually to lower," "gradually to increase," and so on; and Senator Jackson did not demand immediate full freedom of emigration, merely an improvement to the extent of allowing a "benchmark" of some 60,000 exit visas.

The Russians did not, in the end, accept the terms of the Jackson amendment. They did accept those of Helsinki, including, for example, "To facilitate the improvement of the dissemination, on their territory, of newspapers and printed publications, periodical and non-periodical, from the other participating States." Nothing of the sort has taken place. On the contrary, the Western failure to press the issue has gone with—no doubt partly been the cause of—a notable increase in repression over the past year. If one believes that present Western tactics may begin to have some effect, as promised, one must surely ask for at least the beginnings of fulfillment of Basket Three. It was recognized that change is hard, and liable to be fairly slow at first, especially in rigid cultures; but this is not to say that we must accept gestures barely visible to the naked eye, without any sort of genuine and substantial improvement. A Western statesman who puts these human rights clauses into a treaty and then makes no attempt to see to their fulfillment seems, on the face of it, to be collaborating with the Soviet Union in deception—and so to be deceiving his own constituents. This is particularly the case if he adduces Soviet willingness to accept such clauses as an authentic sign of change in the Kremlin. Indeed, such inculcations of delusion can only confuse and weaken the Western will to resist.

THE IMPORTANCE OF HUMAN RIGHTS

To secure no change on human rights must be disastrous in the longer run. It is true, as we have said, that the differences between political cultures are as persistent as they are profound; that they have enormous intrinsic momenta and cannot be rapidly turned in new directions. But they can be turned. There have been despotisms in transition to civicisms, as in prerevolutionary Russia. Even apart from the possibility of a catastrophic breakdown—by no means impossible—slow and firm pressures and inducements from our side might eventually lead first to the abandonment in practice of the Soviet struggle *à l'outrance* with the West, and later to its virtual abandonment even in principle. But our situation is dangerous, and a slow erosion through trade and cultural contacts while giving up all attempt at serious political leverage, could not conceivably have any adequate effect in the period of international danger which looms immediately ahead.

Ideologies do evolve. They evolve under pressure. When the disadvantages of pursuing aggressive policies are clear, and the advantages to be gained by concession are present as a continual bait, then and only then is there any reasonable prospect of slow but substantial change. Lack of firmness is a certain guarantee that the Kremlin, having no inducement to change, will retain its present condition of hostility in both principle and practice. Those who call themselves "realists" and argue that the rulers cannot be expected to make concessions and so should not be pressed to do so, surrender in advance and thereby encourage aggressiveness, while failing to erode in any way its continuation through the foreseeable future. One is tempted to say of them, as Orwell said of appeasement-minded intellectuals in another context, that one doesn't know which to despise more, their cynicism or their shortsightedness.

What one asks of the Kremlin, after all, is no more than we practice, or are willing to practice, ourselves. So long as they maintain a siege mentality, in a state of declared and active hostility to all other ideas, the fuse of war remains primed. A siege mentality is, moreover, no more than the obverse of a sortie mentality.

We can exert pressures by effective military and political blocking of aggression while maintaining the constant offer of true peace. Above all, we may chart any progress of the Soviet rulers away from their total hostility by their attitude toward human rights. For the USSR will indicate its cooperative membership in the world community when its rulers cease their intransigeant intolerance of all that the West stands for. Their progress can be most easily checked in the one area where they are free to tolerate or suppress our ideas as they feel fit—the USSR itself. For the present the answer is clear. "Détente" has been accompanied by repression.

The West's only sane attitude remains one of military strength and diplomatic unity and forcefulness adequate to deter and rebuff expansionism—of which every successful example serves only to encourage more. We must refuse simply to strengthen the Soviet economic (and therefore military) machine without any return; and we must maintain a constant vigilance—combined with a continual offer of real détente as soon as the Russians prove their bona fides by implementing Basket Three. Meanwhile, a stable truce based on mutual distrust is preferable to delusions of friendship accompanied by and encouraging political and military initiatives by the Kremlin, which increase the dangers of both war and totalitarian victory.

The human rights issue remains the key test of their animus against *us*, a test of the basic motivations of their foreign policy.

12

LEONARD SCHAPIRO

The Effects of Détente
on the Quality of Life
in the Soviet Union

In addition to other objectives, Western policymakers have hoped that "détente" would reduce political tensions and encourage Soviet leaders to run a more liberal and humane society. They hoped, in short, that the policy would help improve the quality of life for Soviet citizens. This chapter will consider some of the results which this phase in Western-Soviet relations may have had on internal conditions in the USSR.

DÉTENTE AND MILITARY EXPENDITURES

Reduced military expenditures could have an enormous effect on the standard of living of the Russian people, for in the past the Soviet consumer's needs have continually been sacrificed to the demands of heavy industry (which includes armaments). However, at the May 1972 Moscow summit meeting, it was unclear whether the Soviet leaders expected that détente would lead to a reduced military budget. The one clear benefit that emerged from the meeting was the agreement to limit development of the enormously expensive antiballistic missile (ABM) defense installations. Although the Soviet Union may, arguably, have benefited more than the U.S., the saving to both sides was very great.[1]

The more general agreements on ceilings for certain types of nuclear weapons, on the other hand, can scarcely have had any effect on Soviet military spending, since both sides have concentrated since 1972 on developing technically more sophisticated weapons which, if anything, must be more costly than the weapons covered by the ceilings.

This fact is born out by recent Soviet military budgets which, according to the latest estimate of the British Ministry of Defense, have grown for some years at a rate of 4 percent a year.[2] According to the ministry's study, in 1975 the Soviet Union spent 50 billion rubles on arms of all kinds—or nearly three times the figure specified in the Soviet budget. The discrepancy results from the Soviet practice of camouflaging military spending in their budgets under a whole variety of ostensibly civilian headings. The study now estimates that the USSR spends between 11 and 12 percent of its gross national product on the military—in contrast to a 6.7 percent figure for the U.S. last year. This recent British estimate is far higher than the previous one of 7 percent, and, since these official estimates have repeatedly proved to be too low, it is probably still an underestimate.

At the recently held 25th Congress of the Communist Party of the Soviet Union (CPSU) General Secretary Brezhnev ridiculed the suggestion that the Soviet Union presents any kind of military threat. He did not, however, explain either the rapid growth of Soviet military expenditure, or the predominant superiority in conventional weapons which the Warsaw Pact has built up opposite the NATO powers in the past few years.[3]

We are not concerned here with the problem of the growing Soviet military might vis-à-vis the United States,[4] but with how Soviet military policy affects the material quality of life of Soviet citizens. Clearly détente has had no effect upon conventional arms spending, which has been steadily increasing; and, according to Albert Wohlstetter's discussion in chapter 8, it has not likely influenced expenditures on nuclear weapons—except possibly for the ABM agreement already referred to.

Nor has official Soviet military thinking changed on nuclear weapons. Soviet military analysts at the highest level do not assume the impossibility of nuclear warfare;[5] and for some time, quite unaffected by détente, the USSR has devoted considerable energy and resources to a civil defense program to defend against a nuclear attack. The rationale for this effort is that imperialism remains aggresive and that a nuclear attack therefore remains possible.

Soviet authorities argue that the growing forces of socialism will help stop the imperialists from unleashing war, and Mr. Brezhnev recently encouraged them to do so. However, the task of stopping the imperialists is not limited to socialists. To forestall a nuclear strike many Soviet military analyses stress the need for surprise, for a preemptive strike.[6] This explains why Soviet military writers accept the possibility of nuclear war and concentrate on the question of how to win one. It also explains the Soviet authorities' efforts to prepare their population psychologically and physically for defense in a potential war.[7] There is little in this to suggest any serious intention to limit its nuclear arms program.

DÉTENTE AND CONSUMER EXPENDITURES

The reasons for Soviet economic backwardness are numerous; but this is not the place to discuss them.[8] Whatever the general behavior of their economy, the Soviet consumer is very much affected by the steady growth of the military budget, which takes priority over civilian expenditure.

Soviet statistics of the dynamics of Soviet economic growth for the period 1971–1975 reveal that the planned figure of 46 percent growth of Group "A" projects (i.e., heavy industry, including defense) was fulfilled. In contrast, the consumer Group B planned figure of 49 percent —which caused incredulity at the time because of the traditional preference that Soviet plans had hitherto allocated to Group "A"—was only fulfilled to the extent of 35 percent. Nor does the growth planned for 1976–1980 offer much consolation to the consumer: 38–42 percent for Group "A"; 30–32 percent for Group "B"—which is even lower than the actual achievement of 1971–1975. According to statements made by the Soviet Minister of Finance, in 1974 more than 16 billion rubles were allocated for consumer goods and services and in 1975 the allocation was 2.4 billion rubles less. In contrast, the allocation to heavy industry (which includes defense industry) was 11.6 billion rubles more in 1975 than in 1974.[9]

SOVIET MOTIVES FOR DÉTENTE

Two factors in Soviet economic and political development in past years are very relevant in considering Soviet motives for détente: the growing recognition of the claims of the consumer and the collapse of the 1965 economic reform. Both are political in nature.

After Stalin's death it became clear that the Soviet leaders were no longer prepared to submit the Soviet consumer to privations the stern dictator had imposed without hesitation. Khrushchev's period or rule— and notably his decision in 1963 to purchase grain from the West to meet shortfalls in Soviet production—provided ample evidence of this new attitude toward the consumer. His successors have continued the policy.

There are a number of reasons for the change. One is certainly the decline in terror that the government—meaning the collective party leadership—is prepared to exercise. Another is undoubtedly the in-security and uncertainty the leadership felt about its own hold over the country—which was reinforced by well-authenticated but unpublicized incidents of quite serious riots caused by food prices and shortages. And perhaps one should not exclude some genuine concern for material wel-fare—particularly in the changed climate since Stalin's death and, even more significantly, because of the Soviet leaders' understanding that the Soviet system is judged by others on its ability to provide a reasonable standard of living for the Soviet population.

The economic reform of 1965 was designed to create incentives for the managers of individual manufacturing enterprises to produce goods for consumer demand and satisfaction. This was done by liberating the managers to some degree from the highly centralized control of the state plan. Production of goods was to become related to what people actually wanted to buy and not, as hitherto, solely to fulfill the plan.

But the reform soon ran into difficulties. The main opposition to it came from the Communist party, which feared that decentralization of economic control might lead to decentralization of political control—and thus imperil the traditional grip of the party on the life of the country. The events of 1968 in Czechoslovakia provided a warning that the de-mand for economic reform—which is how the Czech "spring" had begun —was only a step removed from the demand for political reform. There may also have been opposition to the 1965 reform from some managers of enterprises who had become accustomed to working under the old cen-tralized system with a minimum of risk to their own positions, and who were reluctant to countenance change.

In any event, it was quite clear by the 24th Congress of the CPSU in 1971 that the 1965 reform was as dead as the dodo. It was around this time that U.S. moves toward détente opened up better prospects to the Soviet leaders for improving the unsatisfactory state of the country's economy without running the risk of losing party control that the 1965 re-form seemed to them to involve.

DÉTENTE AND WESTERN ECONOMIC AID

There was nothing new in the Soviets seeking economic aid from the non-Communist West in order to build up their ultimate ability to overpower the West. Lenin had written of this policy in 1921:

Speaking the truth is a petty, bourgeois prejudice. A lie, on the other hand, is often justified by the ends. The capitalists of the whole world will shut their eyes to the kind of [subversive] activities on our side I have referred to and . . . will open up credits for us which will serve us for the purpose of supporting communist parties in their countries. They will supply us with the materials and the technology which we lack and will restore our military industry which we need for our future victorious attacks upon our suppliers.[10]

Thus it is not hard to imagine the alacrity with which the Soviet leaders welcomed U.S. détente proposals which opened the prospects of obtaining from the U.S. both the credits and the technological assistance which they hoped would invigorate their economy. (It is significant that before 1971, apparently regarding the expansion of economic relations with the U.S.A. as hopeless, they had concentrated heavily in their propaganda on the supposed advantages to the European Economic Community of economic partnership with the Soviet Union in preference to partnership with the U.S.A.) When discussions took place in May 1972 the Soviet aim of closer economic relations with the U.S.A. met with a ready response.

As Gregory Grossman shows in Chapter 5, Soviet import of technology is not new. Moreover, structural weaknesses in its economy, combined with the imitative rather than inventive nature of Soviet industry, make it likely that Soviet reliance on Western technology will continue to increase rather than diminish.

At the same time, it is a mistake to conclude that the import of technology will go entirely to civilian purposes and is irrelevant to the development of military strength. Imported technology enables Soviet managers to transfer scarce technical skills and resources to military industry. Moreover, as recent émigrés from the USSR have shown, a great deal of Soviet military equipment is manufactured in civilian factories, though it is subject to a much higher standard of inspection. The famous Likhachev plant, for example, produces far more for military than for civilian purposes.

As Professor Grossman notes, Soviet hopes of substantial economic benefit from détente have been disappointed. It is clear that the Soviet Union placed great hopes on U.S. participation in long-term projects for the exploitation of natural gas; and the joint communiqués issued at the conclusion of the June 1973 Nixon-Brezhnev summit meeting in Washington may well have encouraged these hopes. But the project came to nothing by the end of 1974 owing to objections in Congress—very wisely, in this writer's opinion—to a transaction which could have put the United States at the future mercy of the Soviet government for energy supplies. The other major disappointment came around the same time with the refusal of Congress to underwrite further large credits to the USSR. The greatest benefit which the Soviet Union derived from détente was undoubtedly the grain deals with the U.S.A. and Canada which rescued the country from a threat of severe food shortage caused by a combination of harvest failure and breakdown of the state procurement system.

In the final analysis, "the bill for the mismanagement of Soviet agriculture was in effect paid by the American taxpayer to the tune of some 300 million dollars, for the Russians were allowed to buy the wheat at a subsidized price of 1.60 dollars per bushel, whereas in 1973 the price went up to 4.30 dollars." Indeed, at a later stage the United States was "buying back through world market channels some of the wheat she had sold cheaply to Russia, at high prices." [11]

DÉTENTE AND THE IDEOLOGICAL STRUGGLE

If many Soviet citizens hoped—even if they dared not say so—that détente was intended to lead to a reduction in military expenditure and international tension, and hence to improved living conditions, the hopes were soon dashed. Events in the Middle East, in Portugal, and in Southern Africa have shown that whatever détente may have meant on the Soviet side, it did not mean a change in its world posture. Brezhnev made this very clear within a week of the May 1972 summit when he said at a dinner in honor of Castro: "While pressing for . . . the principle of peaceful co-existence, we realize that successes in this important matter in no way signify the possibility of weakening the ideological struggle. On the contrary, we should be prepared for an intensification of this struggle." [12] Official Soviet statements have repeatedly elaborated this theme since that date. Brezhnev restated it at the recent 25th Congress of the CPSU, adding that the Soviet Union "sees in 'détente' a way towards the creation of more favorable conditions for the peaceful construction of socialism and communism." [13] This view was not in itself new. As far back as May

1973, for example, the East German leader Honecker had described Communist détente policy as trying to create "the most favorable external conditions for the building of socialism and communism."

Insofar as détente may have deluded Western countries into believing that the Soviet threat has diminished, opportunities increase for Soviet subversive activities. It was no doubt with this in mind that the Soviet Union has since 1972 substantially increased the number of its intelligence officers, at least in Eastern Europe—from 118 to 150 in France and from 50 to 75 in Austria, for example.[14]

Both the Soviet Union (in its propaganda) and the United States (if for different reasons) presented détente as an epoch-making change in foreign policy. However, there is some circumstantial evidence that the policy aroused apprehensions in Soviet circles. The military leaders seem to have feared that détente might have the effect of reducing their budget allocation. If so, their budgets in the past few years must have allayed their suspicions. At the 25th Congress Brezhnev also referred to "left-wing chatter" about the danger that peaceful coexistence would help capitalism or would freeze the existing territorial status quo; but Brezhnev quite rightly pointed to recent revolutionary developments in Communist favor as evidence rebutting the criticism. He also laid renewed emphasis on the continuing Soviet intention to give aid, as in Angola, to "wars of liberation"—a policy which he apparently considers consistent with détente.[15]

There may also have been some apprehension in party circles that détente could lead to a slackening of internal vigilance or to tolerance of foreign "capitalist" interference in Soviet affairs. The privileged party bosses always oppose this kind of relaxation for fear that their privileges in the midst of want—all recently depicted so graphically by Hedrick Smith in *The Russians*[16]—might be endangered by the comparative equality, openness, and legality associated with Western democracy. Soviet policy toward dissenters and, more recently, toward the Helsinki Conference results (and Helsinki was after all a direct product of détente) must by now have dispelled any fears they may have felt on this score.

DÉTENTE AND THE DISSIDENT MOVEMENT

Since its emergence Soviet authorities would have preferred to deal with the dissent movement by all-out repression, but they have felt constrained to pursue a dual policy—tolerating it on the one hand while using the resources of the KGB to persuade, cajole, and intimidate; indulging on the other in periodic bouts of repression—including staged trials with savage penalities, arrests, and confinements to psychiatric institutions. The repression has been limited in part by adverse publicity about repressive measures to the outside world (including foreign governments and foreign Communist parties) and in part by some fears that extreme repressive measures might be difficult to put through under collective leadership of a kind.

Increased Repression

Soviet authorities seem to have used the anticipation of détente as an occasion to test particularly the U.S. reaction to an intensified attempt to suppress dissent. The motive can be found in the kind of internal fears that détente provokes among the leading elite. It was to reassure such critics that Brezhnev at the 25th Congress of the CPSU was careful to emphasize that the maintenance of public order was an essential part of Soviet democracy: "For us that is democratic which serves the interests of the construction of communism." [17]

Despite attempts to disguise their intent, in late 1971 Soviet authorities made a decision to suppress dissent and *samizdat*, in particular to put an end to the "Chronicle of Current Events" which the dissent movement published abroad as a record of KGB repression and of the dissenters' activities. Many dissenters believe that this decision was encouraged by assurances that the U.S. government would not protest or make an issue of it. There is no way of knowing whether such an assurance was in fact given; but the fact remains the U.S. government has made no public protest on this issue, and Secretary Kissinger has frequently asserted that suppression of dissent is an internal Soviet affair which the U.S. may deplore but cannot make the subject of intervention.[18]

The campaign to suppress the "Chronicle" and its counterpart in the Ukraine was initially successful, especially after the KGB had forced two well-known dissenters, Yakir and Krasin, into collaboration. (Krasin, who is now in Canada, has told of the grim methods by which this collaboration was achieved.) Although the suppression was initially successful, others took the place of those imprisoned or exiled, *samizdat* protest continued—and continues to this day—and the "Chronicle" eventually resumed publication in New York with materials supplied by the dissenters in the USSR.[19]

The most instructive feature about this campaign was not its success but the highlight of its failure in the autumn of 1973. Beginning in September the KGB launched a campaign—obviously a prelude to arrest and trial—against the world-famous dissenters, Sakharov and Solzhenitsyn. This evoked a storm of worldwide protest in the West—and although the U.S. government remained silent, the National Academy of Sciences sent a strongly worded protest to the president of the Soviet Academy of Sciences.[20] The Soviet campaign was abandoned. It was revived later in the year against Solzhenitsyn when the first volume of *Gulag Archipelago* was published; in February 1974 he was forcibly deported, but some of his supporters inside the USSR continued to be persecuted. Since then, if less dramatically, many of the most prominent Soviet dissenters have been "permitted" to emigrate, often by threats.

Response to Pressure

The moral of the 1973 incident with Sakharov is clear. For the Soviet authorities the treatment of dissent is a commodity, to be traded like any other. When an attempt to silence Sakharov—which must be the KGB's dearest wish—threatened to cause a breakdown in U.S.-Soviet scientific collaboration which would have included the loss of the technological information exchanges, the KGB was forced to retreat.

All experience suggests that the Soviets regard détente not as an opportunity for more relaxed and peaceful relations with the West, but as a policy which can yield concrete advantages to the USSR—technology, trade, credits. This is borne out, for example, by Soviet policy toward Jewish emigration. Stimulated by the Six-Day War, the Jewish protest movement attracted Jewish support in the West, especially the U.S., and Soviet authorities were faced with a dilemma: to repress ruthlessly and risk antagonizing the U.S. Jewish lobby (whose influence is probably much exaggerated in Soviet thinking), or to lose face and antagonize the Arabs by permitting emigration. They chose the latter course, though mitigating it in their own minds by staged trials of Jews, savage sentences, persecution and obstruction of would-be emigrants, and an intensified anti-Semitic campaign thinly disguised as anti-Zionism.

To date 112,000 Soviet Jews have been allowed to emigrate, though the numbers have steadily fallen off since 1973; but this decline may be due in part to difficulties of absorption in Israel, reports of which deter would-be emigrants. The assertion sometimes made that emigration of Jews was reduced because of Soviet resentment at the exchange of letters between Secretary Kissinger and Senator Jackson which led to the dropping of the Jackson amendment is totally fallacious. The Soviet Union went back on the arrangement and repudiated the trade agreement with the U.S. only *after* the Congress some months later had shown its unwillingness to extend extensive credits to the USSR.

Treatment of Dissidents

Other instances are recorded where a Soviet emigration decision can be clearly linked to a cold-blooded calculation of national advantage. Such was the case of the dancer Panov, when Soviet authorities responded to an intervention by the British prime minister in the hope that this would help to increase their share of British trade. Similarly, the recent decision to release Leonid Plyushch from a psychiatric institution and permit him to emigrate resulted from an international campaign of unusual intensity which the French Communist party, mindful of its image with French electors, supported. Yet the release of Plyushch was particularly damaging to the Soviet authorities. Only a short time before, evidence purporting to prove his insanity and the humane and correct nature of his medical treatment was adduced in a Soviet court at the trial of one of the most active participants in the Russian human rights movement, the biologist S. A. Kovalev. As is usual in cases against dissidents, Kovalev was accused of anti-Soviet activity and was sentenced to seven years of labor camp and a three-year exile. Part of his "anti-Soviet activity" had been to assert that some dissenters were being kept in psychiatric institutions and subjected to inhuman treatment. When Plyushch arrived in the West it was evident for all to see, first, the appalling effects on him of the treatment to which he had been subjected, and after he had recuperated, that the allegation of insanity was completely fraudulent.[21]

In December 1975 Kovalev became the first member of the Amnesty International Adoption Group (which was formed inside the USSR by dissidents) to be sentenced. A few months later, on 15 April 1976, the secretary of the group, Andrei Tverdokhlebov, was sentenced to five years of internal exile for "dissemination of fabrications known to be false which defame the Soviet state and social system." Vigorous protests in the West followed his arrest and arraignment for trial, and they may have been responsible for his comparatively mild sentence. But neither Amnesty International nor foreign journalists were allowed to attend Tverdokhlebov's trial.

Around the same time, in another political trial aimed at silencing dissent, a thirty-two-year-old Crimean Tatar named Mustafa Dzhemilev was sentenced in Omsk to two-and-a-half years of strict regime imprisonment on a charge of circulating—while imprisoned in a labor colony on an earlier charge—information allegedly slandering official Soviet policy toward the Crimean Tatars, who for years have been denied the right to return to the homelands from which they were ejected on admittedly false charges during World War II.

The failure of these intensified efforts to suppress dissent, which were stimulated by détente, is shown by the recent (May 1976) formation in the USSR of a human rights committee to monitor Soviet implementation of the Final Act signed at Helsinki.

So much is now known in the West of Soviet repression of political and religious dissidents that one may wonder whether the Soviet leaders have given up hope of maintaining the pretense—dating since the time of Lenin—that human rights are better protected in Soviet Russia than in any other country. They may have decided that they must rely on the fact that Western governments, and especially the U.S., will not permit dislike of Soviet internal repression to interfere with détente—or with the advantages the USSR hopes to gain from détente (such as a new grain deal).

The explosive exposures in Solzhenitsyn's *Gulag Archipelago* require no comment. For some years Keston College in England has accurately documented the persecution of believers in its publication "Religion in Communist Lands." Most recently Amnesty International has assembled evidence on political prisoners, based entirely on Soviet sources and on accounts supplied by the victims of persecution—which, the Amnesty report says, exhibit such a "high degree of mutual corroboration" that "to ascribe this corroboration of fact to coincidence would be naive." The report gives a harrowing picture of the hardships and indignities to which Soviet prisoners of conscience are subjected, in violation even of the harsh provisions of Soviet law. It also deals with the even more reprehensible practice of placing sane dissidents in psychiatric institutions and there subjecting them, in the guise of treatment, to what amounts to a form of torture by drugs and other means—a practice that is beyond question a blot on the conscience of the Soviet medical profession. Amnesty estimates the total number of political and religious prisoners today as "at least 10,000." [22] Amnesty also estimates that since 1969 there have been about a hundred fifty cases of sane people certified and detained as insane for their political views, many of them since released. The list of such cases "adopted" by Amnesty contains twenty-five names, but the total of sane dissidents detained as allegedly insane may well be higher.[23]

In May 1976 a group was formed inside the USSR, headed by Dr. Yurii Orlov, to monitor the observance by the Soviet authorities of the

human rights provisions of the Helsinki Final Act. Nothing in the activity
of the group contravenes Soviet law; but Soviet authorities are little
concerned about legality, and the KGB have subjected Dr. Orlov and
other group members to considerable harassment. Soviet censorship naturally precludes publication in the USSR of the investigation results. But
several of its reports, fully documented and authenticated, have been
published by *samizdat* and have found their way abroad. They show that
in such matters as postal and telephonic communication between Soviet
citizens and persons abroad and the reunion of divided families—which
are specifically referred to in the Final Act—Soviet authorities have done
nothing to implement their government's undertaking at Helsinki.

The official Soviet reaction to the human rights provisions of the
Helsinki Final Act further reveals the leaders' confidence that the U.S.
interpretation of détente increases their freedom to pursue a policy of repression at home. Soviet leaders may be worried about the evidence provided by *samizdat* that dissidents now frequently cite the Final Act to
support their defense of human rights. The Soviet government has reacted by hedging this evidence with qualifications imported from Soviet
arguments at the conference which were rejected and not incorporated
into the Final Act. Thus, for example, the Director of the Soviet-U.S.A.
Institute recently argued that the West is trying to use Helsinki as a
wedge to interfere in Soviet internal affairs, that the Soviet Union has no
intention of flinging open its doors to anti-Soviet propaganda, that it is far
ahead of other countries in implementing the Final Act, and that after
Vietnam and Watergate the U.S.A. has no "moral right" to talk about
"eternal values of freedom and democracy." [24]

HUMAN RIGHTS: ONLY AN INTERNAL ISSUE?

Leaving aside the impertinent jibe about "moral right" (has *any* great
power ever subjected itself to merciless self-criticism as the U.S.A. has
done?), one must ask whether the U.S. and other Western governments
are justified in their failure in what many people regard as their moral
duty to give all the support they can to the valiant efforts of Soviet individuals to stand up for human rights? It is said that the way in which a
state treats its population is an internal affair. The memory of the Second
World War is still fresh. Was Hitler's treatment of the Jews and other
minorities and opponents irrelevant to the decision of Great Britain and
the United States to resist Hitler with force?

Moreover, a strong case can be made for the proposition that the Declaration of Human Rights and other similar documents, including the Helsinki Final Act, have taken the whole question of human rights out of the sphere of domestic jurisdiction and into international law. The Final Act indeed specifically states that respect for human rights and fundamental freedoms "is an essential factor for the peace, justice and well-being necessary to ensure the development of friendly relations and cooperation among [the signatories] . . . as among all states."

Sakharov has stated the position in even more practical terms. Rapprochement with the Soviet Union without democratization, he said, would mean "capitulating in the face of real or exaggerated Soviet power." This would "enable the Soviet Union to bypass problems it cannot resolve on its own and to concentrate on accumulating further strength." [25]

And finally one may ask: has a single simple benefit accrued to the West, or a single risk been avoided, by the self-denying ordinance our governments have imposed upon themselves in refraining from defending the principles for which Western civilization stands?

CONCLUSION

A balance sheet of the effect of détente on the quality of Soviet life looks something like this:

1. The burden of military expenditure, which falls on the population, has not been reduced, and has indeed increased since 1972.
2. Some technological help has perhaps benefited the Soviet consumer, but at the price of bolstering Soviet military effort.
3. Large scale industrial development schemes based on extended credits have not materialized as the Soviet authorities had hoped.
4. At no cost in political concessions, the Soviet Union has been rescued from acute grain shortages.
5. Except in certain individual cases, violations of human rights and repression of dissidents have increased because of the Soviet interpretation of the Western—and particularly the U.S.—attitude to human rights as a purely internal Soviet matter.

Détente might have done much to improve the quality of life in the Soviet Union. In actual fact it has done little, if anything, to improve living conditions for ordinary Soviet citizens. Increasing military budgets have reduced opportunities to improve living standards while repression of dissidents has actually increased under the protective mantle of détente. During this period, basic rights and liberties have deteriorated; and, to that extent at least, the quality of life in the Soviet Union has deteriorated with them.

NOTES

1. The limitation may have benefited the Soviet Union since it would have found it a more crippling burden to finance an ABM system than would the much wealthier U.S.A.

2. *The Times* (London), 19 May 1976.

3. *Strategic Survey 1975* (London: International Institute for Strategic Studies [IISS]), p. 63. According to the most recent IISS statement, the Warsaw Pact has twice the number of tactical aircraft and three times the number of main battle tanks. For details, see Edward Luttwak's discussion of conventional forces in Europe, chapter 9 of this book.

4. For an analysis of the situation, see James R. Schlesinger, "Testing Time for America," *Fortune* 93, no. 2 (February 1976).

5. See Paul Nitze, chapter 7 of this book.

6. For one of the very few discussions of this uncomfortable subject, see Leon Goure, Foy D. Kohler, and Mose L. Hervey, *The Role of Nuclear Forces in Current Soviet Strategy* (Miami, Fla.: University of Miami Press, 1974), pp. 102–12.

7. *Soviet World Outlook* 1, no. 2 quoting *Communist of the Armed Forces* (November 1975).

8. For a more extensive consideration of Soviet economic problems, see Gregory Grossman's discussion in chapter 5 of this book.

9. *Pravda*, 13 December 1973; *Pravda*, 19 December 1974.

10. This unpublished but undoubtedly authentic memorandum by Lenin, dated 1920 or 1921, is reprinted in G. R. Urban, ed., *Detente* (London: Universe Books, 1976), pp. 337–38.

11. Ibid., pp. 15–16.

12. *Pravda*, 28 June 1972.

13. Ibid., 25 February 1976.

14. *Foreign Report*, 4 February 1976 (London: The Economist, 1976).

15. *Pravda*, 25 February 1976.

16. Hedrick Smith, *The Russians* (New York: Quadrangle, 1976).

17. *Pravda*, 25 February 1976.

18. Henry A. Kissinger, *New York Times*, 27 September 1973: "We have taken the position [on human problems in the USSR] that we would not as a government take a formal public position."

19. Peter Reddaway, "The Development of Dissent and Opposition," in *The Soviet Union Since the Fall of Khrushchev*, edited by Archie Brown and Michael Kaser (London: Free Press, 1975), pp. 133–35.

20. *New York Times*, 11 September 1973.

21. Tatyana Khodorovich, ed., *The Case of Leonid Plyushch* (London: Westview, 1976).

22. Amnesty International, *Prisoners of Conscience in the USSR: Their Treatment and Conditions* (London: Amnesty International, 1975).

23. Information supplied to the author by Amnesty International Adoption Group.

24. *Izvestia*, 3 September 1975, summarized in *New York Times*, 8 October 1975.

25. Andrei D. Sakharov, *Sakharov Speaks* (New York: Random House, 1974), p. 204.

IV

Epilogue

13

PAUL SEABURY

Beyond Détente

A political concept is a strange creature: when loosed into a world of action, its influence may grow even as its meaning becomes blurred, distorted, or (as Orwell taught us) reversed. Semantical hijacking in our time is a sophisticated art: powerful words may be seized and used as slogans for purposes their creators did not have in mind.

What do we do about this? Abandoning to others a concept whose meaning has been corrupted by them means losing ownership of it. The word *peace*, in our time, has been preempted by those who do not have its interests at heart; so our current word, *détente*, may suffer the same fate. The game now entails a struggle as to what meanings should attach to the word. To abandon *détente* as code word for a set of benign attitudes and policies risks the obloquy of being regarded as opposed to cordiality, improved relations, and friendly ways of living (coexisting!) with adversaries on the great spaceship earth.

Yet, while we should treat valuable concepts as servants, we easily can become their slaves. Since they rearrange our ways of looking at the world, they can easily become our masters, crippling our capacity to sense the nature of the conditions we face, and perhaps misrepresenting them.

Thus a dilemma: shall we retain, and so define, this word *détente* (and the policy which it implies) in ways congruent with our basic interests, or shall we discard it as hopelessly incompatible with them and seek other ways of arranging our thoughts and actions?

I

In its generic sense, of course, *détente* means relaxation; it implies a precedent state of tension. We have used it to describe a set of East-West relations and Soviet-American relations in particular. Since 1969, when the idea began to creep into our language of discourse, most of us have taken it to be a quite nice proposition. As condition or policy, it means *relax.*

Relaxation itself is an ambiguous guide to foreign policy. Let us clarify the possibilities of it: does it mean a relaxed *relationship?* Or a relaxed *posture?* Is it reciprocal or unilateral? Does it arise from calculation and reason, or from necessity? Does it spring from some clear, correct recognition that world conditions warrant it, or does it—as a pessimist might say—arise from some newfound awareness that America's world position has been so weakened by events that a prudent course should be to play low, while pretending to be in charge?

The Soviet view of the relationship, if we may take their views seriously rather than try not to notice, has been somewhat easier to understand than ours; a core aspect of it—which we share with them—has been to avoid major, direct, general war. This meant for them, as for us, a serious concern with the management of bilateral relations—what they call "state-to-state relations"—so as to avoid circumstances which might lead to open military conflict between our two nations. For their own reasons, which others in this volume have explored, the Soviets have also wished détente to encourage our economic assistance. For them, also, peaceful coexistence (an expression more consonant with their general strategy) is an occasion and a span of time in which conflict and competition are expressed in ways other than by direct frontal attack. Soviet hostility has diminished in rhetoric, in the sense that the crude, blatant manifestations of it have been toned down, and it has diminished in action as well: we must, after all, recognize that we are dealing with an expansionist superpower which exploits an ideology, Marxism-Leninism, to gain imperial ends. The force of this ideology can be instrumentally manipulated, and synchronized with other instruments of influence. But we must not forget that only the United States remains in the way of the Soviet quest for global hegemony.

Thus the Soviets' pursuit of a "correct" policy of peaceful coexistence for them but not for us has meant redoubled emphasis on the acquisition of new military power, the enlargement of armed forces, the spread of their naval deployments, enhanced doctrinal vigilance at home, and continued sponsorship of so-called national liberation movements and self-styled revolutionary states. The Angola adventure is only a recent manifestation of this careful expansionism by force of arms and diplomacy.

We may better understand the wellsprings of this expansionism if we discard or at least reexamine some of our own conventional assessments of the modern world. Some of us deem the contemporary world to be one in which competitive struggle is now obsolete and atavistic. Force, gunboat diplomacy, and the like recall the quaint and odd activities of nineteenth-century imperialism. The age of imperialism is over. But could it be that the Soviet leadership—and even perhaps large parts of the new managerial society of modern Russia—listen to a different drummer, obstinately unaffected by liberal ideas about interdependence, convergence, and all the forthcoming planetary bargains the future has in store? I am not a specialist in Soviet behavior, but nevertheless hazard the guess that the current Soviet outthrust as a truly global power is considerably more popular within the official class of Russia than we give it credit for. Perhaps we can better understand the Soviet state if we lay aside both Marxist and liberal categories and look at Prussian Germany in the late nineteenth century. A place in the sun is a nice aspiration for a people long locked up in an icebox. If the Soviet Union now is well on its way to becoming the world's preponderant military and naval power, it would at least be worth noting that this tendency is more apparent after seven years of détente than it was before that process commenced in the early Nixon years.

II

There is nothing peculiar in this, save the odd fact that to dwell upon these Soviet activities, and to take note of their implications, is to risk being called a Cold Warrior. We have so long been informed that the cold war is over that to insert a suspicion that it is not introduces the annoying note that there are some self-delusions abroad. And indeed there are. We have been led into these delusions by our recent chastisement of ourselves.

Time and space here do not permit a careful rehearsal of the reasons why the American position in world politics has declined in the past ten years, but candor requires us to observe some fundamental features of the situation. Let us for a moment revisit the late 1960s, the time of transition from Johnson to Nixon. When that shift of authority took place, the incoming administration confidently gave us to believe that an era of confrontation was ending and an era of negotiation was about to begin. This new era, the new president said, would be one in which the burden sharing between America and its allies would be readjusted; old commitments would remain, but more would be required of America's allies than before. The Guam doctrine was tailored originally for Vietnam, but its implications were soon to be duly accepted as global. The new administration, if one may look at its brighter side, sought to combine multipronged diplomatic initiatives with alliance readjustments so as to obtain a new structure of peace. As Nixon in 1972 observed, this structure of peace would depend upon the coordinated responsibilities and self-restraints of five centers of power in the world: America, Russia, China, Japan, and Western Europe. The most immediate aim of the Nixon administration was to hasten the achievement of peace in Vietnam. The agility with which these initiatives were pursued relentlessly and in so many venues is a tribute to the force, flexibility, and imagination of Henry Kissinger. Not the least of Nixon's achievements was the breakthrough to Peking and the enlivenment of a triangular relationship of Moscow-Washington-Peking which was to have far reaching practical benefits for the United States. Détente became the covering umbrella for all of these activities.

III

These prefatory remarks about the origins of détente, however, do not address the central question which faced the Nixon administration at the beginning: how could the basic requirements of America's secure position in the world be adjusted to a nation wracked and tormented by profound civic commotions? We now have such a short attention span, and the attention of our media has wandered so far from the problems of the 1960s, that most of us now prefer to regard those recent episodes in our history at best as an aberrational nightmare; a nightmare it was, the likes of which the nation had never previously experienced.

Why did there develop in the 1960s this extraordinary cleavage in our culture, of such a nature as to threaten the very civic basis of it? What was the nature of that beast, which Robert McNamara saw slouching toward Bethlehem? In all of the life-style revolution which Dylan and the

Lennons commenced, which Hoffman and Rubin augmented, and which the Weathermen and the SLA consummated, what was signified? The Watts riots, the drug craze, the not-so-innocent flower children, the campus rebellions and prison uprisings, the communal back-to-nature movements, the assassinations of the Kennedys and King, the political show demonstrations of Chicago in 1968, the Ellsberg caper, the hijackings and random bombings, the soaring crime rates, and all the multifarious liberation groups—if one added all of these together, what did they mean, other than some extraordinary time of trouble whose causes sprang from obscure sources, but which joined together into a flood tide, provoking harsh reactions from those who were surprised and horrified by them and eliciting from others a remarkable responsive eagerness to join in the fun? That the Vietnam war came to be the seemingly endless backdrop to these events, intensifying and fueling them, should not cause us to think that they were brought on by the war. It should be remembered, for instance, that the U.S. student rebellion broke out in Berkeley in 1964, at a time when scarcely a student, much less any other American, could have located Vietnam on a map. But Vietnam certainly was the agency of their perpetuation and their enlargement; so the antiwar movement became the cover under which these disparate elements came to be arranged, in a far-flung, broad coalition of the violent and the peaceful, the activists and the passivists, the militants and the flower children, the repressed and the liberated. By and large it had its roots in a strange generational upheaval of the youth of the upper middle classes.

These things do not come to pass independently of powerful and infectious ideas; but then, how do ideas become powerful and infectious? How, for instance, had the less widespread and threatening McCarthy anti-Red craze of the 1950s arisen? Some aspects of this wild 1960s episode do relate to quite traditional ideas. The leveling elements of it were caricatures of an old American fondness for equality; the anti-institutional elements had some traces of more traditional American skepticism about authority; Thoreau also had a part in it, insofar as his civil disobedience doctrines were twisted to justify gigantic street movements; the assertion of rights of all sorts of estranged clienteles was not wholly without traditional roots. But what was unusual in so much of this was that elements fusing swiftly together were focused upon a *new* generation of the American middle class out of which, one might have supposed, the new leadership of the nation would be expected to come. Despite obvious contradictions (how to reconcile Ho Chi Minh with Thoreau, or guns with flowers?), what was one to read into all of this? The major reorientations in value—the turning away from achievement, from traditional definitions of individualism toward new communal forms and styles, and away from technological infatuations—these in combination were nevertheless signs of an antisystemic rebellion which included a revolt against obligation and against a discipline which bespeaks a known acceptance of maturity. (One ironic event of that decade was that the Apollo space mission, conceived eight years before in a time of exhilaration and optimism and requiring exquisite combinations of discipline, controlled imagination, and daring, finally was consummated amidst the riotous confusions of 1969, when heroes were upstaged by antiheroes in the American media.)

Considering these aspects of America in the late 1960s, any sober observer would have been moved to ask: had too much been attempted and expected in the 1960s? Were the rhetorical flourishes of this period impossible in their assertion of what was possible? Were there during this time, in its early stages, some fundamentally flawed notions as to what had become possible in America?

In a very large sense, we must see that the most fatal combination of the 1960s—one which may have some qualities of a Greek tragedy—was the fact that the United States found itself engaged in a two-front war, against two foes which were seemingly intractible: the war on poverty and the Vietnam war. As Lyndon Johnson, in a moment of candor, reportedly said to a confidante,[1]

I knew from the start that I was bound to be crucified either way I moved. If I left the woman I really loved—the Great Society—in order to get involved with that bitch of a war on the other side of the world, then I would lose everything at home. . . . But if I left that war and let the Communists take over South Vietnam, then I would be seen as a coward and my nation as an appeaser.

But there was probably a lot more than that going. What Johnson, being an ordinary person, realized all too late was that there was also a third front for which nothing in his experience had prepared him; this was the intellectual front, where quite different ideas were being generated. Not the least of these were products of philosophers and social scientists who had come to think, for a variety of reasons, that America was on the brink of escaping from history. The original slogan for all of this was "post-industrial America"; this became bowdlerized into "the greening of America." The new condition of America was seen to be one in which traditional constraints of hardship, scarcity, labor, self-control, were matters of the past. The historical rat race was over. A folksong composer, Malvina Reynolds, wrapped the matter up in a ballad, "Ticky-Tacky," a sarcastic critique of bourgeois life cycles which consisted in working and saving money to buy little ticky-tacky houses, to have children who would go to college and then also go out and buy little ticky-tacky houses: a life cycle not thought to be notably commendable. What was *assumed* was that objective material conditions had so changed as to make escape from necessity possible. Were this so, then the remaining hardships could be blamed upon systemic flaws; the new America, whatever difficulties it might pose, offered the prospect of liberation from responsibilities and the luxurious pursuit of self-fulfillment. It was from the ranks of those who accepted these premises that the furies of the 1960s emerged. Self-gratification, scorned by those who saw things otherwise, rose in idealistic revolt when told that something, after all, was expected.

I detail these matters since the combination of them accounts perhaps almost wholly for the vast civic difficulties which afflicted America in the late 1960s. "Liberation" was the theme of the action which—arising out of such premises as these—spread throughout the institutions of America. We do not yet know how to measure adequately the spread and the intensity of these developments which weakened the traditional fabric of civic America. In their less admirable features we may see the diminution of constraints as closely related to the extraordinary increase in brutal crimes: what criminal would not be encouraged to know that whatever he did there were enough people around who would not hold him responsible for what he did? But in more respectable ways, the atmosphere of liberation made it possible for more and more new groups to coalesce —around whatever flawed aspect of human existence they could establish their identities—to ask that society recompense them for the oppressions which they had experienced.

IV

I spend so much time on this digression from foreign policy if only to suggest that our understanding of the *American* initiatives for détente were directly related to a not reprehensible object of cooling the nation down. The early Nixon foreign policies were less aimed at adapting America to new international circumstances than they were at reducing the level and compass of American overseas commitments to ones which domestic circumstances would tolerate. If the level and comprehensiveness of American overseas commitments could be diminished while the nation recovered from its self-inflicted wounds, the country and the world perhaps might be better off; and thus it was that the Nixon administration commenced its quest for the generation of peace. We ought to give it credit; there is no absolute way of knowing how causality works in the larger affairs of men, but we do know now that cities no longer burn; that riots stopped long ago; that the student rebellions are over; that hijackings on U.S. airliners are rare. The mention of law and order no longer suggests that the speaker is a closet Nazi; Thomas Hayden occasionally wears a necktie; and the American flag is rarely used to patch the bottoms of blue jeans. The country seems on keel again. The Nixon strategy, and Kissinger's agile implementation of it, may not have appreciably improved the state of the world, but the country is the quieter for it. America, if it could speak, would say, as the Abbé Sieyès said of himself after the French Revolution: it survived.

V

That we have paid costs, and severe ones, to purchase this time of civic renewal is certain. We have suffered a humiliating defeat in war, the implications of which have been enlarged by the known fact of our abandonment of an ally—and the further known fact that the defeat was, after all, self-inflicted. America's credibility as an ally has accordingly been impaired; we are held in contempt by the Chinese, who know better perhaps than the American public what the psychological consequences of this disaster are. The waning of faith in America's commitments enlivens the attempts of some allies to go their separate ways and, in several instances, also to go thermonuclear. The "lesson" of Vietnam, to large numbers of Americans, now means that no limited engagement of American will and resources in areas of contention is worth further effort. We have well shielded ourselves from an awareness of these reputational changes.

The lessening of our influence may be seen in the amazing OPEC oil price hike of 1973, which an administration crippled by its own foolishness and by overzealous investigators could do nothing to anticipate or to restrict. To compound matters, we have shielded ourselves from a recognition of our reputational decline by our failure to take full note of these matters. The executive branch—led by a president with no mandate and no constituency other than that of Grand Rapids—has been hobbled by congressional legislative constraints. The "lesson of Angola" was clear enough: it was not so much a matter of whether the United States should have intervened—a matter of some dispute—as it was a matter that, by congressional veto, no significant U.S. intervention was possible at all. And—most to the point—what is most peculiar is that this chain of events has not figured in public debates even in an election year.

VI

Is it then too much to suggest that the crucial question about Soviet–American relations is not so much the matter of Soviet actions, intentions, and capabilities as it is the matter of American staying power in a long and obdurate game; and that détente is as much an American domestic problem as it is a flawed superpower relationship? One hardly can cavil about the assumptions which underlay the original Nixon-Kissinger design, nor about the general ways in which it has been pursued. What we should complain of, however, are the public delusions which the pursuit of these policies has encouraged. We accepted with relief the notion that the cold war was ended, but few of us took care to notice that the Soviet view was that the struggle is still very much on, merely rechanneled into areas of opportunity and benefit, where the risks of grave confrontation were minimal. The original policy after all was based upon the notion that *détente should rest upon pillars of strength. The corrupt interpretation of it is that détente warrants the dismantling of such supports.* How else can we explain, for instance, the enthusiasm of parts of the American business community to lend its capital, technology, and expertise to the development of the economic base of the Soviet war machine?

Perhaps no administration could fare well in making these foreign-policy adjustments were it to inform the public that the central reason for such adjustments was to allow the country to mend its civic wounds by demanding less of itself. Nor could any administration admit, in the hearing of our adversaries, that détente in large measure arose from well-founded doubts as to what the American public in its current mood would tolerate. The stability of any superpower détente surely must minimally proceed from, and continue to be based upon, the very structures and wills which give promise of permanently sustaining it. Yet the rhetoric of détente ironically has convinced all too many Americans that these structures and such will no longer are needed.

It is to be assumed, with certainty, that the Soviet leaders never have been under such illusions. In fact they have gone out of their way to inform their own citizens that such illusions are false. They might conceivably have done differently; they might have scuttled their expansionist activities and abandoned their ideological view that the world conflict was moving into a new and more auspicious phase of intensified onslaughts against the bastions of their enemies. But they have not done so. Nor is there any reason to suppose they will.

VII

The investigative and reformist zeal with which American institutions have recently been ransacked to purge them of vestiges of cold war abuses can only be understood, perhaps, when we assume that there are certain illusions about the international world in which the United States today exists. Whence comes such a feeling of security? Does security signify an objective condition of safety or does it mean a subjective feeling of carefreeness? We ordinarily today take the word to have the former rather than the latter definition.

But this has not always been so. The *Oxford English Dictionary* in its primary definition of *security*, informs us that it means "feeling no care or apprehension." This was the pejorative sense of the word in a more vigilant historical period. Before being burned at the stake, the sixteenth century English divine, Latimer, chided his flock: "But we be secure and uncarefull, as though false Prophets could not meddle with us." Another clergyman of the same time cautioned his congregation in the same fashion: "When the Devil brings thee Oyle, bring thou Vinegar. The way to be safe, is never to be secure." The English diarist, Evelyn, in the seventeenth century wrote of his conversation with a captain of arms: "He told me 10,000 men would easily conquer all the Spanish Indies, they were so secure."

So, security can be a frame of mind and a mood, not a condition; and the mood provides the occasion in some quarters for a focus of vindictiveness and culpation against America's imperfect allies, its imperfect leadership, and its imperfect institutions. There is essentially nothing wrong about a ceaseless vigilance about the state of liberties which Americans should enjoy, a concern for the quality of life in other nations which have escaped Communist control, and an affirmation of the ideals which inform a free society. But if such vigilance is needed, why then is it accompanied so frequently by a silence as to the conditions which afflict freedom elsewhere and the grave deterioration of the position of the free democracies in the world? If détente were to come to mean, as it has to many, that its health necessitates a careless tolerance of evil institutions and practices in the camp of our known adversaries, we may be in trouble far greater than we know.

VIII

Those who in alarm now draw parallels between the American mood of isolationism in the 1930s and that of today would do well to further note one singular contrast between these two times: in the 1930s American isolationism meant American detachment from an existing, if crumbling, system of peace. A chief argument then was that it was none of America's business to shore up such a corrupt system.

Things are very different now: for what it is worth, since 1945 America has been the heart, the middle point, of the system; it has been the point of reference to which all have referred who have been genuinely concerned with the condition of human freedom. How then can America isolate itself from itself? Whether we like it or not, the present structure of world politics is such that America is now the *only* major power with resources sufficient to play the serious game of power politics with adversaries who hold the values of our system in open contempt. Europe and Japan, our central allies, are civic cultures acclimatized to a condition of protection which has enabled them to tailor and diminish their roles in the world to modest civilian and regional ones. This is now simply a fact of life; yet today it goes almost unmentioned. It should be an embarrassment to us that we have to be reminded of this fact by an heroic emigré from a country where such freedom does not exist.

IX

A new American leadership might use this occasion of renewal to draw a line in the path of time and to declare, as the saying goes, that this is the first day in the rest of the life of the republic. The merit of attempting this would be that it would both permit some teaching and learning about the new "correlation of forces" in the world and present the face of an America purposefully moving again. Our estimate of ourselves might be considerably improved. As Francis Bacon once wrote, "for he that is used to go forward, and findeth a stop, falleth out of his own favor, and is not the thing that he was."

It may be an odd time, when the art of commitment in America has come to be regarded by so many as antique, to suggest that it is, after all, quite necessary—as necessary in personal terms as in larger ones which are dealt with in this book. Strangely, the avoidance of commitment in relationships in contemporary America often comes in the happy guise of a search for freedom or fulfillment. But the significance of any relationship depends upon the prior commitment to it. It might do us some good now, when civic freedom is generally not doing well in other parts of the world, to remember the poem of larger commitment which Archibald MacLeish wrote in 1941, in days far darker than these.[2] It concluded:

> Lift up O land O land lift clear
> The lovely signal of your skies.
> If freedom darkens eastward here
> Here on the west let freedom rise.

NOTES

1. Quoted in Doris Kearns, "Who *Was* Lyndon Johnson?" *Atlantic* (June 1976), p. 65.

2. *The Free World, A Monthly Magazine* 1, no. 1 (October 1941):6. Copyright © 1941 by Archibald MacLeish.

Index

ABM (antiballistic missile), 217, 218
Aden: Great Britian and, 52; Soviet Union and, 55
Afghanistan, 49
Africa, xii; conference of Communists of, 28; Soviet influence in, 11, 27–30; *see also specific nations*
Agriculture, Soviet, 6, 74, 76, 80, 222; United States, 74, 78
Aircraft, 33, 58, 117, 123; nuclear propelled, 168; tactical, 178–80; tanker, 148; *see also* Bombers
Aircraft carriers, 31, 196
Air Force, U.S., predictions on Soviet strategic forces by, 128–29
Algeria: France and, 52; Soviet Union and, 11, 53, 55
Amendola (Italian Communist), 40, 41
Amnesty International, 227; Adoption Group of, 226
Angell, Norman, 51
Angola, 25–30; Cuban presence in, 7, 10, 28–30; détente and, 15, 16, 18; Guinea and, 27; Soviet Union and, 7, 10, 19, 28–29, 223; United States and, 240–41
Anti-Semitism, Soviet, 225
Antisubmarine forces, 180
Antonov Cock 22S ships, 33
Apollo space mission, 238
Appeasement, 3–4, 7–8, 15–16; *see also* Détente
Arbatov, Georgi, 9
Arab-Israeli wars: of 1948–1949, 50, 52–54; Six Day War, 57; Yom Kippur War, 11–12, 60
Arab nationalism, 52–54
Arms race, 87–88, 111–23; measures of relative destruction area and, 139–41; net effect of qualitative change in, 24–26, 84–85, 157–62; number of strategic warheads and, 138–39; offense and defense budgets and, 141–57; stereotypic

views of, 111–15; total explosive energy and "overkill" and, 136–38; United States estimate of Soviet capabilities and, 116–35; *see also* SALT
Army, U.S.: in NATO forces, 177; predictions of Soviet strategic forces by, 128
Aspin, Lee, 198–99
Aswan Dam, 53
Atlantic Treaty Association, 50, 63; *see also* NATO
Atlas ICBM, 148
Austria, 223
Autarky, 69–72
Authoritarianism, 169; *see also* Repression

B–29 bombers, 148
B–36 heavy bombers, 148
B–47 medium bombers, 148
B–50 bombers, 148
B–58 supersonic bombers, 148
Backfire bombers, 194
Bacon, Francis, 244
Badger bombers, 194
Balance of payments, 67
Balance of power, change in, 9, 16, 23, 31, 50; comparative attitude toward, 84–85
Balkans, 49
Ball, George, 44–45
Baltic States, 213
Barnet, Richard J., 166
"Basic Principles of Relations Between the United States of America and the Union of Soviet Socialist Republics," (Moscow Summit, May 72), 5, 8, 18, 59; violation of, 10, 11, 61
Belgium, 186; former colonies of, 50; in NATO armies, 177, 182
Bentham, Jeremy, 51
Berlin airlift, 50
Berlinguer (Italian Communist), 39, 41

Bettiza, Enzo, 44
Bicentennial, xi
Binder, David, 36
Blainey, Geoffrey, 89
Blechman, Barry, 167
Bohemia, 3
Bohler, Charles E., 88
Bolshevik Central Committee, 207
Bomarc area defense missiles, 148
Bombers: Soviet, 123, 194; United States, 148
Bottome, Edgar, 114
Boumédienne (Algerian President), 11
Brezhnev, Leonid, 6, 17–18, 69, 201; on democracy, 224; on détente, 8, 9; as military man, 189; on Mutual Balance Force Reductions, 183; Nixon and, 222; on Soviet Union as military threat, 218–19; on Yom Kippur War, 11
Brodie, Bernard, 167
Brookings Institute, 144–45, 156, 167
Brooks, Harvey, 115
Browne, H. Monroe, ix
Brzezinski, Z. 26, 43
Bulgaria: Soviet Union and, 170; in Warsaw Pact armies, 175, 177
Bull, Hedley, 166
Bulletin of Atomic Scientists, 110
Bury, J. B., 91
Butterfield, Herbert, 89
Byrd, Harry F., Jr., 11, 16

Cambodia, 59
Canada, 175, 177, 182
Carillo, Santiago, 38, 40
Carlyle, Thomas, 46
Carpatho-Ukraine, 3
Carriers, 31–32, 196
Castro, Fidel, 29, 222; United States sympathies for, 44
Catherine the Great, Empress of Russia, 211
Catholic authoritarianism, 169
Causes of War, The (Blainey), 89
Centurian tanks, 175
Central Intelligence Agency (CIA), 79
Chamberlain, Neville, 3, 4, 19
CHAMPUS (Civilian Health and Medical Program of the Uniformed Services), 144

Chemical-Biological-Radiological (CBR) defense capabilities, 200
Chieftan tanks, 175
China, 22, 50; Ghana and, 28; influence in Africa of, 28, 29; Korean War and, 12; Soviet Union and, 36, 44, 63, 64; United States and, 58–60, 240
Christian Science Monitor, 135
Christianity and History (Butterfield), 89
"Chronicle of Current Events," 224
Civil defense, 104–105
Clifford, Clark, 133; *see also* Defense budgets
Cobden, Richard, 112
Cold war, xiii, 4, 13, 16; Middle East and, 49; nonstrategic world order and, 90; United States condition during, 83–84, 92; *see also* Arms race
Columbo, Sri Lanka nonaligned conference (1976), 36; *see also* Third world
Comité d'études regionales et sociales (CERES), 42
Command-Control-Communications (C³) defense capabilities, 200
Commentary (magazine), 15
Commodities, United States need for key, 67–68
Communist of the Armed Forces (periodical), 99
Communists: African, 28; Soviet failure to support, 24; Western European, 37–48; *see also* Soviet Union; Warsaw pact
Compromisso historico, 32
Conquest, Robert, viii, xiii, 90, 205–16
Conscription, 182–83; *see also* NATO
Consumer goods: doctrine of progress and, 93; Soviet demand for, 72–73, 219–21; United States and, 93
Containment policy, 84, 91
Contingencies of war, 82–83
Counterforce and countervalue capabilities: assessment of, 100–2; strategy and, 107–108; *see also* Arms race
Credit, international, 83
Crimean Tatars, 205, 226–27
Crimean War, 49
Crop failures, Soviet, 73, 74
Cruise O'Brien, Conor, 36
Cruisers, 193–94
Cuba: Angola and, 10, 28–30; at nonaligned conference, 36; Soviet Union and, 32, 44; troops of, in Africa, 23

Cuban missile crisis, 84, 191
Cultural exchange, 17–18, 211
Currie, Malcolm, 200
Cyprus: conflict over, 55, 172; Turkey and, 31
Czechoslovakia: economic reform in, 220; German invasion of, 3–4, 60; multiparty system in, 39–40; Soviet domination of, 170; in Warsaw Pact armies, 177; Warsaw Pact invasion of, 32, 207

Days of Sadness, Years of Triumph (Perrett), 92
Declaration of Paris (1973), 59
Defeatism, 94; *see also* Public opinion
Defense Department Program I, 141–43
Defense budgets, 141–56
Democracy, decline of, 52; Western European Communism and, 38–39, 44–46
Denmark, 173, 186; in NATO armies, 177, 182
Depression, economic, 91
Détente, ix; alternatives to, 15; anticolonialism and, 25–26; appeasement in guise of, 15–16; consumer expeditures and, 219; crisis of, 18–20; cultural exchange and, 18; definitions of, 4–8, 233–35; dissident movement and, 223–28; economic aid and, 221–22; human rights and, 228–29; ideology and, 22–23, 171, 222–23; incentives theory in, 7; increase in international danger and, 16; linkages concept of, 5; military aspects of, 217–19, NATO and, 172, 185; political aspects of, 5–14; repression and, 16–18; Soviet motives for, 6–8, 72–74, 219–20; Soviet view of, 9–11, 59–61
Dinerstein, Herbert, 4
Disarmament, *see* SALT
Dissidents, Soviet, 223–28; increased repression of, 224–25; treatment of, 226–28; *see also* Détente, Human rights
Doty, Paul, 115
Draper, Theodore, vii, 3–21
Dulles, John Foster, 53
Dylan, Bob, 236
Dzhemilev, Mustafa, 226–27

East Germany: human rights in, 213; multiparty system in, 39–40; Soviet domination of, 170; in Warsaw Pact armies, 175, 177
Eastern Europe: Soviet policy in, 8; *see also specific nations*
Economic aspects of détente, 5–14, 65–80, 219–22; autarky and, 69–72; balance of payments and, 67; decline in Soviet growth and, 72–73; employment effect of, 67; key commodities and, 67–68; Western technology and, 69; United States policy and, 76–77
Economic reform, 219–20
Economic self-sufficiency, 69–72
Egalitarianism, national security and, 93
Egypt: Communist Party of, 24; Soviet Union and, 49–55; United States and, 23
Eisenhower, Dwight D.: Middle East policy of, 52; strategic budget of, 142
Electro-Magnetic Pulse (EMP) defense capabilities, 200
Ellsberg, Daniel, 237
Ellul, Jacques, 158, 161
Embargoes, oil, 55
Employment effect of détente, 67
Energy, *see* Oil
Enlightenment, 89
Entente, 4
Environmentalists, technology and, 58, 158
Equivalent megatonnage, *see* Nuclear weapons
Epstein, William, 114
Espresso, L' (newspaper), 43
Ethiopia, Italian invasion of, 51
European Economic Community (EEC), 38, 40, 41
Evelyn (English diarist), 242
Export-Import Bank, 76

Fail-safe techniques, 159
Falcon missiles, 139
Fallout, 105
Feld, Bernard, 114
Festinger, Leon, 113
Fighters, Soviet, 178–79
Finland, 46, 56
Fishing fleet, Soviet, 196
Five Year Plans, 70, 74–76
Ford, Gerald R., 90; on détente, ix, 15; Solzhenitsyn and, 17–18

Foreign Affairs (magazine), 98
Fostinger, Leon, 166
Fractional identities, 93–94
France, 185; appeasement and, 4, 15; Communist Party of, *see* French Communist Party; former colonies of, 25, 26, 50; in Middle East, 52; NATO and, 170, 177, 182; 1974 elections in, 24; Siberian natural gas and, 68; Socialist Party of, 38, 42; Soviet intelligence officers in, 223; Soviet Union and, 51; in World War II, 63
Franco, Francisco, 169
French Communist Party, 24, 32–33, 170, 171; authoritarian structure of, 39; doctrinal changes in, 37, 38, 40; political strength of, 42
Fulbright, J. William, 4, 12

Garwin, Richard, 109
Gelb, Leslie, 113
Geneva Conference (1954), 52
Germany: invasion of Czechoslovakia by, 3–4, 60; Soviet Union and, 51, 159, 188; *see also* East Germany, West Germany
Ghana: China and, 28; Soviet Union and, 27–28, 30, 55
Giornale Nuovo, Il (newspaper), 44
Giscard d'Estaing, Valery, 24
Goldman, Marshall I., 6–7
Gorshkov, S. G., 188; influence on Soviet navy, 194–96, 199, 200
Great Britain, 186; appeasement and, 3–4, 15; former colonies of, 25, 26, 50; Labour Party of, 44; in Middle East, 50, 52; NATO and, 46, 175, 177, 182; Siberian natural gas and, 69; Soviet Union and, 51; in World War II, 58, 63, 159, 188
Grechko, Andrei, 188
Greece, 50; in NATO armies, 177, 182
Grey, Lord, 111, 112
Gromyko, Andrei, 85, 87
Gross national product (GNP), defense spending as proportion of, 143
Grossman, Gregory, vi, 65–80, 221
Ground forces, of NATO armies, 175–77
Guam doctrine, 236
Guinea: Angola and, 27; North Vietnam and, 27, 30

Gulag Archipelago (Solzhenitsyn), 225, 227
"Gulliverisation," 46

Halperin, Morton, 113, 114
Hard Rock Silo project, 168
Haselkorn, Avigdor, 36
Hassner, Pierre, 47
Hayden, Thomas, 240
Heavy bombers: Soviet, 123; United States, 148
Helicopter carriers, 194, 196
Helsinki Agreement: Final Act of, 227–29; human rights and, 208–10, 213–14; international law and, 229
High-quality foodstuffs, Soviet demand for, 74
Hiroshima, 136
Hitler, Adolf, 3–4, 52, 60
Ho Chi Minh, 237
Hobson, 51
Hoffman, Abbie, 237
Hoffman, Stanley, 113
Holland, 186
Holloway, James L., III, 190, 198
Holy Roman Empire, 22
Holzman, Franklyn D., 80
Honecker (East German leader), 223
House of Representatives: Appropriations Committee of, 198; Armed Services Committee of, 198
Human rights, 205–16; détente and, 228–29; Helsinki Agreement and, 208–10, 213–14; importance of, 215–16; international law and, 228–29; Kissinger on, 16–18; negotiations on, 208–10; psychological disarmament and, 212; Russian state tradition and, 206–8; South Africa and, 43
Hungary, 175; multiparty system in, 39–40; Soviet domination of, 170; in Warsaw Pact armies, 177
Huntington, Samuel P., 159–60
Hydrofoil missile ships (PHM), 190

ICBMs (intercontinental ballistic missile launchers), 116–24, 128–29, 132–33
Iceland, 45
Idea of Progress, The (Bury), 91

Ideology, 88; détente and, 18, 171, 222–23; divisions among Western European Communists on, 38–43; evolution of, 215; peace and, 88–91; as strategic weapon, 24–26

Il Mondo (newspaper), 44–45

Imperialism, economics of, 50–51; Soviet development of, 8, 28–30

Incentives, *see* Détente

Inchon, naval assault on, 191

Indochinese wars, 26, 51; *see also* Vietnam war

Inflation, defense spending and, 150–51

Ingrao, 41

Inherent nature of peace, belief in, 89

International Court of Justice of the United Nations, 56

International credit, 83

International law, 228–29

International Monetary Fund, 22

Iran, 49, 50

Iraq: Communist Party of, 24; Soviet Union and, 53, 55

IRBMs (intermediate range ballistic missile launchers), 116–17

Isolationism, 243

Israel, 63; League of Nations and, 53; occupation of Arab territories by, 57; Soviet Jewish emigration to, 225; Suez Canal and, 54; *see also* Arab-Israeli Wars

Italian Communist Party, 169, 171; authoritarian structure of, 39; American attitudes toward, 44–46; doctrinal changes in, 38, 40; NATO and, 41; Soviet Communist Party and, 40–42

Italy, 51, 173, 186, 188; Christian Democratic Party of, 41, 45; politics of, 46; Communist Party of, *see* Italian Communist Party; invasion of Ethiopia by, 51; in NATO armies, 173, 177, 182; Socialist Party of, 45

Ivory Coast, 29

Izvestia, 10

Jackson, Henry, 163; Kissinger and, 225

Jackson amendment, 76, 209, 214

Japan, 50; economic prosperity in, 25; oil needs of, 33; Soviet Union and, 63; United States facilities in, 32; in World War II, 188

Jarring, Gunnar, 59, 60

Jews, Soviet, 205, 209–10

Johnson, Lyndon Baines, 236, 238

Jordan, 50, 63; British intervention in, 52; Egypt and, 53, 54

Juenger, Friedrich, 158

Junta Democratica, 40

Kara cruisers, 194

Kashin-class missile destroyers, 194

KC–29 tanker aircraft, 148

KC–97 tanker aircraft, 148

Kennan, George F., 4

Kennedy, John F., 237

Kennedy, Robert F., 237

Keston College, 227

Key commodities, 67–68

KGB (Soviet State Security Committee), 177; dissidents and, 224–28

Khrushchev, Nikita, 40, 69, 117, 220; economic conditions under, 73; Soviet navy and, 188–89, 194

Kiev (carrier), 31

Kiev VSTOL carriers, 196

Kim Il Sung, 36

King, Martin Luther, 237

Kissinger, Henry, 47, 80, 164; achievements of, 236, 240; on Angola, 19; on détente, ix, 4, 5, 8, 12, 14, 60; "gulliverisation" concept of, 46; on human rights, 16–18; Jackson and, 225; on military technology, 110; on nuclear weapons, 12–13; on SALT I, 5; on Soviet dissidents, 224; on Soviet Union as superpower, 18–20; on Western European Communism, 47; on Yom Kippur War, 11–12

Kistiakowsky, George B., 5–6, 115

Koestler, Arthur, 212, 214

Korea, 49

Korean War, 50, 136; China and, 12; strategic budget during, 142, 144; United States fleet during, 188

Kovalev, S. A., 226

Krasin (Soviet dissident), 224

Kresta I cruisers, 194

Kresta II cruisers, 194

Kurds, 24

Kuznetsov, N. G., 188, 200

Kynda-class cruisers, 193–94

Laos, 59
Laqueur, Walter Z., vii, 37–48
Latimer (English divine), 242
League of Nations: Covenant of, 89; Israel and, 53
Lebanon, 53, 54, 63; United States intervention in, 52, 191
Legum, Colin, 36
Legvold, Robert, 36, 80
Leites, Nathan, 88
Lend-lease repayments, Soviet obligation and, 77
Lenin, V. I., 51, 52, 69, 207, 214, 227; on power, 25; on Western economic aid, 221
Leninism, 24, 39, 99
Lennon, John, 237
Lennon, Yoko, 237
Libya, 49; Soviet Union and, 30, 53, 55
Lift capabilities, 33
Linkage, 5; economic, 77; *see also* Détente
Lipton (author), 158
London *Times*, 4, 39
London *Tribune*, 212
Luddite view of technology, 114–15, 158–59
Luttwak, Edward N., 169–86
Luxemburg, Rosa, 207

McCarthy, Eugene, 4
McCarthy, Joseph, 237
MacLeish, Archibald, 244
McNamara, Robert, 113, 116, 166, 236; predictions of Soviet strategic forces by, 129–33
Machel, Samora, 29
Mahon, George, 198
Malaysia, 30
Manned Orbiting Lab, 168
Mao Tse-tung, 52
Marchais, George, 38, 39
Margelov, V. F., 195
Marshall, Charles Burton, vii, xiii, 80–94
Marx, Karl, 207
Marxism, 24
Marxism-Leninism, 28, 99; world view of, 206, 207
Mazzini, Giuseppi, 46

Medium bombers: Soviet, 123; United States, 148
Megatonnage, 137
Merchant fleet, Soviet, 196
Meskhetians, 205
Middendorf, J. William, II, 196
Middle East, as key to Europe, 48–51; détente and, 8, 11, 15; peace in, 64; Soviet influence in, 11–12, 23, 24, 48–64; United States influence in, 48–64; *see also specific nations*
MiG–17 fighters, 178, 179
MiG–19 fighters, 178
MiG–21 fighters, 178
MiG–23 fighters, 179
Military aspects of détente, 5–14, 217–19
Military technology, 110
Millerites, 134
Milton, John, xiii, 209
Minerals, 32
Minorities, 93–94
MIRVs (Multiple Independent Re-entry Vehicles), 106, 107, 129
Minuteman missiles, 106, 108
"Missile gap," 116; overcorrection of, 129–32; *see also* Nuclear Weapons
Missiles, 106, 108, 139, 148, 164; submarine-launched, 122–23, 132
Mitterand, François, 24, 44
Mondo, Il (newspaper), 44–45
Mongolia, 23
Monroe Doctrine, 50
Montreux convention, 31
Moravia, 3
Morocco, 52
Moscow Summit, 5; *see also* Basic Principles
Moskva class helicopter carriers, 194, 196
Mozambique, 29
MPLA (Angolan Popular Liberation Movement), 27, 30; Nigerian support for, 28
MRBMs (medium range ballistic missile launchers), 116–17
MRVs (Multiple Re-entry Vehicles), 129
Munich agreements, 3–4, 15, 60
MURFAAMCE (Mutual Reduction of Forces and Armaments and Associated Measures in Central Europe), 184–85
Mutual Balance Force Reductions (MBFR), xii, 183–85
MX missiles, 108

Nagorski, Z., 43
Nacht, Michael, 114
Nasser, Gamal Abdul, 52–54, 57, 62
National Academy of Sciences, 225
National liberation movements, xii, 10–11
National security, 81–94; Atlantic Alliance and contingencies of war and, 82–83; doctrine of progress and, 91–93; ideology and, 88–91; nuclear warfare and, 83–87; strategic equilibrium and, 87–88
Nationalism, Arab, 52–54
NATO (North Atlantic Treaty Organization), 32, 169–86; air forces of, 178–80; armies of, 173–77, 179–80, 182–85; communications system of, 32; Middle East and, 31, 53, 55; navies of, 187–88, 198; Nuclear Planning Group of, 45; Portugal and, 28; sealift for, 180–81; Turkey and, 31; weaknesses of, 31, 181; Western European Communism and, 32, 38, 45–46
Natural gas, *see* Oil
Navajo ramjet intercontinental missiles, 168
Naval balance, 187–201; aftermath of Cuban missile crisis and, 193–96; historical perspective on, 187–89; Vietnam War and, 189–93
Navy, Soviet, 193–96
Navy, U.S., 187–201; as "projection" fleet, 191–93; predictions of Soviet strategic forces by, 128
Necessity for Choice, The (Kissinger), 17
Nehru, Jawaharlal, 54
Netherlands, 186; in NATO armies, 177, 182
New Deal, 91–92
New Republic (magazine), 134
New York Times, 43, 44, 75, 93–94, 134, 212
Newhouse, John, 114
News media, defense spending and, 149–54; *see also* Public opinion
Nicholas I, Tsar of Russia, 207
Nigeria, 28, 29
Nike-Hercules missiles, 139, 148
Nitze, Paul H., viii, 97–109
Nixon, Richard M., 18; achievements of, 236, 239–40; Brezhnev and, 222; China trip of, 58; on détente, 10–11, 59, 60, 63; Moscow visit of, 59, 61

Nkrumah, Kwame, 28, 54
Non-aligned nations, 36
Nonstrategic world order, *see* Peace
North Atlantic Treaty Organization, *see* NATO
"North Star" natural gas project, 68
North Korea: Iraq and, 23; non-aligned status of, 36
Norway, 186; coastal submarines of, 198; in NATO armies, 177, 182
Nuclear propelled aircraft, 168
Nuclear weapons: assessment of capabilities of, 100–3; cold war and, 84; détente and, 12–14; defense strategy and, 106–7; distinction between counterforce and countervalue capabilities of, 107–8; fallout from, 105; measure of relative destructive area (EMT) of, 139–41; number of strategic warheads of, 138–39; "overkill" of, 136–38; possibility of European use of, 181–82; Soviet attitude toward use of, 84–87, 97–100, 218; total explosive energy of, 136–38; warheads of, 138–39
Nutter, Warren G., 80

Offense budgets, 141–56
Oil: economic détente and, 68; foreign policy and, 55–56, 79, 82, 240; reserves of, 32, 33
OPEC oil price hike, 240
Operational codes, 88–91
Orlov, Yurii, 227–28
Orwell, George, 163, 164
Ostpolitik, 171, 182, 185
Ottoman Empire, 49
Overhead allocations, 143–44
"Overkill," 136–38
Oxford English Dictionary, 4, 242

Pajetta, Gian Carlo, 39
Palestine, 49, 50
Pan-Arabism, 54
Panov (dancer), 226
Patrol frigates, 190
Peace, belief in inherent nature of, 89–90
"Peaceful coexistence," xiii, 9–10, 72
Permissive Action Links, 159

Perrett, Geoffrey, 92
Persian Gulf, 33, 34
Peter I, Tsar of Russia, 187, 211
Petroleum, *see* Oil
Philippines, United States facilities in, 32
Plyushch, Leonid, 226
Poland, 56; Mongolia and, 23; multiparty system in, 39–40; popular disturbances in, 74; Soviet domination of, 170; in Warsaw Pact armies, 177
Political aspects of détente, 5–14; dissident movement and, 223–28; ideological struggle and, 22–23
Polmar, Norman, viii, 186–201
Ponomarev, 213
Portugal: Communist Party of, 26, 36; former colonies of, 25, 50; Guinea attacked by, 27; in NATO armies, 177; Soviet Union and, 55
Poseidon submarines, 105
Potsdam agreement, 51
Pravda, 10
Price, Melvin, 198
Progress, doctrine of, 91–93
Psychiatric incarceration, Soviet, 226–28
Psychic satisfaction, demand for, 93
Psychological disarmament, 212
Public opinion: defense and, 81–94, 212; Korean War and, 51; Middle East and, 62–64; Vietnam War and, 60, 237–39
Puerto Rico, 24

Rapprochement, 4
Rascal missiles, 168
Raskin, Marcus G., 166
Rathjens, George, 115
RB–36 heavy bombers, 148
RB–47 medium bombers, 148
Regulus II missiles, 168
"Religion in Communist Lands" (Keston College), 227
Repression, Soviet, 205–12; détente and, 17–18, 224–25; *see also* Human rights
"Reverse engineering," 69
Reynolds, Malvina, 238–39
Richardson, Lewis Fry, 111, 112
Ridder, Walter T., 93–94
Rodberg, Leonard, 113, 114, 158
Roosevelt, Franklin D., 91
Rostow, Eugene V., vii, 49–64, 90

Rubin, Jerry, 237
Rumania: repression in, 39; Soviet Union and, 170; in Warsaw Pact armies, 174, 177
Rusk, Dean, 4
Russell, Bertrand, 111
Russia, *see* Soviet Union; Tsarist Russia
Russians, The (Smith), 17, 223

Sadat, Anwar, 60
Sakharov, Andrei, 17, 225, 228
Samizdat movement, 17, 224; *see also* Dissidents
SCAD Armed Decoys, 168
Schapiro, Leonard, viii, 217–30
Schlesinger, James R., vii, xi–xiii, 36, 63
Schmidt, Helmut, 45
Schneider, William, Jr., 36
Scholarly exchange program, 18
Schumpeter, Joseph A., 94
Scientific American (magazine), 135
Scoville, Herbert, 113
Sea control ships (SCS), 190
Seabury, Paul, viii, 233–44
SEATO, 59
Security, 81–82; illusions of, 242–43; *see also* National security
Senate: Armed Services Committee of, 198; Foreign Relations Committee of, 4
Shanghai communique, 58
Shulman, Marshall, 4, 12
Siberian natural gas, 68
Sieyès, Abbé, 240
Six-Day War, 57; Soviet Jews and, 225
Sixth Fleet, U.S., 52
Skybolt missile, 168
SLBMs (submarine-launched missiles), 122–23, 132
Slovakia, 3
Smith, Hendrick, 17, 223
Snark intercontinental cruise missiles, 148
Solod (Soviet ambassador), 27
Solzhenitsyn, Aleksandr, 17–18, 225, 227
Somalia, 30, 32, 33, 35
Sonnenfeldt, Helmut, 7–8
South Africa, 213
South Vietnam, 33; *see also* Vietnam War
South Yemen, 30
Soviet Academy of Sciences, 225; Institute of the U.S.A. of, 9

Soviet Union: African influence of, 27–30; agriculture in, 6, 74, 76, 80; Algeria and, 53, 55; Angola and, 7, 10, 19, 223; alliance system of, 23, 30–31; assessment of nuclear capabilities of, 100–3; attitude toward nuclear warfare of, 84–87, 97–99, 218; autarky and, 69–72; Border Troops of, 177; Bulgaria and, 170; carriers of, 32; China and, 36, 44, 59; civil defense program of, 104–105; in cold war, 84; Communist Party of, 38, 39; conditions of peace viewed by, 90–91; consumer expenditures in, 72–73, 219; Cuba and, 32, 44; decline in growth rate of, 6, 72–76; defense strategy of, 106–7; détente and, xi–xii, 5–20; domination of Eastern Europe by, 5, 170, 213–214; economic reform in, 75–76, 219–20; economic relations of United States and, 6–8, 65–80; emigration of Jews from, 225–26; estimation of capabilities of, 116–35; Five Year Plans of, 70, 74–76; human rights issues and, 205–16; imperialism and, 28–30, 51–52; intelligence officers of, 223; Kissinger on, 18–20, 47; Middle East and, 33, 49–64; military expenditures of, 217–19; national liberation movements and, 10–11, 24–25, 69; NATO and, 169–86; naval strength of, 34–35, 58, 187–201; nullification of trade agreement by, 76–77; "peaceful coexistence" concept of, xiii, 9–10, 72; repression in, 16–17, 39, 205–12, 224–28; strategic offensive forces of, 116–35; strategic use of ideology by, 24–25; submarines of, 181, 187–89; technology of, 69; third world influence of, 22–35; Turkey and, 31; Vietnam War and, 58–60; in Warsaw Pact armies, 177; West Germany and, 72; Western European communism and, 38–43; Western technology and, 69, 73, 221–22

Spain, Communist Party of, 32–33; authoritarian structure of, 39; doctrinal changes in, 38, 40; political strength of, 42–43

Spanish Socialist Workers Party, 38, 39, 171

Spartan missiles, 139

Spengler, Oswald, 158

Spirit of Camp David, 63

Sprint missiles, 139

SS–18 missiles, 107

SS–19 missiles, 107

Stalin, Josef, 39, 52, 69; death of, 220; Western technology and, 211

"Static" indicators of nuclear capabilities, 100

Steinhoff, General Johannes, 32

Stennis, John, 198

Stone, Jeremy, 113, 114

Strategic arms budgets, 141–56

Strategic Arms Limitation Talks (SALT), xii, 5, 102, 112, 148, 159

Strategic arms race, *see* Arms race

Strategic equilibrium, 87–88

Student rebellion, 237

Su–7 fighter-bombers, 178

Su–17/20 (Fitter C) fighter bombers, 179

Su–19 fencer fighters, 179

Submarines: Norwegian, 198; Soviet, 181, 187–89

Suez Canal: Great Britain and, 52; Israel and, 54

Sukarno, 54

Supersonic bombers, 148

Surprise Attack Conference, 161

Suslov, 213

Sutton, Antony C., 79

Sverdlov-class cruisers, 194

Symbionese Liberation Army (SLA), 237

Syria, 23, 53–55

T–34/85 tanks, 175

T–62 tanks, 175

Tactical air power, 178–80; *see also* Aircraft

Taft, Robert, 198, 201

Tanker aircraft, 148

Tanks, 175–76

Tatars, Crimean, 205, 226–27

Technology, 211; civilian, 158; instabilities brought about by, 112; military, 110–11, 157–62; political control of, 163; Soviet Union and, 69, 73, 221–22

Terrorism, 82

Thailand, 30; United States bases in, 34

Thatcher, Margaret, 44

Third world: projection of Soviet power into, 22–35; *see also specific nations*

Thompson, W. Scott, vii, 22–35
Thoreau, Henry David, 237
Thorez, Maurice, 39
Times of Zambia (newspaper), 30
Titan I ICBN, 148
Tito, Josef, 54
Togliatti (Italian Communist), 39
Touré, Sékou, 27
Trade, *see* Economic aspects of détente
Treaty of Westphalia, 22
Trident submarine, 108
Trident II missiles, 108
Tripartite Declaration, 52–53
Trudeau, Pierre, 29
Truman, Harry S., 90
Tsarist Russia: colonies of, 26; despotism of, 206–8; expansionist policies of, 49–50; Western capital and technology in, 68–69
Tu–16 medium bombers, 179
Turkey, 49, 50; Greece and, 172; in NATO armies, 174, 177, 182; strategic importance of, 31
"Turnkey" projects, 69
Tverdokhlebov, Andrei, 226

Ukraine, dissidents in, 224
UNITA (National Union for Total Independence of Angola), 29
United Nations, 22; Charter of, 57, 89, 90; International Court of Justice of, 56; Israel and, 53, 56; Security Council of, 53, 57, 59, 61–62; use of veto power in, 35–36
United States: alliances of, 63–68, 235–37; Angola and, 240–41; assessment of nuclear capabilities of, 100–3; China and, 58–60, 240; in cold war, 83–84, 92; Communist Party of, 75, 218, 220, 222, 223; decline in military capabilities of, 31–32, 34, 55–56, 58; decline in nuclear capabilities of, 135–41; defense strategy of, 106–107; détente and, 5–20; doctrine of progress in, 91–93; economic policy of, 6, 76–79; Egypt and, 23; estimation of Soviet capabilities by, 116; fractional identities in, 93–94; ideology in, 15, 25, 58; key commodities needed by, 67–68; Middle East policy of, 23, 52–53, 56–

57, 61–62, 83; NATO and, 170–71, 173, 177, 180, 183; military strength of, 33–34, 98; national interest of, 56–57, 65–68; naval strength of, 187–201; offense and defense budgets of, 141–57; operational codes of, 88–91; projection of power by, 31–35, 83–84; Security Council of, 136; strategic defensive forces of, 138–39; strategic offensive forces of, 82, 111, 135–56; Western European Communism and, 43–48
Union of Soviet Socialist Republics (USSR), *see* Soviet Union

Vertical/short take-off and landing (VSTOL) aircraft, 190
Vietnam: Algeria and, 23; non-aligned status of, 36
Vietnam War, xi, 23, 59, 92, 240–41; lessons of, 26–27, 237–238; naval balance and, 189–93; nuclear weapons and, 12; Thai bases in, 34; youth rebellion and, 237–39
Vladivostok agreement, 163; *see also* SALT
Volga Germans, 205

Waldeck-Rachet (French Communist), 39
War, contingencies of, 82–83
Warheads, nuclear, 138–39
Warnke, Paul, 113, 145, 167
Warsaw Pact: airforces of, 178–80; armies of, 173–77, 179–80, 182–85; Soviet dominance of, 32; weaknesses of, 181
Washington Post, 37, 44
Watergate scandal, 60
Watts riot, 237
Weathermen, 237
West Germany: NATO and, 46, 175, 177, 182; *Ostpolitik* of, 171, 182, 185; Siberian natural gas and, 68; Social Democratic Party of, 44; Soviet Union and, 72
Western Europe: alliance system of, 23; Soviet Union and, 32–33; *see also* NATO; *specific nations*
Western European Communists, 37–48; American attitudes toward, 43–46; Catholic authoritarianism and, 169–70; ideological divisions in, 38–43

Wiesner, Jerome, 113–15, 144
Wildavsky, Aaron, 93
Wilhelm II, Kaiser of Germany, 52
Wohlstetter, Albert, viii, 110–68, 218
World War II, 49, 83, 90, 92, 136, 141, 159, 189, 201
"Worst case" dynamic, 113, 163

XB–70 bomber, 168

Yakir (Soviet dissident), 224

Yalta agreement, 51
Yom Kippur War, 60; Brezhnev on, 11; Soviet violation of "Basic Principles" during, 11–12
York, Herbert, 115
Youth rebellion, 237–39
Yugoslavia, 50; repression in, 39; Soviet Union and, 44

Zäire, 29
Zambia, 29; Angola and, 30
Zevi, Sabbatai, 134
Zumwalt, Elmo R., 190, 197, 200